# POLITICS AND
## STATE BUILDING
### IN SOLOMON ISLANDS

# POLITICS AND STATE BUILDING IN SOLOMON ISLANDS

SINCLAIR DINNEN AND STEWART FIRTH (EDS)

ANU
THE AUSTRALIAN NATIONAL UNIVERSITY

E PRESS

Asia Pacific Press
The Australian National University

# ANU

## E PRESS

Copublished by ANU E Press and Asia Pacific Press
The Australian National University
Canberra ACT 0200 Australia
Email: anuepress@anu.edu.au
This title is available online at http://epress.anu.edu.au/solomon_islands_citation.html

Asia Pacific Press
Crawford School of Economics and Government
The Australian National University
Canberra ACT 0200
Ph: 61-2-6125 0178 Fax: 61-2-6125 0767
Email: books@asiapacificpress.com
Website: http://www.asiapacificpress.com

Studies in State and Society in the Pacific, Number 2
State, Society and Governance in Melanesia Program, The Australian
National University, Canberra. The financial support of the Australian
Agency for International Development (AusAID) is gratefully
acknowledged.

*State*
Society *and*
Governance *in*
Melanesia

National Library of Australia Cataloguing-in-Publication entry

| | |
|---|---|
| Author | Dinnen, Sinclair. |
| Title: | Politics and state building in Solomon Islands / authors, Sinclair Dinnen, Stewart Firth. |
| Publisher: | Canberra, A.C.T. : Asia Pacific Press, 2008. |
| ISBN: | 9780731538188 (pbk.)<br>9781921313660 (online) |
| Notes: | Includes index. |
| Subjects: | Solomon Islands--Economic conditions.<br>Solomon Islands--Politics and government. |

Other Authors/Contributors: Firth, Stewart, 1944-

Dewey Number: 995.93

Cover image: AAP Image/Rob Griffith
Cover design: ANU E Press

# Contents

## *Provincial Perspectives*

# Tables

# Figures

# Preface

This collection originates in a one-day conference organised jointly by the State Society and Governance in Melanesia (SSGM) Program and the Pacific Centre at the Australian National University on 5 May 2006. The conference—Solomon Islands, Where to Now?—was held shortly after serious disturbances in the Solomon Islands capital, Honiara, in April 2006. This was a timely opportunity to reflect on these events and what they meant for Solomon Islands, as well as for the substantial Australian-led Regional Assistance Mission to Solomon Islands (RAMSI). As well as Australian-based scholars, several colleagues from Solomon Islands and other parts of the region accepted our invitation to contribute their observations and analysis of developments in Honiara.

The crisis that gripped Solomon Islands in April 2006 started when newly elected parliamentarians chose Snyder Rini as prime minister-elect. People expressed outrage, peacefully at first but then in a riot that destroyed Chinese-owned stores in the capital. Australia, New Zealand and Fiji sent troops and police to join those already there under the regional mission. RAMSI was deployed initially in mid-2003 at the request of the Solomon Islands government. Law and order was restored quickly and peacefully after four debilitating years of 'ethnic tensions', endemic lawlessness, economic decline, and a progressive paralysis of the central government. The disturbances in April caused extensive damage to Honiara's Chinatown district—though fortunately no fatalities occurred—and caught most observers completely off-guard. While these events did not derail the regional mission, they inevitably raised questions about some of the earlier assessments. Before they occurred, many experts were hailing RAMSI as an unqualified success. Some saw it as a model for 'cooperative intervention' in 'failing states' worldwide. In light of April's developments, RAMSI's success appeared less certain and its model more problematic.

Shortly after the disturbances, a new government was established in Solomon Islands under the leadership of Manasseh Sogavare. In the following fifteen months relations between the governments of Solomon Islands and Australia deteriorated dramatically as they struggled over the control and direction of the regional mission. While some of the contributions, notably the introductory chapter, allude to these subsequent developments, most are focused on the events surrounding the April disturbances. While by no means a definitive account, this book explores a significant crisis moment in recent Solomon Islands history. Contributors examine what happened when unrest engulfed the capital of the small Melanesian country in 2006, the role of members of the local Asian community in business and politics, and why the crisis is best understood in the context of the country's unique blend of traditional and modern politics.

Chapter One situates RAMSI in the setting of international state building and the particular social and historical context of state building in Solomon Islands. Chapters Two and Three look at the politics underlying the disturbances and the Asian involvement in Solomon Islands politics and economics. Chapters Four, Five and Six examine the workings of the formal political and electoral process and, in particular, the 2006 election and process of government formation. Some of the challenges facing the regional assistance mission are examined in Chapter Seven. While most contributors focus on developments in the national capital, Chapters Eight and Nine offer some different perspectives from the provinces. Chapter Ten provides some broader reflections on the challenges facing Solomon Islands in the years ahead. Appendix 1 is an Australian government perspective on the events in Honiara in April 2006, while the terms of reference for the Solomon Islands government Commission of Inquiry into these events are reproduced in Appendix 2. Appendix 3 contains the terms of reference for the subsequent Pacific Islands Forum Review of RAMSI. Chapters Five and Nine are reproduced with permission from the 2007 Special Issue on Solomon Islands of the Journal of Pacific History.

We would like to acknowledge the support of the State, Society and Governance in Melanesia Project of the Australian National University, in particular Ms Sue Rider, and the Pacific Centre at the Australian National University in helping organise the conference in May 2006, as well as AusAID for their financial assistance. Sincere thanks to all our patient contributors and, last but by no means least, to Debra Grogan and her team at the Asia Pacific Press.

Sinclair Dinnen and Stewart Firth
Canberra, February 2008

# Contributors

**Sam Alasia** graduated in Political Science from the University of the South Pacific in Fiji in 1982 and worked in the civil service before being elected to the Solomon Islands Parliament in 1989. He was Minister of Education from 1990–1993 and then Minister of State in the Prime Minister's office from 1994–1997. He left politics in 1998 and became Special Adviser to the Prime Minister from 2000–2001. He was also Political Adviser to Prime Minister Sogavare. As well as writing about Solomon Islands politics, Sam has produced several creative works including poems, a novel, and a collection of short stories.

**Matthew Allen** is a Postdoctoral Fellow with the Resource Management in Asia Pacific Program (RMAP) at the Australian National University. His background is in political anthropology and human geography. His recently awarded PhD thesis investigated the 1998–2003 conflict in Solomon Islands from the perspective of ex-militants. Matthew has also worked in Papua New Guinea and Vanuatu.

**Transform Aqorau** is from Roviana, New Georgia, in Western Province of Solomon Islands. He studied in Papua New Guinea, Canada and holds a PhD in Law from the University of Wollongong in Australia. He has worked as legal adviser to the Solomon Islands Ministry of Foreign Affairs and the Pacific Islands Forum Secretariat. He is currently working as legal counsel to the Pacific Islands Forum Fisheries Agency. He has also been appointed Senior Visiting Fellow at the Centre for Maritime Policy at the University of Wollongong.

**Anita Butler** is a career officer with the Department of Foreign Affairs and Trade, currently serving as Australia's Consul General in New Caledonia with responsibility for French Polynesia and Wallis and Futuna. Ms Butler was Deputy Head of Mission in Honiara (2002–05), Director, Pacific Bilateral Section (2007), Director, Solomon Islands Section (2005–07) and Second Secretary in Hanoi (1999–2002). She has also held positions in the South and South East Asia, and International Organisations and Legal Divisions. Ms Butler holds a Bachelor of Arts (Hons) from the University of Adelaide, a Masters of Arts (Foreign Affairs and Trade) from Monash University, and a Master of Arts (Applied Linguistics) from the University of New England.

**Sinclair Dinnen** is Senior Fellow in the State, Society and Governance in Melanesia Program, Research School of Pacific and Asian Studies at the Australian National University. He previously taught law at the University of Papua New Guinea, and was a Senior Research Fellow at Papua New Guinea's National Research Institute. He has undertaken extensive research and policy work in Melanesia and was an adviser to the Solomon Islands Peace Process in 2000. He is author of *Law and Order in a Weak State: Crime and Politics in Papua New Guinea* (University of Hawai'i Press, 2000); and co-editor of *Reflections on Violence in Melanesia* (Hawkins Press and Asia Pacific Press, 2000) and *A Kind of Mending—Restorative Justice in the Pacific Islands* (Pandanus Books, 2003).

**Stewart Firth** is Head of the Pacific Centre, ANU, and was Professor of Politics at the University of the South Pacific, 1998–2004. He has published widely on the history and politics of the Pacific Islands. His most recent books are *Australia in International Politics: an introduction to Australian foreign policy* (Allen & Unwin, 2005), and two edited collections, *Globalisation and Governance in the Pacific Islands* (ANU E Press, 2006) and (with Jon Fraenkel) *From Election to Coup in Fiji: the 2006 campaign and its aftermath*, Asia Pacific Press, 2007. In *Engaging our Neighbours: Towards a new relationship between Australia and the Pacific Islands* (Australian Strategic Policy Institute, 2008), he reported the deliberations of an independent task force on Australia's Pacific policy.

**Jon Fraenkel** is a Research Fellow in the State, Society & Governance in Melanesia Program, Research School of Asian and Pacific Studies at the Australian National University. He has researched widely on electoral systems in the Pacific Islands, and recently edited a special issue of *Commonwealth & Comparative Politics* on this subject. He is author of *The Manipulation of Custom: from uprising to intervention in the Solomon Islands* (Victoria University Press & Pandanus Books, 2004). His research and publications focus on the economic history of Oceania, electoral systems and contemporary Pacific politics, and he regularly covers contemporary Pacific issues in both the local and international media.

**Tarcisius Tara Kabutaulaka** is a Fellow at the East-West Center's Pacific Islands Development Program in Honolulu, Hawai'i. He holds a PhD in political science and international relations from the Australian National University. His research interest is on issues of governance, development, natural resource development, conflicts, international interventions and post-conflict reconstruction. He is also interested on the impact of the rise of China on Pacific island countries. He previously taught history and political science at the University of the South Pacific in Fiji and wrote opinion columns for regional magazines like *Islands Business* and *Pacific Magazine*. He is a Solomon Islands citizen.

**Clive Moore** has taught at James Cook University, University of Papua New Guinea and University of Queensland, where he is now Professor of Pacific and Australian History. His major and rather eclectic publications have been on Australia's Pacific Island immigrants, the Pacific labour reserve, Australian federation, masculinity, gay Queensland, New Guinea, and most recently the Solomon Islands. His most recent book is *Happy Isles in Crisis: the Historical Causes for a failing state in Solomon Islands, 1998–2004* (Asia Pacific Press, 2005). President of the Australian Association for the Advancement of Pacific Studies (2006–2008), his major current research projects are a history of Malaita Province in Solomon Islands and an historical dictionary of Solomon Islands.

**Mary-Lousie O'Callaghan** is a commentator and long-term resident of Solomon Islands. In her former capacity as the Pacific correspondent for *The Australian* newspaper she was awarded a Gold Walkley. She is the author of *Enemies Within: Papua New Guinea, Australia and the Sandline Crisis* (Doubleday, 1999) and currently works as the Public Affairs Manager for the Regional Assistance Mission to Solomon Islands.

**Jaap Timmer** is a Research Fellow in the Van Vollenhoven Institute for Law, Governance and Development at Leiden University and Project Manager for an Access to Justice Project in Indonesia. His early research explored the dynamics of cultural change and the invention of tradition in Indonesian Papua but his more recent work focuses on indigenous constitution production in Solomon Islands and Indonesian Papua, legal aid in Indonesia, and access to justice and political ecology in East Kalimantan. Until recently, Timmer worked in the State, Society and Governance in Melanesia Project at the Australian National University that supported his recent research in Solomon Islands and in Indonesia. He is the author of *Living with Intricate Futures: Order and Confusion in Imyan Worlds, Irian Jaya* (Centre for Pacific and Asian Studies, Nijmegen, 2000).

**Ian Scales** is an anthropologist and independent development consultant who has worked extensively in Solomon Islands and Bougainville. His PhD fieldwork was undertaken in Kolombangara in the Western Solomon Islands. Dr Scales is an Associate of the State Society and Governance in Melanesia Program at the Australian National University.

# Maps

---

**Map 1**          **Solomon Islands**

---

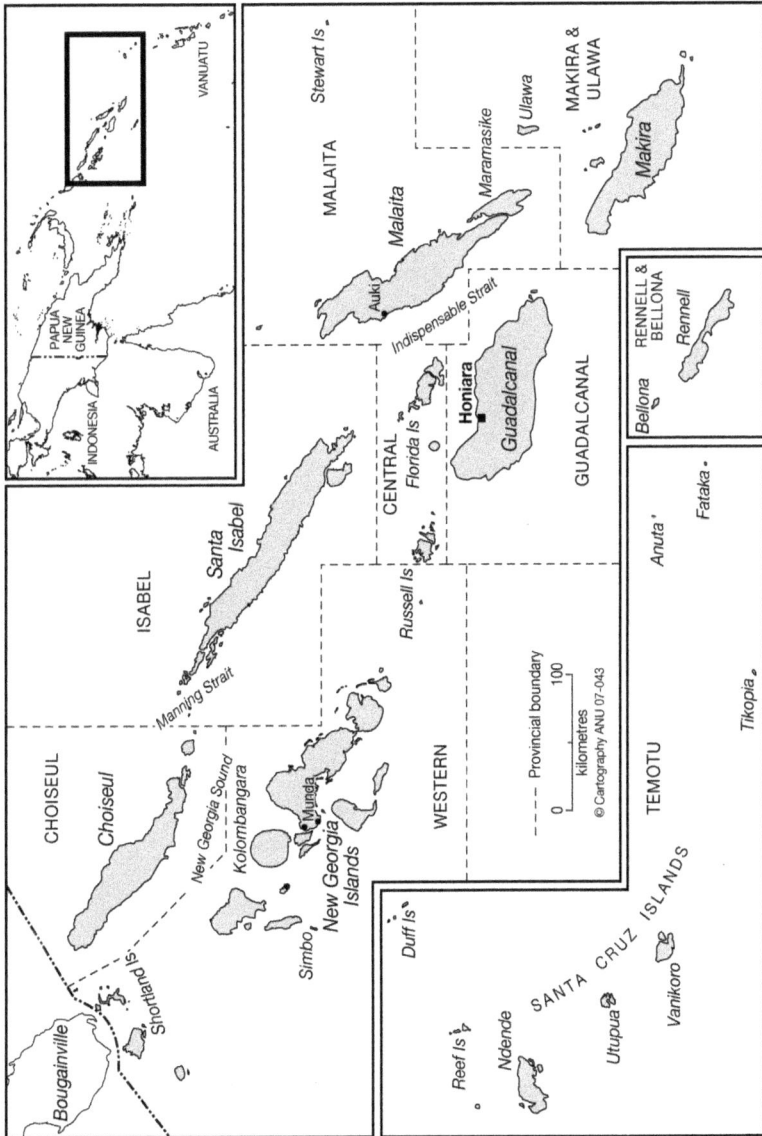

Map 2        Guadalcanal

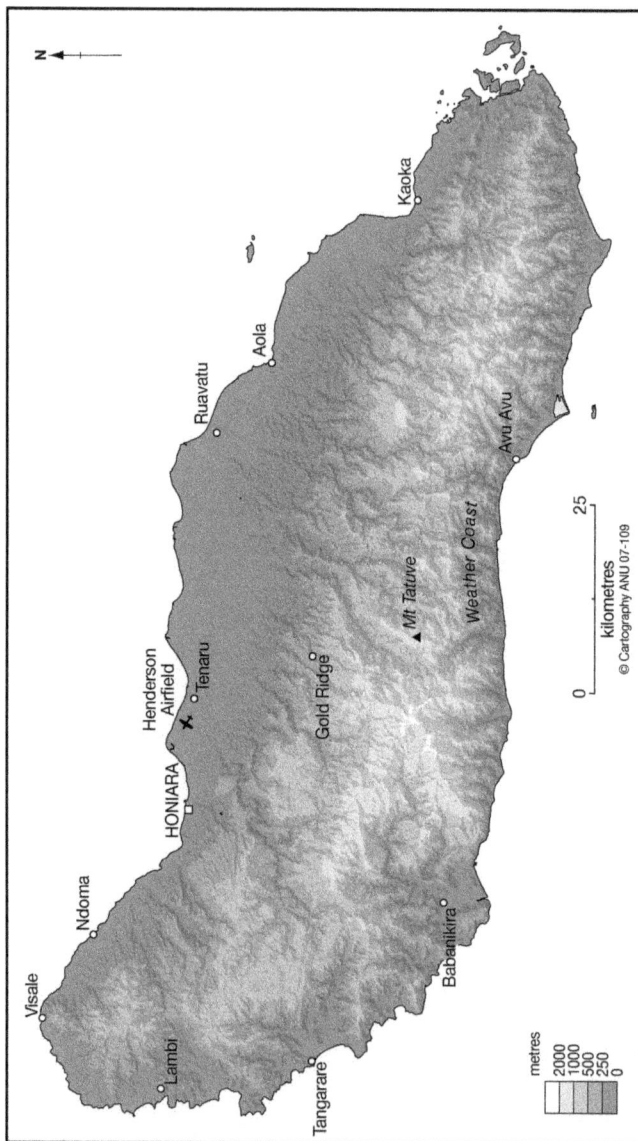

**Map 3**    **Western Province**

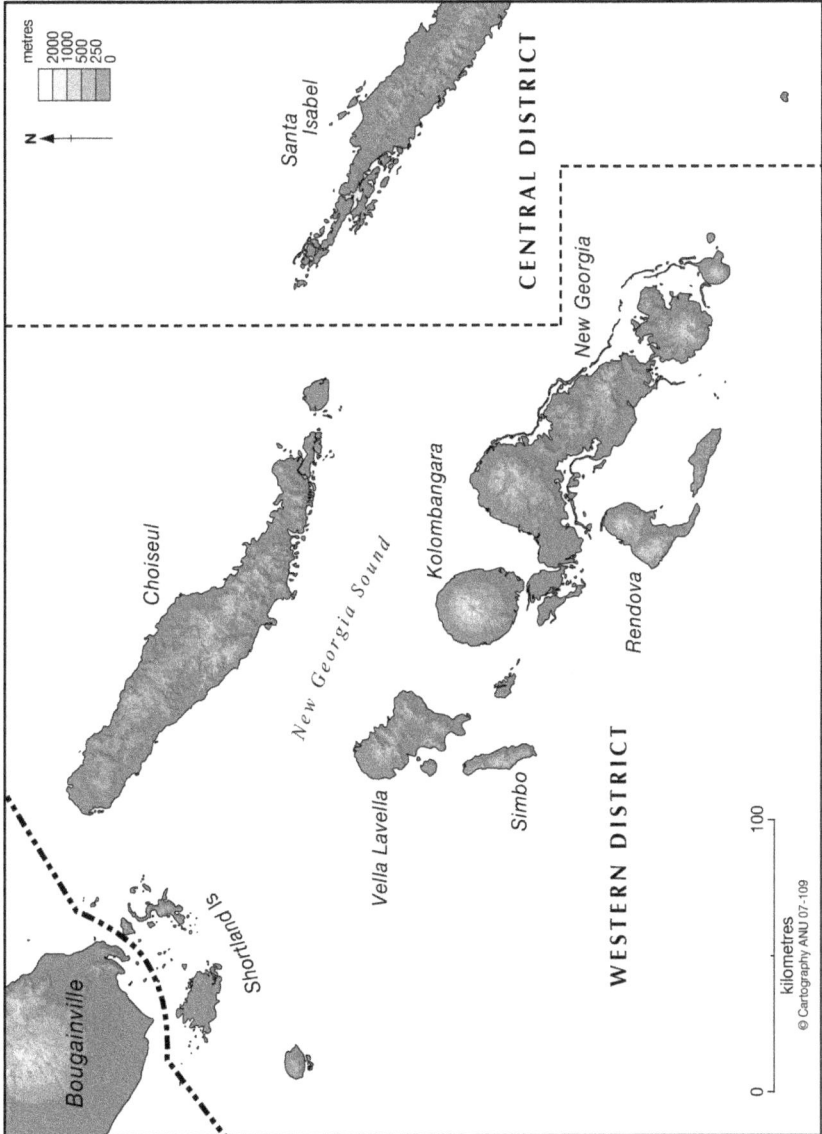

Map 4        Malaita

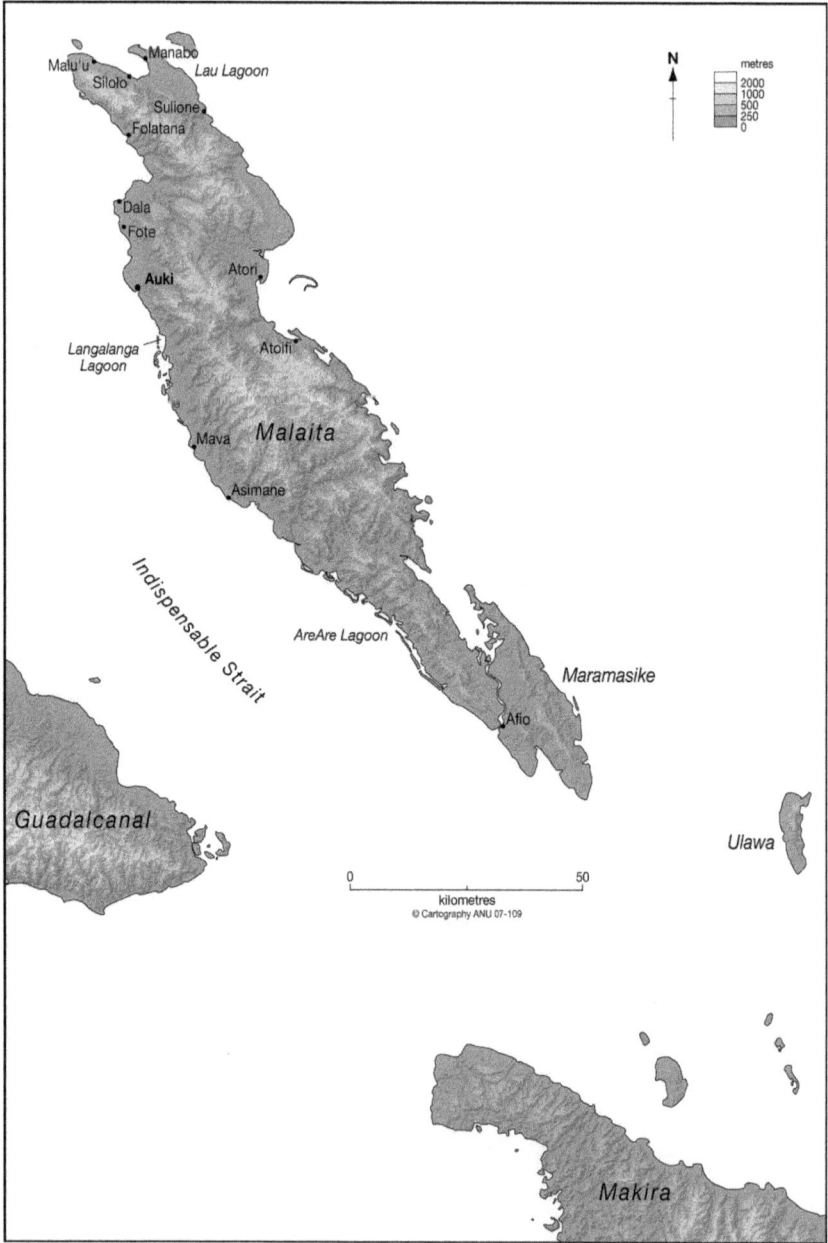

# Chapter 1

## Dilemmas of intervention and the building of state and nation

Sinclair Dinnen

Even by the momentous standards of recent times, 2006 was an eventful year in Solomon Islands. The first general elections since the deployment of the Regional Assistance Mission to the Solomon Islands (RAMSI) were held at the beginning of the year. In view of RAMSI's early achievements in restoring security and stabilising the economy, voters had high expectations of continuing progress. The elections led, in turn, to the first change of government since 2001. Despite its unpopularity, the outgoing government of Sir Allan Kemakeza (2001–06) was the first since independence to survive a full term in office. July 2006 also marked RAMSI's third anniversary.

The events most widely reported were not, however, the passing of these milestones but the public disturbances in Honiara after the announcement of Snyder Rini as prime minister-elect and the subsequent deterioration in relations between Solomon Islands and Australia under the new Sogavare government. Two days of rioting and opportunistic looting on 18 and 19 April 2006 reduced much of Honiara's Chinatown district to ashes, and overseas military and police reinforcements were needed to restore order in the national capital. For most observers, the unrest came as a complete surprise, not least because of the success of the regional mission in the previous three years. What lay behind the April disturbances and the souring in bilateral relations, and what did they signify in terms of Solomon Islands' post-conflict recovery?

After the disturbances, Rini quickly lost support among members of the new parliament and resigned after failing to secure the votes needed to survive a vote of no-confidence. In his place, Manasseh Sogavare became the new prime minister. In contrast with the compliant role adopted by Sir Allan Kemakeza in his dealings with RAMSI and the Australian government, Sogavare began to openly challenge various aspects of the mission. Many of his fellow citizens and Australian officials have viewed his more combative stance—undertaken in the name of reasserting Solomon Islands' sovereignty—as a brazen and cynical attempt to undermine reform efforts and protect corrupt political and business interests. The second half of 2006 witnessed an increasingly intense and acerbic struggle between the governments of Solomon Islands and Australia over the control, shape and future of the regional assistance mission.

This chapter locates recent developments in Solomon Islands in the larger context of state and nation building. At the core of RAMSI is an ambitious state-building exercise. Although some of the recent difficulties in Solomon Islands arise from the particularities of local circumstances and political culture, others are shared with state-building interventions in other parts of the world. This chapter examines the contemporary setting of international state building and the particular challenges presented in many post-colonial settings, as well as examining some of the common difficulties facing international interventions and the processes of institutional transfer entailed. The character of RAMSI and its reception in Solomon Islands is analysed before the discussion returns to the events of April 2006 and the ensuing struggle for the control of the mission.

## Contemporary international state-building interventions

Building or rebuilding functioning states capable of providing their citizens with a guaranteed level of physical and economic security has become one of the most pressing policy challenges in international relations today (Chesterman et al. 2005). The frequency and intensity of state-building interventions—usually, though not solely, in post-conflict situations—have increased exponentially since the end of the Cold War. Internal tensions and divisions that were effectively suppressed during that era resurfaced after its demise, as demonstrated in growing levels of, in particular, intra-state conflict and internal instability in different parts of the world (Kaldor 1999). The attacks against the United States on 11 September 2001 and the ascendancy of the 'war on terror' have given rise to powerful, though contested, arguments linking issues of security with those of state capabilities. In the process, they have imbued today's external state-building efforts with a sense of urgency and pronounced concern for security.

Whereas the international community once viewed state failure after internal conflict primarily in humanitarian terms, the war on terror embarked on by the United States and its 'coalition of the willing' has recast this phenomenon as a major threat to security. Moreover, this threat is not confined to the unfortunate citizens of the state in question but extends to those in neighbouring states and, indeed, the broader region. Building effective states is now viewed as the necessary antidote to real and potential failure and its contagious effects (Hippler 2004). Western governments contend that the principal threat to international peace and stability comes not from powerful and aggressive states but from failed and failing ones with limited capabilities.[1] The result, as Francis Fukuyama puts it, is that '[s]uddenly the ability to shore up or create from whole cloth missing state capabilities and institutions has risen to the top of the global agenda' (2004:xi).

The limited capabilities of the small independent Melanesian states of the southwest Pacific, including Solomon Islands, have been apparent for many years, not least to Pacific islanders themselves. They have manifested themselves in the difficulties experienced in fulfilling the most basic tasks of modern statehood, including the maintenance of internal security, the provision of essential services (such as health, education, transport and communication) and prudent economic management. International development assistance from Australia and other donors has been directed at a wide range of capacity-building activities with Pacific island states throughout most of the post-independence period. Despite substantial amounts of aid, donors have been disappointed with the limited impact of traditional approaches to development assistance in strengthening weak recipient institutions and improving living standards. As well as reflecting changes in the international strategic environment, Australia's more robust engagement with its Pacific neighbours in recent years has been driven by the need to realise more tangible outcomes in transforming the capabilities of these states. One feature of this more hands-on approach has been the direct insertion of Australian personnel—including police and seconded public servants—into 'line', as well as advisory, positions with key government agencies and departments in recipient countries. In addition to Solomon

Islands, this approach is evident, albeit on a lesser scale, in Australia's efforts to strengthen Nauru and in the Enhanced Cooperation Program (ECP) in Papua New Guinea under which Australian officials—including, for a short time, Australian police—have been deployed to build the capacity of recipient government agencies.

The influential report on Solomon Islands by the Australian Strategic Policy Institute, *Our Failing Neighbour*, offers an early articulation of the strategic thinking behind Canberra's changing policy. Published several weeks before RAMSI's deployment in July 2003, the report labelled Solomon Islands a failing state and warned of the dire security and humanitarian consequences if vigorous and prompt remedial action was not taken. It proposed a 'sustained and comprehensive multinational effort' to undertake rehabilitation work with the consent of Solomon Islands. The restoration of law and order would provide the initial focus, followed by a long-term state-building exercise designed to 'build new political structures and security institutions and address underlying social and economic problems' (Australian Strategic Policy Institute 2003:39).

While the prospect of Solomon Islands becoming an incubator for terrorism and transnational crime is, to say the least, remote (Greener-Barcham and Barcham 2006), positioning the troubled archipelago within this larger strategic framework bolstered the initial case for intervention, particularly among a domestic Australian audience with little familiarity or interest in the travails of Pacific island micro-states. Beyond the emotive rhetoric of failed states and terrorist threats, RAMSI has focused on issues of governance and, in particular, strengthening the capacities of key state institutions. The intervention has also provided an important source of learning for further engagements, notably in the larger and more challenging context of Papua New Guinea. Australian Prime Minister, John Howard, revealed another strand informing Canberra's change in policy in his reference to Australia's special responsibilities towards the struggling states in 'our patch' (Sydney Morning Herald 2003b). Not only was Australia expected to provide leadership as the major regional power, there was the risk that others, with China and Taiwan already active in the Pacific, might adopt a more prominent role if Canberra did not.

Although broad agreement exists about the potential consequences of lack of state capabilities, there is less certainty about how to build effective states in divided societies. As Payne (2006:606) states, 'The dirty little secret of nation building is that *no one knows how to do it.*' In the literature generated by recent interventions, the terms 'state building' and 'nation building' are often used interchangeably. This has confused different, though related, processes of political development. Most interventions in the name of nation building have focused on strengthening state institutions, or, in some cases, are aimed at achieving political goals of regime change or transition to democratic government. They have relatively little to do with nation building in the literal sense of developing a shared sense of identity or community among the population of a given state. Using these terms interchangeably has also obscured the highly contingent relationship between nation and state in historical processes of state formation and consolidation. These processes have complex, diverse and lengthy histories in different parts of the world, dating back, at least, to the emergence of the first European nation-states.

## Post-colonial state building

Although it is unwise to generalise given the wide variations across time and space, building the modern nation-state in Europe was different to the more recent experiences in much of the so-called developing world, including the Melanesian states of the southwest Pacific. In the former case, processes of state formation often took place over centuries rather than years, they were not the outcome of well-intentioned international interventions and they frequently entailed extensive conflict as the forces of centralisation confronted and overcame rival sources of power at local and regional levels (Tilly 1992; Cohen et al. 1981). In addition nationalism, constructed around the symbols and ideals of shared community and identity, was a major force in the development of many European states (Guibernau 1996). Nationalism, in this broad sense, often preceded the establishment of states. For example, it contributed to the unification of Italy in 1861 and Germany in 1871, as well as to the subsequent break-up of Austria–Hungary in 1918. The two most widely cited cases of successful international nation building in the twentieth century were the reconstruction of West Germany and Japan by the United States and its allies after World War II (Dobbins et al. 2003). Both countries, however, had long traditions of nationalism and strong state institutions. They were already ethnic and cultural communities, as well as political states, and intervention was primarily about the re-legitimation of their states on a democratic basis.

While the experience of a select few European powers continues to shape much Western thinking about states, the establishment of states in other parts of the world has followed a very different historical trajectory. Many developing states have their origins in the era of colonial expansion by major European powers during the eighteenth, nineteenth and the first half of the twentieth centuries. In the process of annexing large swathes of territory around the world, colonial powers created arbitrary borders and imposed external systems of governance with little, if any, consideration as to their fit with existing polities and other forms of indigenous social organisation. Colonial states were external creations with (initially, at any rate) an inherently non-democratic character.

The building of elaborate state structures and social infrastructure often did not take place until very late in many colonial projects. Before the accelerated institutional modernisation that typically preceded independence, local participation in formal political processes was limited and any hint of emerging nationalism was viewed as a threat to the maintenance of colonial order. Where nationalist movements arose, they were often anti-colonial in character, provoked by opposition to intervention rather than its engineered outcome. Many former colonies were ill prepared for the challenges of independent statehood that arrived in the second half of the twentieth century. In Solomon Islands and Papua New Guinea, the timing of independence was almost as abrupt and unilateral as the original acts of colonial annexation a century before. Modern state institutions began to be assembled only well after World War II, with, as a result, shallow foundations in the local environments they were grafted on to. This lack of embeddedness was manifested not only in limited capabilities as modern states, it was obvious in the low levels of legitimacy accorded them by many of their new 'citizens'. Many post-colonial states were not only weak in an institutional sense, they were incomplete—what some scholars have termed quasi states (Jackson 1990)—with a limited presence in parts of their territories and incapable of delivering basic services, such as education, to all eligible citizens (Nelson 2006). Colonial borders were retained; formal economies remained skewed towards the interests of metropolitan powers and the infrastructure and human resources required to operate a complex bureaucratic state were often in scarce supply. For example, in Solomon Islands, there were only about a dozen university graduates at the time of independence in 1978 (Bennett 2002:7).

There was little sense of shared political community, beyond a tiny urban élite, capable of uniting the citizens of the new state of Solomon Islands. For such citizens, living predominantly in rural communities, bonds of kinship, shared language and ties to ancestral land, along with Christianity, were more likely to constitute the basis for individual identities and allegiance than abstract notions of citizenship or membership of the modern state. Localism prevailed over nationalism in virtually every sphere of social, economic and, significantly, political life. In the absence of a sizeable and unifying anti-colonial movement, formal independence in Solomon Islands—as in many parts of Africa, Asia and the Pacific—created what was, in effect, a state without a nation. Nations, like states, have to be made; they do not exist naturally. Nation building in a country such as Solomon Islands is complicated by the sheer scale of its internal diversity (with more than 84 languages spoken) and its fragmented topography as an archipelago of about 1,000 islands. Jourdan (1995) identifies the most likely 'stepping stones to national consciousness' as the education system; Pijin, the lingua franca; and the growth and spread of an urban-centred popular culture.

The absence of a sense of shared identity makes it hard to fashion the cohesive national community needed for the development of effective and durable state institutions. According to Borgerhoff (2006:104), the 'double task' of state and nation building aspires 'to unify the national community within the state container, with the objective of political stability'. As in many other post-colonial settings, in Solomon Islands, processes of state and nation building have had to be undertaken simultaneously. Unfortunately, they have often worked against each other in practice, thereby contributing to a growing crisis of state legitimacy and the weakening of state institutions in the post-independence period.

## Practical difficulties of international state building

Despite the complex historical reasons behind variations in state capabilities, the latest wave of international state building has been undertaken primarily as a technical and problem-solving exercise. There is scant evidence of learning from the long and diverse history of state making in different parts of the world. The scale and urgency of today's interventions inevitably divert attention away from the need for a sound analytical understanding of the processes involved and the particular ways in which local and global forces have shaped the capabilities of individual states. Yet, unless we know something of the existing state, we are going to have an extremely tough time trying to improve it. Much of the policy discourse has an ahistorical and formulaic flavour, approaching state building in much the same way one might approach the repair of a faulty object. There is little questioning of what state failure or fragility really means and how it has come about in the country concerned. An unquestioning belief in the universality of state structures and the technology of institutional transfer underlies the confidence among international state builders that even the most troublesome state can be rendered effective. The possibility that such a noble goal might not be possible through external intervention, or that such intervention might end up doing more harm than good, is rarely considered. A booming global industry of technical experts devotes its time and energy to the construction of new states and the repair of faulty ones.

In his critique of international state building, Chandler (2006) argues that it constitutes a form of 'empire in denial', allowing Western powers to surreptitiously create what are, in effect, 'phantom states' that depend on international supervision and lack the capacity for self-government. He notes 'the highly depoliticised nature of the discussions of state-capacity building, where concerns of stability and regulation are discussed in a narrow technical and functionalist framework' (Chandler 2006:5–6). Deep-seated political and developmental problems in post-conflict and otherwise fragile national settings have increasingly been recast as technical and administrative challenges. Institutional solutions are almost always derived from donor countries. The current enterprise of state building is founded on the assumed merits and feasibility of one-way processes of institutional transfer from (strong) donor to (weak) recipient countries. Earlier critiques of modernisation theory and, in particular, its underlying premise as to the inexorable and linear direction of historical progress, have been forgotten. Today's cadre of international state builders appears intent on modernising in its own image.

There are many practical difficulties attaching to these processes of institutional transfer. These include the task of managing processes of transfer, as well as more profound questions relating to the appropriateness and sustainability of the institutions being transferred. Another is how the interventions that provide the context for these transfers can be reconciled—in theory and practice—with traditional notions of national sovereignty. As is borne out by Australia's recent experience in Solomon Islands, one of the biggest dilemmas is how to manage successfully relations between external administrations and elected domestic governments.

Although increasing resources have been devoted to international state building, the results of these efforts have been patchy at best (Pei and Kasper 2003). Even in cases viewed as successful (as in Timor-Leste and Solomon Islands) subsequent set-backs, such as the disturbances that occurred in both these countries in April 2006, have led to the qualifying of earlier optimism. Despite this record, the international response continues to be demands for more of the same: more interventions, more institutional transfer and building and more foreign personnel. Francis Fukuyama (2004) recently outlined some of the most common difficulties with institutional transfers in current state-building interventions. Most of these are evident in varying degrees in the Solomon Islands case.

A major issue relates to the fit (or lack thereof) between introduced institutions and the local conditions prevailing in recipient countries. Just as human recipients can reject donated organs, recipient countries can reject institutional transplants. Generally speaking, the greater the social and economic disparities between donor and recipient societies, the less likely it is that such transplants will succeed. Important matters here relate to institutional design and the appropriateness of external models to local circumstances. Questions about the apparent lack of fit between indigenous and Western institutions of governance have long been a source of contention in Solomon Islands, as they have in many parts of the Pacific, and are one of the regularly identified root causes underlying the recent crisis (Morgan and McLeod 2006). Whether these are genuine sources of discontent or simply a pretext for mobilising opposition to intervention, it is difficult for international state builders to do other than promote their own institutional solutions, particularly when most have no previous local experience or knowledge and are deployed for relatively short periods. This tendency to be guided by 'home' experience is likely to be accentuated further by the dominance of foreign personnel and sizeable numbers of public servants seconded from overseas government agencies and departments.

A second and related set of difficulties concerns issues of ownership and the mechanisms of transfer. As development practitioners have long been aware, local ownership is critical for successful institutional transfer. How do international actors generate local demand for reform? This issue continues to perplex development specialists who have traditionally been more concerned with supplying solutions than with stimulating local demand for them. There is also the very real dilemma of how donors can engage in state building in fragile environments without simultaneously 'crowding out' or marginalising local actors who ultimately will have to take responsibility for running the state. This is an obvious challenge in situations where there has been, in effect, no functioning government and where large numbers of foreign officials working to often unrealistic time frames and schooled in foreign operating systems feel as though they have to perform many of the functions themselves if the job is to be done. Early in the Solomon Islands intervention, Kabutaulaka (2004) warned that the dominance of RAMSI in decision making could lead to a debilitating dependency or a perception of foreign occupation. In a later paper (Kabutaulaka 2006), he referred to post-conflict Solomon Islands as a 'crowded stage', comprising a bewildering array of international actors with multiple, sometimes conflicting, agendas and with relatively little space left for local players. The capacity-building paradox is that the more substantial the intervention is, the greater is the risk that it ends up sucking out local capacity rather than building it (Ignatieff 2003).

A third set of issues relates to the challenges external interveners face in charting a course through the unfamiliar and troubled local political contexts where these engagements typically occur. Despite the technical and depoliticised self-image of international state building, the intrusive and unsettling character of such interventions reveals them as profoundly political enterprises that deliberately seek to challenge and transform existing power relations. Just as there were winners and losers in the conflict that gave rise to the intervention (Dinnen 2002), there will be those who stand to gain from the intervention and those who stand to lose. In this respect, no intervention can be politically neutral. The much longer history of interaction between Solomon Islanders and successive waves of interveners (entailing alternating patterns of accommodation and resistance) is, in many respects, echoed in current relations between Solomon Islands' political leadership and the regional assistance mission (and its Australian sponsors).

The focus on restoring law and order is shared by all of today's post-conflict interventions and is manifested in the growing prominence of issues of policing and criminal justice. Rebuilding the security apparatus of weak or failed states through strengthening the rule of law reflects international thinking about the importance of internal security as a prerequisite for all other aspects of state building and development. International systems fail to acknowledge, however, the highly contested character of historical processes of state consolidation and tend to respond to any sign of conflict as a lapse from the normal condition of peace. In asking today's fragile states to consolidate without conflict, they are expecting those states to do something never asked of their European forerunners. Concentrating on suppressing the manifestations of conflict can also mean neglecting their underlying causes. International insistence on rule-of-law solutions in post-conflict settings such as Solomon Islands regularly attracts criticism that the root causes are not being addressed. In addition, the state-centric character of international conceptions of the rule of law can obscure the important role of non-state institutions in the maintenance (and not just the disruption) of order, as well as the resolution of local conflicts, in countries such as Solomon Islands.

## The Solomon Islands crisis and the regional intervention

RAMSI was deployed in July 2003 in response to a plea for help from the Solomon Islands government. In the preceding five years, the country had been gripped by a progressively debilitating internal crisis that manifested itself in serious lawlessness in some areas, the breakdown of essential government services, closure of major commercial enterprises and impending national bankruptcy (Fraenkel 2004; Moore 2004). What began as tensions between the indigenous inhabitants of Guadalcanal and settlers from the adjacent island of Malaita, developed into a low-level armed conflict between opposing ethnic militias and, in its later stages, into a process of 'instrumentalisation of disorder' whereby criminality became a key political instrument (Chabal and Daloz 1999). The latter culminated in the effective capture and ransacking of the state by a relatively small cohort of corrupt leaders, ex-militants and renegade police officers.

The police fractured along ethnic lines. Rogue officers, in collaboration with Malaitan militants, raided armouries in Auki and Honiara and mounted a *de facto* coup in June 2000. After the Australian and New Zealand-brokered Townsville Peace Agreement (TPA) in October 2000, which helped avert an all-out civil war, the Guadalcanal militants—who had forcibly displaced about 30,000, mainly Malaitan, settlers from rural Guadalcanal—turned in on themselves in a series of violent internecine struggles. The most serious bloodshed occurred in the southern Weather Coast and involved the notorious militia leader Harold Keke. By early 2003, it was clear that the beleaguered and heavily compromised government of Sir Allan Kemakeza was incapable on its own of halting the deteriorating situation.

Having declined previous requests for intervention on the grounds that the crisis was an internal matter to be resolved by Solomon Islands authorities, the Australian government agreed to lead a regional assistance mission. Although leadership and most of the resources were provided by Australia, the intervention was undertaken on a regional rather than bilateral basis, largely to enhance its legitimacy. After agreement among Pacific island foreign ministers, it was mobilised under the auspices of the Pacific Islands Forum and, specifically, the Biketawa Declaration on Mutual Assistance of 2000. RAMSI marked the beginning of Australia's new robust model of regional engagement. Labelled as 'cooperative intervention' by the Australian Foreign Minister, Alexander Downer (2003), RAMSI has been described as having 'a unique kind of authority in the world of state building—it has substantial practical influence but works with and inside the Solomon Islands Government, which remains the repository of executive, legislative and judicial authority' (Fullilove 2006b:33).

The mission's design drew on previous Australian and international peace-keeping and post-conflict reconstruction experiences—such as in Kosovo and, in particular, East Timor—but added some new features. With a large military contingent as back-up, the intervention was led initially by police. Approximately 330 police made up the Participating Police Force (PPF) and were drawn mainly from the Australian Federal Police (AFP), but included smaller contingents from Australian state forces, New Zealand and other forum member states.[2] Security was restored quickly and without bloodshed in Honiara and a police presence was extended to other parts of the country. Key militia leaders were arrested and large numbers of weapons and ammunition were removed from the community. By February 2004, more than 50 police officers (including two deputy commissioners) had been arrested and charged with 285 offences (Dinnen et al. 2006:99). More than 400 officers (approximately 25 per cent of the total police force) were removed from the force (Dinnen et al. 2006). Deployed originally in an executive capacity, the PPF has switched progressively into an advisory and capacity-building role, although it remains active in certain operational areas.

The police-building component was always intended as a gateway to a more ambitious exercise aimed at reconstructing the Solomon Islands State (Peake and Brown 2005). As former RAMSI Special Coordinator James Batley (2005) noted, '[a]t its core, RAMSI is a state-building exercise.' Substantial Australian resources have been committed to rebuilding the police force, strengthening the law and justice sector, implementing a range of governance programs, improving financial management and undertaking economic reform. In addition to police personnel, RAMSI includes seconded Australian public servants and private consultants in key departments and agencies of the Solomon Islands government. Overall coordination is exercised by a Special Coordinator's Office in Honiara, headed by a senior Australian diplomat, and through a high-level inter-departmental committee in Canberra.

The speed and peaceful manner in which RAMSI restored law and order and essential services and stabilised government finances attracted considerable praise (Fullilove 2006a). These impressive achievements provided a welcome contrast with the generally disappointing results from other international interventions. RAMSI was commended as 'a model for future deployments' (Watson 2005:37). The disturbances in April 2006, however, and the subsequent deterioration in relations between Australia and Solomon Islands highlighted the premature character of initial appraisals. Even before the April unrest there had been set-backs. An early example was the fatal shooting of a young Australian Protective Services officer, Adam Dunning, while on patrol in Honiara in December 2004. The security clamp-down that followed led to complaints of heavy-handed policing tactics, and gave rise to the first court action to test the constitutionality of the immunity provisions provided to foreign police personnel under the Facilitation of International Assistance Act. Although this and another constitutional challenge were ultimately unsuccessful, they generated anxiety among senior

RAMSI officials. Australian police serving in Papua New Guinea under the ECP had to be withdrawn after a successful challenge in the Supreme Court in May 2005 (Dinnen et al. 2006:103).

While there have undoubtedly been accomplishments (see O'Callaghan, this volume), the progress of capacity development has been slow and uneven. Despite its prominence in the work of post-conflict reconstruction, capacity development remains an imprecise and long-term undertaking. Almost three years after RAMSI's initial deployment, the Australian Commissioner of the Solomon Islands Police Force (SIPF) acknowledged that his force remained 'inadequately prepared and is still not properly equipped to perform the vast majority of policing functions throughout the Solomon Islands'.[3] International police-building experience confirms the uncertainties and slowness of this kind of work (Bayley 2006).

The majority of Solomon Islanders have been supportive of the intervention throughout the past four years. Memories of the insecurity and paralysis of government that preceded RAMSI's deployment remain fresh and many fear the consequences of a premature departure. Criticisms have nevertheless been made and many of these are heard in other interventions. Most have called for adaptation of the mission rather than its total withdrawal. While some concerns have been addressed, others are trickier to deal with. Outright opposition has been confined to a relatively small number of people, such as the ex-militants and separatists in North Malaita who have accused the mission of anti-Malaita bias (see Allen, this volume). Although these views are not shared widely, indigenous sovereignty movements with a strong antipathy towards foreign interference (real or perceived) have long histories in parts of the country (see Timmer, this volume).

The sheer scale of RAMSI in such a small country has predictably given rise to concerns about the dominance of foreign personnel in key government agencies and the risk that Solomon Islands officials could become marginalised. This was the gist of the plea by the Solomon Islands Christian Association (SICA) that RAMSI should respect the need for indigenous leadership and resist the temptation to provide all the answers.[4] Enhancing Solomon Islander participation, particularly in the early stages of the mission, proved difficult for many reasons, not least owing to the shortage of suitably qualified local personnel to take up senior positions.

Concerns about Australian dominance reflect the fact that Australia has provided the bulk of personnel and resources for the mission. Other participating countries have not been in a position to make substantial contributions. A shortage of relevant skills in Pacific island countries has been a significant factor. Indeed, relatively few specialised personnel (from any source country) can claim to be experts in Solomon Islands cultures and languages. RAMSI officials have become increasingly aware of these difficulties and have tried to broaden the regional mix of mission personnel within these practical constraints, while trying to develop more appropriate training for Australian personnel. Concerns about the considerable disparities in pay and conditions between foreign and local personnel have been a source of resentment in some quarters, as they are in all international engagements.

The early focus by mission police on the perpetrators of violence during the so-called tensions prompted criticism that RAMSI was less rigorous in its pursuit of more influential figures, the so-called 'big-fish', widely suspected of having manipulated the conflict for their own political and economic advantage.[5] Despite a series of high-profile arrests and prosecutions during the first two years, including five former cabinet ministers,[6] this sentiment continued well into 2006 and contributed to the anger after Rini's election as prime minister. Indeed, while anti-RAMSI sentiments were not a significant cause of the April unrest, negative feelings were evident in the deliberate targeting of PPF vehicles, as well as in some of the graffiti left behind in the ruins of Chinatown (Allen 2006 and this volume).

As in other cases where interveners are forced to work closely with unpopular domestic governments, a major challenge has been trying to balance the need for political stability, on the one hand, with the appearance of impartial law enforcement, on the other. This was particularly so during the Kemakeza administration, given that many of its members (including the prime minister himself) were widely believed to have been involved in corruption and tension-related wrongdoing. Had all the allegations been acted on, there would have been few leaders left to run the government. Interveners such as RAMSI run the unavoidable risk of becoming tainted in the public eye through their association with discredited governments and leaders. This was evident in respect of the mission's relationship with Kemakeza and his short-lived successor, Rini.

Owing to its high visibility and coercive role, the policing component of RAMSI has attracted more than its fair share of criticism. For example, in early 2005, Terry Brown, the outspoken Anglican Bishop of Malaita, raised a number of concerns about the mission's policing and security activities (Brown 2005). These included the alleged failure to deal with minor crime in the provinces; the Honiara-centred focus; the high turnover of RAMSI personnel; understaffing of provincial police stations; detachment from local people; lack of communication with crime victims; and the shortage of magistrates and consequent delays in court hearings. He warned that without improving its relations with ordinary Solomon Islanders, RAMSI risked being seen as an occupying army.

Although viewed popularly as a unitary entity, RAMSI is a multi-faceted exercise, comprising many different agencies and actors. It is also a dynamic mission that has undergone various phases, ranging from initial peace-keeping and stabilisation to longer-term capacity development with a broad array of local institutions and stakeholders. Its complexity and evolving character are often difficult to discern, let alone fathom, by those outside its innermost circles. In the absence of a well-understood mandate, it is easy for misunderstandings to arise. The mission is also susceptible to deliberate misrepresentation by opponents. Officials regularly point out that certain issues fall beyond the mission's mandate and can be addressed only by local stakeholders. These include the sensitive matter of reconciliation in conflict-affected areas, which, according to mission officials, is the responsibility of community leaders with the necessary local knowledge and standing. The substantial resources available to the mission, especially when compared with those of the Solomon Islands government, have heightened local expectations about its ability to tackle all manner of outstanding problems. Declarations that certain matters fall within the remit of domestic authorities can be interpreted (or misrepresented) as either a failure to appreciate their significance and/or a deliberate unwillingness to help.

High popular expectations have also contributed to feelings among some critics that RAMSI has failed to go beyond the manifestations of conflict to the deeper sources of stress that have undermined the political and social fabric of Solomon Islands in recent years. These are often referred to cumulatively as the 'root causes' of the conflict and, although they include the ethnic tensions between Guadalcanal and Malaita, they cover a myriad other factors, including the poor policies of successive governments; corruption; regional disparities in resources and income; the poor fit between indigenous and introduced institutions; land exploitation; unresolved historical grievances; and long-standing dissatisfaction with the centralisation of political power in Honiara and neglect of the island provinces and rural areas where most Solomon Islanders live (Morgan and McLeod 2006:416).

An Eminent Persons' Group from the Pacific Islands Forum (2005) echoed many of these concerns in its findings of a review of the mission in 2005. Acknowledging RAMSI's considerable achievements, the review also made a number of recommendations concerning its future operation. These included the need to adopt a more development-oriented approach with Solomon Islands as an equal partner; increasing Pacific island representation in the mission's policing and civilian components; developing a clearer strategy for utilising local counterparts; addressing the underlying causes of the conflict; making greater efforts in the areas of reconciliation and rehabilitation; using local chiefs in conflict resolution; improving consultation between central and provincial governments, as well as with non-government organisations; and implementing more effective donor coordination (Pacific Islands Forum 2005). RAMSI officials have subsequently tried to address, within existing constraints, most of these recommendations.

## The April unrest and subsequent developments

The angry response to the announcement of the prime minister-elect on 18 April 2006 indicated, among other things, the deep-seated frustration felt by many Solomon Islanders with the workings of the formal political process. Popular expectations of a decisive break with discredited politics and leaders were high. Two days of rioting and looting injured about 50 police personnel and unknown numbers of civilians, as well as causing extensive damage to Honiara's commercial centre (Hawes 2006).

Disappointment with the naming of the prime minister-elect provided the immediate setting for the disorderly scenes outside the national parliament, but there were many other factors involved. In Solomon Islands, as in Papua New Guinea and Vanuatu, members of the new parliament elect a prime minister in what is, in effect, a second election from which the ordinary voter is excluded. Successful candidates do not require a commanding majority or indeed any support. In the absence of strong party affiliations or significant policy differences, loose blocs of members coalesce around individual leaders rather than ideology. There is usually frenetic manoeuvring by smaller groups seeking to tilt the balance in favour of a particular bloc. The common goal among new members is to secure a place on the government benches and, preferably, a ministerial portfolio. As several elections have demonstrated, the ease with which parliamentarians can change allegiances has meant that prime ministers are particularly vulnerable to outside influences on their colleagues, including overt bribery. Financial and other inducements provided by Asian business interests are believed to have fuelled the formation of new governments in recent years (see Moore, this volume). Given its patently non-transparent and unpredictable character, this process invariably generates intense levels of popular speculation and rumour. The election of Rini—deputy prime minister in the previous government and discredited in the eyes of many—came as a shock to voters and was also taken as evidence of the hidden hand of Asian-backed 'money politics', hence the targeting of Chinatown.

The SIPF and its mentors in the PPF were clearly caught off-guard by the scale and intensity of the disturbances. Public order was restored only after military and police reinforcements were flown in from Australia, New Zealand and Fiji. Several former senior SIPF officers contested claims by the Australian commissioner that there had been no prior intelligence indicating trouble, pointing out that the announcement of a new prime minister should routinely merit special policing measures and that Chinatown was especially vulnerable in the case of unrest in the capital.[7] The speaker criticised mission police for exacerbating the situation by using tear-gas outside parliament (ABC 2006a). Many others viewed the disturbances and lack of police preparedness as evidence of more fundamental shortcomings with the regional mission, including the large communication gap between its personnel and the Solomon Islands population.[8] While most external commentaries and media reports applied a law-enforcement lens (for example, the role of the police and other actors in fomenting or responding to the disturbances), the broader significance of the unrest and what followed lay in the changing political dynamics in Solomon Islands and their implications for the future of the regional mission.

The April unrest tarnished the aura of inviolability that had grown up around RAMSI's early achievements (see Allen, this volume). In doing so, it bolstered the confidence of local critics of the mission, while probably adding to their ranks. The ransacking and destruction of a large part of the national capital seemingly under the helpless gaze of the SIPF and its regional advisers also raised questions about the substantial police-building component of the mission. In addition to spontaneous expressions of anger, there were rumours of deliberate manipulation of the disorder by certain leaders and political interests. These suspicions appeared to be confirmed when two MPs were arrested and charged with inciting the riots. Their detention, however, led to Rini's political opponents accusing mission police of partisanship by depriving them of two critical votes in the proposed vote of no-confidence against Rini (see ABC 2006b). These perceptions, refuted vigorously by the police, were accentuated by the fact that the SIPF commissioner was a seconded member of the AFP. As long-time Solomon Islands observer and current RAMSI employee Mary-Louise O'Callaghan remarked, 'when you've got an Australian Federal policeman as the Police Commissioner of the local police, it's much easier for those accusations to be made.'[9]

The immediate political crisis after Rini's election receded when he failed to secure the numbers needed to survive the vote of no-confidence and resigned. He was replaced by Manasseh Sogavare, who had shifted to the opposition camp on the eve of the vote in return for an agreement to nominate him as prime minister (see Alasia, this volume). Viewed by many Solomon Islanders as the lesser of two evils, Sogavare's assumption of power was a source of disquiet among RAMSI officials and the Australian government. A leaked email written by a senior RAMSI official described the choice between Rini and Sogavare as prime minister as 'depressing'.[10] Sogavare, who had served as prime minister after the 2000 coup, was well known for his critical stance towards the regional mission.[11] His initial assumption of office in 2000 had been facilitated through his close association with elements of the Malaitan Eagle Force (MEF) and influential power-brokers, including Charles Dausabea. Despite hailing from Choiseul in Western Province, Sogavare was seen as being closer to the Malaitan side of the tensions, and appeared to share the antipathy towards RAMSI held by many former Malaitan militants (Allen 2006). Conversely, many Guadalcanal people viewed him with suspicion.

Shortly after being sworn in, Sogavare called for a review of the mission, a clear exit strategy and increased participation of Solomon Islanders in critical decision making (see ABC 2006c). His most controversial act, however, was to announce the appointment of two detained parliamentarians, both members of the prime minister's political faction, as members of his new cabinet. Dausabea was given the sensitive police and national security portfolio, while his fellow accused, Nelson Ne'e, was appointed Minister for Tourism and Culture (The Canberra Times 2006). Australian Foreign Minister, Alexander Downer, expressed his government's deep concern, providing the opening salvo in the increasingly acrimonious exchanges between the two leaders in the months to come (ABC 2006d).

Having been deployed at the request of the Solomon Islands government, RAMSI is dependent on the acquiescence and cooperation of whatever government is in power (see Butler, this volume); this leaves it especially vulnerable to shifting local political allegiances (Wainwright 2005:5). Events since April 2006 have demonstrated the extent of this vulnerability. Former Prime Minister Sir Allan Kemakeza had gone out of his way to accommodate the presence and demands of the regional mission and its principal sponsors, appreciating, no doubt, that RAMSI provided his administration with a legitimacy that it patently lacked among ordinary Solomon Islanders. Indeed, the tacit support of RAMSI was a critical factor in the unprecedented longevity of the Kemakeza administration (see Fraenkel, this volume). Sogavare, on the other hand, had signalled well in advance that he would adopt a very different approach. Cloaking himself in the mantle of defender of Solomon Islands sovereignty, he adopted an openly combative approach, advocating greater local control of the mission and the reduction of Australian dominance. Underlying his personal style has been an unusual degree of suspicion about the possibility of external manipulation of Solomon Islands affairs. Speaking on national radio on 8 May, he stated that

> Australia seemed to have used the provisions of the current partnership as a licence to infiltrate almost all sections of the public sector. By their high-level engagement in senior posts within the government we have a situation where foreign nationals have direct and unrestricted access to the nerve centre of Solomon Islands public administration, security and leadership. This is an unhealthy situation (reported in the *Green Left Weekly* 2006).

Sogavare's rhetoric might have struck a chord with those who felt threatened or otherwise marginalised by RAMSI's dominant presence in most sectors of government; however, it also caused alarm among many of his fellow citizens about the practical consequences of a diminished mission or premature withdrawal. For his critics, Sogavare's assertions of sovereignty concealed a less benign personal agenda aimed at undermining RAMSI's efforts to strengthen the rule of law and the accountability of state institutions that had been eroded after years of corrupt and incompetent leadership.

The prime minister's proposal to revise aspects of the mission, including areas of financial management, met with vigorous opposition from Australia, New Zealand and others, who saw it as a way for politicians to regain unfettered control of public funds and, as such, a recipe for institutionalised corruption. Downer argued that the mission was an integrated package that could not be cherry-picked by the Solomon Islands government (see Appendix 1).[12] Relations deteriorated further after Sogavare announced the setting up of a commission of inquiry into the April disturbances (see Appendix 2). The terms of reference included directions to evaluate the police response, investigate the role of MPs and, most controversially, to examine the circumstances surrounding the detention of the two MPs charged with inciting the riots, in order to establish whether this 'was reasonably justified and not politically motivated' (Solomon Islands Government 2006). While the last term was later dropped, it was viewed by many as a crude attempt to undermine the case pending against Sogavare's two political allies and divert attention on to the police response to the riots.[13] These views appeared to be vindicated when the local media published damning extracts from a leaked cabinet memo. In the document, Sogavare stated that the criminal proceedings against the two MPs were likely to be dropped once the inquiry started (ABC 2006f).

Primo Afeau, the attorney-general, claimed that the inquiry amounted to an 'outrageous case of political interference in the legal process' and instituted legal proceedings challenging the controversial terms of reference. Sogavare responded by accusing Afeau of acting under Australian influence and questioned his suitability for office (Radio New Zealand International 2006a). In the meantime, the prime minister's nominee to chair the inquiry, retired Australian judge Marcus Einfeld, was experiencing legal difficulties of his own after allegedly lying about a speeding offence in Sydney. In an atmosphere of growing paranoia, Sogavare and his closest associates saw the timing of Einfeld's troubles as a deliberate attempt to discredit the former judge and undermine the inquiry.

Bilateral relations hit a new low in early September when the Australian High Commissioner, Patrick Cole, was declared *persona non grata* by the Solomon Islands government for allegedly interfering in local politics. The gist of the allegations was that Cole had been talking with the parliamentary opposition, presumably encouraging it to mount a vote of no-confidence, and had been trying to block funding for the inquiry (Radio New Zealand International 2006b). Downer condemned the diplomat's *de facto* expulsion as outrageous[14] and retaliated by imposing visa restrictions on Solomon Islands politicians seeking entry to Australia (International Herald Tribune 2006). Sogavare responded by accusing Canberra of meddling in Solomon Islands politics. He told reporters that 'the Government and the people of Solomon Islands are concerned about the manner in which the Howard Government has continued to subtly dictate over sovereign issues that are beyond the jurisdiction of Canberra.'

The next, and most bizarre, twist came when it was announced that the prime minister was considering replacing the incumbent attorney-general with a controversial Australian lawyer, Julian Moti (Solomon Star 2006b). Moti had been an associate of Sogavare for many years and was believed to have had a hand in drafting the terms of reference for the inquiry. He had also faced child sex charges in Vanuatu 10 years earlier. According to media reports, Moti was committed to stand trial in Vanuatu's Supreme Court in 1998; however, the Court of Appeal dismissed the case before proceeding to trial on technical grounds. The case was returned to be heard before another magistrate, but was again dismissed amid rumours that Moti had paid off the magistrate (The Australian 2006). After Moti was linked with the attorney-general's position in Solomon Islands, it emerged that he was wanted for questioning by the AFP regarding his earlier activities in Vanuatu and would be arrested when the opportunity arose. The circumstances and timing of the AFP investigation confirmed Sogavare's suspicions that Australian authorities were prepared to use every means possible to block his chosen candidate for attorney-general. Moti was subsequently arrested while in transit in Papua New Guinea at the request of Australian authorities seeking his extradition (ABC 2006g).

After failing to turn up to his scheduled court hearing, Moti was granted refuge at the Solomon Islands High Commission in Port Moresby, sparking further angry exchanges between Honiara and Canberra. Sogavare denounced Moti's arrest as a serious violation of Solomon Islands' sovereignty, while Australian leaders denied accusations that the arrest was politically motivated (ABC 2006h). The bilateral dispute now drew in PNG authorities and, in particular, Prime Minister Sir Michael Somare, a veteran of many acrimonious exchanges with his southern neighbour.[15] Somare accused Australia of bungling the extradition and causing diplomatic embarrassment to Papua New Guinea (ABC 2006i). Moti was then secretly flown to Solomon Islands in a PNG Defence Force aircraft, where he was arrested (Sydney Morning Herald 2006a). Australian officials expressed outrage at Moti's 'escape' from Papua New Guinea, directed in equal measure at the governments of Solomon Islands and Papua New Guinea, who had clearly collaborated on this matter.[16] Although Moti was suspended as attorney-general, Sogavare threatened to end Australia's role in the regional mission if the extradition proceeded (ABC 2006j). Commenting on the tenor of these exchanges between the leaders of Papua New Guinea, Solomon Islands and Australia, strategic analyst Hugh White lamented the reversion to a 'puerile, immature diplomacy' (Sydney Morning Herald 2006b).

Police investigations into how Moti got back into the country, apparently without a passport, led to the arrest of the minister for immigration. The Solomon Islands government responded by threatening to withhold the salary of the Australian commissioner. Shortly after Sogavare left to attend a Pacific Islands Forum meeting in Fiji, police raided the prime minister's office in relation to the same investigation, prompting angry protests from leaders in Solomon Islands, Papua New Guinea and Vanuatu (ABC 2006l). Attempts to rally forum support to Sogavare's side in the stand-off with Australia failed and served to highlight differences between the Melanesian and non-Melanesian member states. A five-point plan presented by Sogavare to overhaul RAMSI and reduce Australian involvement was rejected. The forum nevertheless agreed to review the operations of the mission and establish a new consultative mechanism comprising representatives of Solomon Islands and RAMSI, and the leaders of Papua New Guinea, Fiji and Tonga (see Appendix 3).

As 2006 drew to a close, the Sogavare government again upped the stakes by abruptly declaring the Australian SIPF Commissioner, Shane Castles, an 'undesirable immigrant' while he was on leave in Australia. This had the effect of preventing Castles, who had 20 months of his contract still to run, returning to Solomon Islands to resume his duties. Foreign Minister,

Patteson Oti, stated that Castles' continued presence was considered prejudicial to the peace, defence, public safety, public order, public morality, security and good government of Solomon Islands (Solomon Star 2007a). The Australian government and Solomon Islands opposition immediately condemned Castles' sacking. Castles told journalists that he believed his dismissal was related to SIPF corruption investigations and the continuing Moti affair (Post-Courier 2007). Australian Justice Minister, Chris Ellison, complained of the politics that were continually interfering with Australia's policing efforts in the Pacific (The Australian 2007a).

Sogavare took another swipe at the regional mission in his 2006 Christmas message to his fellow citizens. As well as complaining about the lengthy delays facing detainees awaiting trial for tensions-related offences, Sogavare questioned the retributive foundations of RAMSI's approach to those implicated in the earlier conflict.

> It is worrying that the strategy so far has been very heavily focused on punishing those who have been forced by the environment created during the crisis to commit crime. This is a backward look to addressing our problems. In fact one is fully justified to ask whether the huge investment in this program, that will only financially benefit foreign companies that run our prisons, will address the deep rooted problems of this country (Solomon Star 2006c).

In mid January, Australia's decision to expel Fiji's military contingent from participation in RAMSI after that country's December coup was criticised by foreign ministers from the Melanesian Spearhead Group, revealing the growing animosity among Melanesian leaders towards Australia's regional activism. Minister Oti lambasted Australia's 'dictatorial leadership' of RAMSI (*Solomon Star* 2007b). Further acrimony ensued after it was revealed that Sogavare was planning to re-arm members of the SIPF unit assigned to guard him. Outright opposition to any re-arming of the Solomon Islands police was voiced by Australian and RAMSI leaders, as well as by the opposition and civil society groups in Solomon Islands. Sogavare accused Australia of interfering in local politics by persuading Taiwan to drop the firearms training component in a proposed training scheme with the Solomon Islands police force. He also accused RAMSI of retaliating by withdrawing the mission police assigned to protect him.

Sogavare added to Canberra's frustrations by repeatedly delaying attempts by the newly appointed Australian High Commissioner to Solomon Islands (Patrick Cole's replacement) to present his credentials (The Australian 2007b). Unsubstantiated allegations were also made of RAMSI involvement in prostitution and serious traffic accidents. Another twist in the increasingly surreal tussle between the two governments came with the arrest of a long-time Australian resident, apparently on the basis of a conversation overheard in a local hostelry. He was charged with conspiring to assassinate Sogavare, but the charge was subsequently dropped after being widely criticised, including by the director of public prosecutions, as blatant interference in the criminal justice system. Media reports at the time nevertheless included the unattributed claim that a bounty had been paid to Australian sources to assassinate the Solomon Islands prime minister (Mercer 2007)! Shortly thereafter, a visiting American official urged all parties to 'get away from this kind of boxing match' (Solomon Star 2007c).

In a remarkable departure from normal protocol, an exasperated Alexander Downer sought to go around the government and appeal directly to the Solomon Islands people in a letter published in the *Solomon Star* in early February 2007. In it, he listed and berated various attempts by Sogavare to allegedly undermine the regional mission and appealed to Solomon Islanders 'to go out of your way to encourage your leaders to listen to you, their people, and make wise decisions for the future of your country' (Solomon Star 2007d). In a subsequent interview, Downer claimed that the Solomon Islands prime minister wanted 'to get rid of RAMSI and to go back to the situation where the country was basically run by the Malaita Eagle Force and people like that' (ABC 2007a).

Parts of the western Solomons were devastated by a tsunami and a series of tremors in early April, drawing attention away from the bilateral crisis. These events and Australia's prompt humanitarian response contributed to some thawing in relations (New Zealand Herald 2007); however, this turned out to be a temporary reprieve and the 'boxing match' soon resumed. The Defence Force Board of Inquiry in Port Moresby investigating Moti's flight from Papua New Guinea was uncovering mounting evidence of political involvement at the highest levels in the decision to facilitate Moti's escape. An increasingly petulant Somare sought to have the inquiry disbanded. He also sacked his defence minister and named himself as replacement, thereby ensuring that the report ended up on his desk. Despite Somare's attempts to suppress the publication of the report, *The Australian* newspaper obtained a leaked copy. The report pointed the finger squarely at Somare and recommended that he and several of his civilian and military advisers be investigated for a range of possible offences (The Australian 2007d).

The announcement that a Fijian police officer, Jahir Khan, had been sworn in as the new commissioner of the SIPF in May prompted protests from the Public Service Commission about irregularities in the appointment process (Radio New Zealand International 2007). It was also opposed by local groups who saw it as another attempt by Sogavare to place a compliant person in a critical national post. Khan's appointment was seen as a way of undermining the legal system and the anti-corruption efforts of RAMSI and the police. Groups that had been protesting against the appointment of Moti as attorney-general now added the new commissioner to their list of grievances (ABC 2007b). Unease about this appointment was heightened when Khan announced that he had submitted a supplementary budget to the government seeking US$2.6 million to re-arm elements of the SIPF (SIBC 2007). Moti was formally sworn in as attorney-general on 10 July 2007, despite strident opposition from the Solomon Islands Public Service Commission, the legal fraternity, parliamentary opposition and civil society groups, as well as the governments of Australia and New Zealand (ABC 2007c). Meanwhile, the commission of inquiry into the April 2006 riots, chaired by former PNG judge Brian Brunton, had finally begun in Honiara. As RAMSI marked its fourth anniversary in July 2007, the commission released an interim report (Solomon Islands Government 2007). Among its preliminary findings were that the riots had been politically motivated and that RAMSI police had fallen short in their preparation for and response to the disturbances.

## Conclusions

Despite the mounting difficulties facing RAMSI in the wake of the April 2006 disturbances, it would be premature to predict its impending failure, just as it was to proclaim its success after its early accomplishments. The impact of the intervention will be measured ultimately by what it leaves behind. As well as set-backs, there have been successes that have been largely overshadowed by the disturbances and deterioration in bilateral relations. These have included changes to the taxation system, which have seen Solomons Island government revenue increasing by 170 per cent in RAMSI's first three years, and other reforms that have contributed to growth in the economy and employment opportunities for Solomon Islanders (The Australian 2007c). While falling well short of levels required by the fast-growing population, they nevertheless represent a significant achievement given the disastrous economic situation that existed in mid 2003. Likewise, as O'Callaghan points out in this volume, beneath the high-level jousting between political leaders in Honiara and Canberra, relations between many RAMSI personnel and their Solomon Islander counterparts are very effective. Moreover, retaining overwhelming popular support four years after deployment is unusual among contemporary state-building intervention and remains the mission's principal strength.

That said, the fundamental challenges of implementing and sustaining its reform agenda remain formidable. RAMSI was always much more than a technical and politically neutral exercise. The protracted struggle over its control should serve to dispel doubts about the inherently political character of international state building. Appeals to sovereignty and nationalist sentiments will continue to provide the rationale for strategies of obstruction and resistance by those who stand to lose most from the mission's far-reaching governance and economic reforms. Alexander Downer's persistent objections show no sign of wearing down the resistance. Recent events also demonstrate just how susceptible the language and conceptual framework of intervening authorities are to appropriation by local actors for their justificatory value and then to redeployment against the interveners. This can be seen in Prime Minister Sogavare's objections to the 'injustices' perpetrated against large numbers of Solomon Islanders awaiting trial in Rove Prison. In a similar vein, others have sought to justify Commodore Bainimarama's illegal assumption of power in Fiji in December 2006 by recasting it as the 'good governance' coup. In each case, one version of justice and good governance competes with another.

The domain of law enforcement illustrates the near impossibility of trying to maintain an impartial image in such a politically charged context. AFP Commissioner, Mick Keelty, acknowledged recently the considerable difficulties of working in 'the morally ambiguous' and 'politically challenging' environments of 'imperfectly governed democracies' (Keelty 2006). Having been criticised earlier for neglecting the big fish, police and other legal agencies have increased their vulnerability to political attacks by switching focus onto corrupt officials and leaders. Sogavare's successful efforts to insert his personal appointees into the key posts of attorney-general and police commissioner not only threaten the integrity of the legal system, they drag those who insist on strict adherence to the rule of law into messy political struggles. Appeals to the technical imperatives of neutral and depoliticised law enforcement are unlikely to displace perceptions of underlying power plays, whether real or imagined.

Shane Castles' sacking in December 2006 demonstrates the incompatible nature of a freely elected government and its relationship with an external intervening force. While the intervention makes possible the legitimacy of the government, it cannot ensure or control its behaviour. This goes to the heart of RAMSI's current difficulties. The reforms it seeks to implement demand robust political responses but the nature of its legal foundations— 'cooperative intervention'—severely constrains the extent to which it can engage politically with a resistant government in Honiara. The imperative of cooperation limits the mission's ability to push for deeper political reforms while simultaneously making it more susceptible to entanglement in local politics, as illustrated in the Moti affair and many of the other developments discussed in this volume.

The narrow, technical orientation of the mission's approach to state building and capacity development obscures the social and political dynamics that have contributed to the dysfunctionality of the post-colonial state in Solomon Islands. This is not simply the result of a lack of institutional capacity to be remedied by carefully targeted technical assistance. Rather it reflects the particular history and politics of the post-colonial state and the manner in which it has been shaped by local and global forces. The Solomon Islands state, like all other states, does not stand apart from society as some kind of discrete entity that can be worked on in isolation. Hameiri (2007) has shown how the literature on failed states sets up a dichotomous conceptualisation of state and society by defining institutions primarily in terms of their policy capacity. As a result, 'social and political relationships are not seen as intrinsic to institutions but only as constraints or obstacles to performance' (Hameiri 2007:414). The idealised institutions the interveners are seeking to (re-)build are to be devoid of politics and the pernicious influence of social relations. Despite these noble aspirations, institutions cannot be separated from what Leftwich (2000:9) calls 'the raw processes and practices of politics' that gave rise to them in the first place and that have shaped their evolution ever since. The history of post-colonial states such as Solomon Islands attests to the centrality of politics in their development.

International state builders evaluate their subjects in terms of the extent to which they fall short of the ideals of a modern state. The deficits so identified—for example, the absence of good governance, lack of accountability and transparency, corruption and nepotism, unfavourable investment regimes and inefficient taxation systems—establish the parameters for the remedial work of institution building and capacity development. The imperatives of addressing these 'self-evident deficiencies', often in absurdly short time frames, affords little opportunity to reflect on why these institutions and the individuals that constitute them behave in the particular ways they do. That would require a much deeper understanding of the complex interplay between history, culture, politics and material change that have shaped them. It would entail a search for the rationality in political and institutional behaviour rather than simply dismissing it as inherently irrational or pathological (Chabal and Daloz 1999).

While the Honiara riots involved manipulation by some parties, and while Sogavare has embarked on a personal mission to frustrate important aspects of the regional mission's work, the travails of Solomon Islands in recent decades and the present difficulties faced by RAMSI cannot be reduced simply to the incompetence or mendacity of post-independence governments and a handful of political leaders. While these factors have undoubtedly contributed, they are not in themselves sufficient to explain the profound difficulties of building state and nation in Solomon Islands. Governments and their leaders are significant players within a larger political economy whose roots extend deep into Solomon Islands society and the manner of its engagement with the global economy. The peculiarities of Solomon Islands' electoral politics, process of government formation and volatile system of coalition government cannot be understood in isolation from their encompassing political culture. Nor can they be viewed apart from the mutually transformative character of state–society relations that have configured the political landscape in the past three decades. The relative absence in Solomon Islands of the institutionalisation and functional differentiation between state and society on which Weberian state building is premised, is a reflection of powerful historical and social forces rather than the product of individual or collective pathology.

The entanglement of pre-colonial and colonial pasts remains deeply implicated in the difficulties of the post-colonial present in Solomon Islands. Rather than nurturing shared community, 'the raw processes and practices of politics' in the post-independence period have accentuated localism and divisions within the archipelago. An important message for the interveners is the need for a much stronger appreciation of the importance of nation building, in its literal sense, and the need for a significant broadening of the narrow, technical state-building perspective. In part a consequence of its mandate, RAMSI's state-building efforts have not been embedded in the larger and critical project of nation making, leaving it with little scope to address the deeper causes of the recent crisis. On this point, it is worth concluding that the disturbances in April 2006—viewed widely as a manifestation of state-building failure—might be interpreted more positively. Is it not conceivable that the spontaneous anger of many ordinary Solomon Islanders at the lack of openness and transparency of their government system was itself an example of nation building in the face of state failure? Likewise, an unintended consequence of the months of bitter and debilitating wrangling between Prime Minister Sogavare and his Australian nemeses might be the translation of growing popular concern into a heightened scrutiny of the actions of their own government and leadership. This illustrates the earlier point that the building of political communities is often a messy and contested process. It also demonstrates how nation building is as likely to occur by default as by design.

## Acknowledgments

My thanks to Stewart Firth, Hank Nelson and the anonymous reviewers of an earlier draft.

# Notes

1   In 2002, the United States redefined its National Security Strategy to warn that 'America is now threatened less by conquering states than we are by failing ones' (United States Government 2002).

2   The PPF includes contingents from Australia, New Zealand, Fiji, Cook Islands, Kiribati, Nauru, Papua New Guinea, Samoa, Tonga, Marshall Islands, Federated States of Micronesia, Palau, Tuvalu and Vanuatu.

3   Shane Castles quoted in the *Solomon Star* (2006a).

4   Solomon Star 2005a. See also Roughan 2005.

5   See, for example, Solomon Star 2005b.

6   These included the conviction and imprisonment of a former minister of communication in February 2004 for, among other things, demanding money with menace; the arrest of the former foreign minister in September 2004 on a charge of demanding money with menace; the arrest of the minister for provincial government and constituency development on corruption-related charges in January 2005; the arrest for theft of the minister for police, national security and justice in February 2005; the arrest of two prominent lawyers, including the former MEF spokesperson, in February 2005 in relation to the misappropriation of compensation funds; and the arrest on corruption charges of the former finance minister in April 2005.

7   See the articles by Mike Wheatley (2006), former Assistant Commissioner, RSIP, and Frank Short (2006), former Commissioner, RSIP.

8   See, for example, Roughan 2006.

9   Quote from O'Callaghan 2006.

10  This email was a source of embarrassment to RAMSI and the Australian government. It also described extensive behind-the-scenes lobbying against Rini by Patrick Cole, the Australian High Commissioner (see The Age 2006a).

11  Sogavare was one of the only political leaders to speak against the regional mission during the debates in the Solomon Islands Parliament that preceded its deployment. He warned then that such a mission might lead to 're-colonisation'. See Sydney Morning Herald 2003a.

12  See also ABC 2006e.

13  See *The Age* 2006b. Concerns were also expressed by New Zealand and the European Union.

14  See *The Age* 2006b.

15  This included the diplomatic stoush between Papua New Guinea and Australia after the so-called 'shoe incident' at Brisbane airport in March 2005. Airport security officials insisted that Sir Michael remove his shoes as part of a routine security check. This incident led to public demonstrations in several PNG towns. Somare has been an open critic of Australia's new interventionism and has taken great offence to the labelling of Papua New Guinea as a weak or failing state.

16  Alexander Downer subsequently announced a ban on ministerial visits from Papua New Guinea to Australia (see ABC 2006k). The collaboration between the two governments was later confirmed in the leaked report from the PNG Defence Board of Inquiry.

# References

Allen, M.G., 2006. 'Dissenting voices: local perspectives on the Regional Assistance Mission to Solomon Islands', *Pacific Economic Bulletin*, 21(2):194–201.

Australian Broadcasting Corporation (ABC), 2006a. 'Speaker critical of RAMSI response to crisis', *Pacific Beat*, ABC Radio Australia, 19 April. Available from http://www.abc.net.au/ra/pacbeat/stories/s1618650.htm.

——, 2006b. 'Labour party warns of perception that RAMSI supported Rini', *Pacific Beat*, ABC Radio Australia, 27 April. Available from http://www.radioaustralia.net.au/pacbeat/stories/s1625001.htm.

——, 2006c. 'Solomon Islands: new PM says RAMSI's operations will be reviewed', *Pacific Beat*, ABC Radio Australia, 5 May. Available from http://www.abc.net.au/ra/pacbeat/stories/s1631306.htm.

——, 2006d. 'Downer condemns Solomon Cabinet decision', ABC Radio Online, 6 May. Available from http://www.abc.net.au/news/newsitems/200605/s1632243.htm.

——, 2006e. 'Australia fears Sogavare wants to "cherry pick" RAMSI', *Pacific Beat*, ABC Radio Australia, 22 May. Available from http://www.abc.net.au/pacbeat/stories/s1644352.htm.

——, 2006f. 'Memo heightens Honiara riots inquiry fears', ABC News Online, 18 September. Available from http://www.abc.net.au/newsitems/200609/s1743850.htm.

——, 2006g. 'Solomons AG faces extradition to Australia, Downer says', ABC News Online, 30 September. Available from http://dsl.optus.net.com.au/news/story/abc/20060930/09/domestic/1752566.inp.

——, 2006h. 'Ellison denies Moti case politically motivated', ABC Online, 4 October. Available from http://www.abc.net.au/news/newsitems/200610/s1755118.htm.

——, 2006i. 'PNG: prime minister backs Honiara over Moti case', *Pacific Beat*, ABC Radio Australia, 5 October. Available from http://abc.net.au/ra/pacbeat/stories/s1756413.htm.

——, 2006j. 'Solomon Islands government threatens to expel Australians', ABC News Online, 13 October. Available from http://www.abc.net.au/news/newsitems/200610/s1764670.htm.

——, 2006k. 'Downer suspends ministerial contact with PNG', ABC News Online, 15 October. Available from http://www.abc.net.au/news/newsitems/200610/s1765093.htm.

———, 2006l. 'PNG, Vanuatu condemn raid on Solomons PM's office', ABC Online, 23 October. Available from http://www.abc.net.au/cgi-bin/common/printfriendly.pl.

———, 2007a. 'Appeal for RAMSI to be saved', *Pacific Beat*, ABC Radio Australia, 12 February. Available from http://www.abc.net.au/ra/pacbeat/stories/s1845775.htm.

———, 2007b. 'Civil society groups to protest over Julian Moti', *Pacific Beat*, ABC Radio Australia, 31 May. Available from http://www.radioaustralia.net.au/pacbeat/stories/s1939039.htm.

———, 2007c. 'Moti sworn in as Solomons A-G', ABC News Online, 10 July. Available from http://www.abc.net.au/news/stories/2007/07/10/1975046.htm.

Australian Strategic Policy Institute (ASPI), 2003. *Our Failing Neighbour: Australia and the future of Solomon Islands*, Australian Strategic Policy Institute, Canberra.

Batley, J., 2005. The role of RAMSI in Solomon Islands: rebuilding the state, supporting peace, Paper presented at the Peace, Justice and Reconciliation Conference, Brisbane, 31 March–3 April. Available from http://www.dfat.gov.au/media/speeches/department/050331_ramsi_paper_by_james_batley.html.

Bayley, D.H., 2006. *Changing the Guard: developing democratic police abroad*, Oxford University Press, New York.

Bennett, J., 2002. *Roots of conflict in Solomon Islands. Though much is taken, much abides: legacies of tradition and colonialism*, Discussion Paper 2002/5, State, Society and Governance in Melanesia Program, Research School of Pacific and Asian Studies, The Australian National University, Canberra.

Borgerhoff, A., 2006. 'The double task: nation and state-building in Timor-Leste', *European Journal of East Asian Studies*, 5(1):101–30.

Brown, T., 2005. 'RAMSI, the police and the future', *Solomon Star*, 18 January 2005.

Chabal, P. and Daloz, J.-P., 1999. *Africa Works: disorder as political instrument*, James Currey and Indiana University Press, Oxford and Bloomington, Indiana.

Chandler, D., 2006. *Empire in Denial—the politics of state-building*, Pluto Press, London.

Chesterman, S., Ignatieff, M. and Thakur, R. (eds), 2005. *Making States Work: state failure and the crisis of governance*, United Nations University Press, Tokyo, New York and Paris.

Cohen,Y., Brown, B.R. and Organski,A.F.K., 1981. 'The paradoxical nature of state making: the violent creation of order', *American Political Science Review*, 75(4):901–10.

Dinnen, S., 2002. 'Winners and losers: politics and disorder in Solomon Islands 2000–2002', *Journal of Pacific History*, 37(3):285–98.

Dinnen, S., McLeod,A. and Peake, G., 2006. 'Police-building in weak states: Australian approaches in Papua New Guinea and Solomon Islands', *Civil Wars*, 8(2):87–108.

Dobbins, J., McGinn, J.G., Crane, K., Jones, S.G., Lal, R., Rathmell, A., Swanger, R.M. and Timilsina, A.R., 2003. *America's Role in Nation-Building: from Germany to Iraq*, Rand Corporation, Santa Monica.

Downer, A., 2003. Our failing neighbour: Australia and the future of the Solomon Islands, Speech delivered at the launch of the *Australian Strategic Policy Institute Report*, Sydney, 10 June. Available from http://www.foreignminister.gov.au/speeches/2003/030610_solomonislands.html

Fraenkel, J., 2004. *The Manipulation of Custom—from uprising to intervention in the Solomon Islands*,Victoria University Press,Wellington.

Fukuyama, F., 2004. *State-Building: governance and world order in the twenty-first century*, Profile Books, London.

Fullilove, M., 2006a. 'The testament of Solomons: RAMSI and international state-building', *Analysis* (March), Lowy Institute for International Policy, Sydney:1–32.

——, 2006b. 'RAMSI and state building in Solomon Islands', *Defender*, Autumn:31–5.

Greener-Barcham, B.K. and Barcham, M., 2006. 'Terrorism in the South Pacific?Thinking critically about approaches to security in the region', *Australian Journal of International Affairs*, 60(1):67–82.

Green Left Weekly, 2006. 'Solomon Islands: new PM criticises Australian domination', *Green Left Weekly*, 24 May. Available from http://www.greenleft.org.au/back/2006/668/668p19.htm.

Guibernau, M., 1996. *Nationalism: the nation-state and nationalisms in the twentieth century*, Polity Press, Cambridge.

Hameiri, S., 2007. 'The trouble with RAMSI: re-examining the roots of conflict in Solomon Islands', *Contemporary Pacific*, 19(2):409–41.

Hawes, R., 2006. 'Rocks and renewal—a new phase for the Solomon Islands', *Platypus Magazine*, 91(June):3–6.

Hippler, J. (ed.), 2004. *Nation-Building: a key concept for peaceful conflict transformation?*, Pluto Press, London and Ann Arbor.

Ignatieff, M., 2003. 'The burden', *New York Times Magazine*, 5 January:162.

International Herald Tribune, 2006. 'Australia suspending favourable visa treatment for Solomon Islands politicians', *International Herald Tribune, Asia-Pacific*, 13 September. Available from http://www.iht.com/articles/ap/2006/09/13/asia/AS_GEN_Australia_Solomon_Islands.php.

Jackson, R.H., 1990. *Quasi-States: sovereignty, international relations and the Third World*, Cambridge University Press, Cambridge.

Jourdan, C., 1995. 'Stepping-stones to national consciousness: the Solomon Islands case', in R.J. Foster (ed.), *Nation Making: emergent identities in postcolonial Melanesia*, University of Michigan Press, Ann Arbor:127–49.

Kabutaulaka, T.T., 2004. '"Failed state" and the war on terror: intervention in Solomon Islands', *Asia-Pacific Issues*, 72:1–8.

——, 2006. 'Crowded stage: actors, actions and issues', in J. Henderson and G. Watson (eds), *Securing a Peaceful Pacific*, Canterbury University Press, Christchurch:408–22.

Kaldor, M., 1999. *New and Old Wars: organized violence in a global era*, Polity Press, Cambridge.

Keelty, M., 2006. Policing in a foreign policy space, Address to the National Press Club, Canberra, 11 October.

Leftwich, A., 2000. *States of Development: on the primacy of politics in development*, Polity Press, Cambridge.

Mercer, P., 2007. 'Australia denies Solomons plot', BBC News, 31 January. Available from http://news.bbc.co.uk/1/hi/world/asia-pacific/6316319.stm

Moore, C., 2004. *Happy Isles in Crisis: the historical causes for a failing state in Solomon Islands 1998–2004*, Asia Pacific Press, The Australian National University, Canberra.

Morgan, M.G. and McLeod, A., 2006. 'Have we failed our neighbour?', *Australian Journal of International Affairs*, 60(3):412–28.

Nelson, H., 2006. *Governments, states and labels*, Discussion Paper 2006/1, State, Society and Governance in Melanesia Program, Research School of Pacific and Asian Studies, The Australian National University, Canberra. Available from http://rspas.anu.edu.au/melanesia.

New Zealand Herald, 2007. 'Solomons PM to soften anti-Australian stance', *New Zealand Herald Online*, 30 April. Available from http://www.nzherald.co.nz/feature/story.cfm?c_id=621&objectied=1.

O'Callaghan, M.L., 2006. Presentation given at 'Australia and the South Pacific: roles and responsibilities', seminar at Australian Institute of International Affairs, Sydney, July. Available from ABC Radio

National *Background Briefing* transcripts http://www.abc.net.au/rn/ backgroundbriefing/stories/2006/17062.

Pacific Islands Forum, 2005. *Mission helpem fren. A review of the Regional Assistance Mission to Solomon Islands*, Report of the Pacific Islands Forum Eminent Persons' Group, Pacific Islands Forum, Suva, May:1–36.

Payne, J.L., 2006. 'Does nation building work?', *The Independent Review*, X(4):599–610.

Peake, G. and Brown, K., 2005. 'Police-building: the International Deployment Group in the Solomon Islands', *International Peacekeeping*, 12(4):520–32.

Pei, M. and Kasper, S., 2003. *Lessons from the past: the American record on nation building*, Policy Brief 24, Carnegie Endowment for International Peace, Washington, DC:1–8.

Post-Courier, 2007. 'Castle [*sic*] to fight case', (PNG) *Post-Courier*, 11 January.

Radio New Zealand International, 2006a. 'Solomons PM says he will speak to Australian PM about alleged interference in judicial system', Radio New Zealand International, 4 September. Available from http://www. rnzi.com/pages/news.php?op=read&id=26540.

——, 2006b. 'Australian diplomat expelled from Solomon Islands', Radio New Zealand International, 12 September. Available from http://www. rnzi.com/pages/news.php?op=read&id=26756.

——, 2007. 'Solomons police commissioner not chosen in transparent way', Radio New Zealand International, 21 May.

Roughan, J., 2005. 'Voices of civil society', in J. Henderson and G. Watson (eds), *Securing a Peaceful Pacific*, Canterbury University Press, Christchurch:423–9.

——, 2006. 'RAMSI failed us!', 22 May. Available from http://www.scoop. co.nz/stories/HL0605/S00326.htm.

Short, F., 2006. 'Honiara riot warrants formal inquiry', *Pacific Islands Report*, 22 May. Available from http://archives.pireport.org/archive/2006/ May/05-24-com.htm.

Solomon Islands Broadcasting Corporation (SIBC), 2007. 'Government to arm two sections of the police', SIBC, 25 June. Available from http:// www.sibconline.comsb/story.asp?IDThread=46&IDNews=19519.

Solomon Islands Government, 2006. Establishment of Commission of Inquiry into April Civil Unrest, Press release, Solomon Islands Government, Honiara,13 July.

——, 2007. *First Interim Report of the April Riot Commission of Inquiry,* Solomon Islands Government, Honiara. Available from http://www.pmc.gov.sb (accessed 25 July 2007).

Solomon Star, 2005a. 'SICA wants RAMSI focus on longer term', *Solomon Star*, 1 February.

——, 2005b. 'RAMSI, the "big fish" and Solomon Islands sovereignty', *Solomon Star*, 31 July.

——, 2006a. 'Police chief replies to criticisms', *Solomon Star*, 19 May.

——, 2006b. 'Moti is likely to be new AG', *Solomon Star*, 22 September.

——, 2006c. 'Detainees win PM's heart', *Solomon Star*, 28 December.

——, 2007a. 'I'm still the boss: Castles', *Solomon Star*, 3 January.

——, 2007b. 'Acting High Commissioner disappointed at criticism', *Solomon Star*, 16 January.

——, 2007c. 'Get out of boxing match', *Solomon Star*, 6 February.

——, 2007d. 'A letter to the people of Solomon Islands from the Hon. Alexander Downer, Minister for Foreign Affairs, Australia', *Solomon Star*, 12 February.

Sydney Morning Herald, 2003a. 'Ex-Solomons PM fears colonisation', *Sydney Morning Herald*, 10 July. Available from http://www.smh.com. au/text/articles/2003/07/09/1057430278743.htm.

——, 2003b. 'Howard: Solomons could have become haven for terrorists', *Sydney Morning Herald*, 23 July.

——, 2006a. 'Moti in custody but for how long', *Sydney Morning Herald*, 11 October.

——, 2006b. 'Talks will show if Howard acted too tough', *Sydney Morning Herald*, 23 October.

The Age, 2006a. 'Leaked email shows hand of Canberra in Honiara', *The Age*, 1 May. Available from http://www.theage.com.au/news/national/leaked-email-shows-hand-of-canberra/2006/04/30.

——, 2006b. 'Meddle fears over Solomons riot trial', *The Age*, 11 September. Available from http://www.theage.com.au/news/world/meddle-fears-over-solomons-riot-trial/2006/09/10.

The Australian, 2006. 'Child rape trial was quashed', *The Australian*, 3 October. Available from http://www.theaustralian.news.com.au/story/0,20867,20515140-601,00.html.

——, 2007a. 'Pacific instability knocks police efforts', *The Australian*, 9 February. Available from http://www.theaustralian.news.com.au/story/0,25197,21013229-2702,00.html.

——, 2007b. 'SI PM accused of snub', *The Australian*, 9 February.

——, 2007c. 'Careful planning puts archipelago in the sun', *The Australian*, 15 June. Available from http://ww.theaustralian.news.com.au/story/0,20867,21906994-758.

——, 2007d. 'Scrambling for cover', *The Australian*, 30 July. Available from http://media.theaustralian.com.au/pdf/070802-pngr2.pdf.

The Canberra Times, 2006. *The Canberra Times*, 8 May.

Tilly, C., 1992. *Coercion, Capital, and European States, AD 990–1992*, Blackwell, Cambridge, MA.

United States Government, 2002. *The National Security Strategy of the United States of America*, Washington, DC. Available from http://www.whitehouse.gov/nsc/nss.html.

Wainwright, E., 2005. *How is RAMSI faring? Progress, challenges and lessons learned*, Strategic Insights 14, Australian Strategic Policy Institute, Canberra:1–12.

Watson, J., 2005. *A model Pacific solution? A study of the deployment of the Regional Assistance Mission to Solomon Islands*, Working Paper No. 126, Land Warfare Studies Centre, Department of Defence, Canberra:1–37.

Wheatley, M., 2006. 'RAMSI Tuesday wasn't to do with intelligence failure', *New Matilda*, 24 May. Available from http://www.newmatilda.com.

# Chapter 2
## Politics of disorder: the social unrest in Honiara

Matthew Allen

The rioting and looting that broke out in Honiara, the capital of Solomon Islands, immediately after the parliamentary election of the new prime minister in April 2006, and the national election two weeks earlier, highlight the deep-seated structural issues that continue to plague this fledgling independent South Pacific nation. The prime minister-elect, Snyder Rini, resigned a week after he was elected in the face of a parliamentary vote of no confidence and was succeeded in the nation's top position by Manasseh Sogavare. Two Members of Parliament were arrested on charges relating to the riots, parliamentary sittings were 'locked down' by the commissioner of police, parliamentarians travelled to and from Parliament House under heavily armed Australian and New Zealand police and military escorts and the Regional Assistance Mission to Solomon Islands (RAMSI) and the Solomon Islands Police Force (SIPF) were criticised by MPs for interfering with the political system.

This chapter examines the 2006 national election and seeks to offer some explanation for the social unrest that saw the looting and destruction of numerous Chinese-owned businesses in Honiara. The election, which was declared fair and free by international observers, exhibited all of the elements that have come to characterise elections in the independent Melanesian countries. It was contested by a large number of candidates, meaning that seats were won with very small 'majorities', and by a large number of parties and independents with weak or incoherent policy platforms. There were allegations of vote buying (or 'bag rice' politics) and the bankrolling of electoral campaigns by local and foreign interests. There were also reports of corruption among electoral officers and problems with the electoral roll. Moreover, although a record number of women candidates contested, none were elected.

After the election, we saw the inevitable 'numbers game' in the lead up to the formation of a new government and the parliamentary ballot for the prime ministerial position. Parties and independents coalesced to form rival political camps based in the capital's leading hotels and vied to lure one another's members. As has been the case in previous elections, there were widespread allegations that local business interests, particularly Asian businessmen, were closely involved in this political manoeuvring. And, as in the past, there was a sharp disjuncture between the politics of campaigning at the local level and the character of the government that ultimately assumed power.

This last process is perhaps the greatest cause of frustration for the electorate in Solomon Islands and, indeed, for voters elsewhere in independent Melanesia. In the context of an extremely weak party system, election outcomes are essentially indeterminable from the voter's perspective. This, perhaps more than any other factor, was the primary cause of the ostensibly spontaneous riots that broke out after the announcement of the outcome of the parliamentary ballot for the prime minister, particularly as the same coalition that had held the previous government of Sir Allan Kemakeza was returned to power. The electorate had become exasperated with the Kemakeza administration and the inability or unwillingness of RAMSI to arrest the so-called 'big fish' within that government, including Kemakeza himself.

The riots can also be located in the long-standing tradition of Solomon Islanders' resistance to 'alien' and centralised authority (Keesing 1992; Akin 1999). In two previous episodes of rioting and looting in Honiara, in 1989 and 1996, the rioters were Malaitans seeking compensation from the central government for acts of swearing committed by Bellonese (in the 1989 incident) and Reef Islanders (in 1996). These ultimately successful claims saw the invocation of Malaitan *kastom*, particularly the 'traditional' practice of compensation, as a form of symbolic resistance to the government. There is some evidence to suggest that former members of the Malaita Eagle Force (MEF), disgruntled about having never received the rehabilitation provided for them under the Townsville Peace Agreement (TPA) and later promised to them by the Kemakeza government, deliberately targeted Chinatown as a way of 'lodging a claim against the government' (Stritecky 2001:230). The apparent targeting of RAMSI during the riots could also be understood in the context of resistance to perceived foreign hegemony.

Other elements contributing to the social unrest include latent anti-Chinese sentiments in the context of deepening socioeconomic inequalities and the growing numbers of unemployed young men in Honiara; growing opposition to, and frustration with, RAMSI; alleged mismanagement of the situation by police, particularly the mission's Participating Police Force (PPF); the particular dynamics of the crowd in Melanesia; and suspected attempts by MPs to incite social disorder for political ends. This last element resonates, somewhat alarmingly, with the situation at the beginning of the so-called 'ethnic tension' in 1998–99, when it was argued by then Prime Minister, Bartholomew Ulufa'alu (deposed in the coup of June 2000) that the parliamentary opposition was stirring up ethnic violence deliberately in order to destabilise his government. In that case, the alleged ethnic manipulation drew on long-standing structural grievances to pit Guales against Malaitans, while in the present case it is the Asian business community that has fallen victim to the racial card.

The events in Honiara in 2006 would therefore appear to be another example of a process of instrumentalisation of disorder, which has been used to describe continuing political and social instability in parts of Africa (Chabal and Daloz 1999) and which has been adopted by some commentators to explain the violence and lawlessness that plagued Solomon Islands between 1998 and 2003 (Dinnen 2002; Fraenkel 2004). Moreover, as has been the case since the early 1990s, and in spite of the best efforts of RAMSI's economic governance and the machinery of government programs, the drama of politics in Honiara continues to unfold against a backdrop of systemic corruption in the key export sectors of forestry and fisheries. It is these lucrative but non-renewable resources that continue to provide the bulk of spoils of the politics of disorder in Solomon Islands.

## The 2006 national election and the formation of government

The national election of 5 April 2006, and the subsequent formation of government, exhibited many of the characteristic elements of elections and national politics in the post-colonial Westminster-style democracies of Melanesia, particularly Papua New Guinea, Solomon Islands and Vanuatu (for a summary of these characteristics, see Reilly 2004 and Morgan 2005). A record 453 candidates, including 26 women, contested the 50 parliamentary seats, making an average of about nine candidates for each constituency. As a consequence, seats were won with small majorities: an average of about 31 per cent of the vote, with more than half of all elected MPs polling less than 30 per cent of the vote. As observed by Jon Fraenkel, a factor contributing to the unprecedented number of candidates was the increasing use of dummy candidates, who were engaged by candidates to split rivals' supporters (Solomon Star 2006g).[1]

A record 12 political parties also contested the election, although of the 50 elected MPs only 16 had submitted a party affiliation with their nominations (Solomon Star 2006g). There was a high turnover of MPs, with only 50 per cent of incumbents holding their seats. No women candidates were successful. The turnover rate varied across the country: it was lowest in Western and Choiseul provinces and highest in Honiara and Isabel Province (Solomon Star 2006g). As in previous elections, and as is frequently the case in Melanesia, party policy platforms were weak or non-existent and campaigns were focused mostly on specific local issues. Throughout the election campaign, the local media reported allegations of candidates providing 'gifts' to constituents and the bankrolling of electoral campaigns by local and overseas interests, particularly local Asian businessmen and the Republic of China (Taiwan).

While the election was declared free and fair by international observers, domestic observers, candidates and voters reported a number of problems. Domestic observers in the three Honiara constituencies complained about problems with the voter registration lists, whereby significant numbers of voters who had claimed to be registered correctly were unable to find their names on the lists and were turned away from polling booths (Solomon Star 2006b). It was also reported that some voters were able to remove the so-called indelible ink that was placed on voters' fingers to prevent them from voting more than once. In the Central Kwara'ae constituency (Malaita Province), complaints were made in relation to the poor printing and layout of ballot papers, which made it difficult for illiterate voters to associate candidates' names with their symbols (Solomon Star 2006c). In the Gela constituency (Central Province), it was alleged that some candidates' symbols were not present on the ballot papers (Solomon Star 2006d).

Perhaps the most serious allegations relate to the rigging of electoral rolls and interference by candidates in the selection and appointment of electoral officials. Complaints were made about the rigging of electoral rolls in the Gela and Central Honiara constituencies (Solomon Star 2006d, 2006f) and in Gela it was also alleged that the winning candidate had hand-picked the electoral officers (Solomon Star 2006d). On a more positive note, the move from a multiple to a single ballot-box voting system was reported widely as having simplified the voting process and very few invalid votes were recorded.

Events after the national election exemplify the fluidity of party politics in Solomon Islands. A week after the election, three camps had formed and were vying to woo one another's members (Solomon Star 2006e). A coalition comprising the National Party, Liberal Party, Solomon Islands Social Credit Party (Socred), Solomon Islands Party for Rural Advancement and a number of independents were camped at the Iron Bottom Sound Hotel. The Association of Independent Members of Parliament (AIMP) was camped at the Honiara Hotel, which was owned by the association's president, Sir Thomas Chan. The third grouping—comprising the People's Alliance Party of caretaker Prime Minister, Sir Allan Kemakeza, and his previous coalition partner, Lafari—were based at the prime minister's residence at Vavaya Ridge. Five days later, on the eve of the parliamentary election for the new prime minister, the People's Alliance Party had joined the AIMP camp at the Honiara Hotel, while Sogavare's Socred Party had left the Iron Bottom Sound Hotel camp to form a new coalition with the One Nation Party and members of the Lafari Party, basing themselves at the Pacific Casino Hotel, reportedly with the backing of local businessman Bobo Dettke (Solomon Star 2006f). There were widespread rumours circulating in Honiara that vested interests, particularly local Asian businessmen, were offering bribes and inducements to MPs in relation to the formation of coalitions in the lead up to the election of the new prime minister.

Three candidates went into the parliamentary vote for the prime minister's post on the morning of Tuesday 18 April, a day now referred to locally as 'Black Tuesday'. Job Dudley Tausinga, MP for North New Georgia and leader of the Solomon Islands Party for Rural Advancement, represented the Iron Bottom Sound Hotel camp; Manasseh Sogavare, MP for East Choiseul, represented the Pacific Casino Hotel camp; and Snyder

Rini, MP for Marovo and leader of AIMP, represented the Honiara Hotel camp. Sogavare was eliminated in the first round of voting and Rini defeated Tausinga in the second round and was declared the new prime minister.

## Black Tuesday: the aftermath of the parliamentary ballot

The crowd that had gathered outside Parliament House greeted the announcement of the new prime minister, made about midday, with anger. Prime Minister Rini's statement to the crowd was met with insults, jeers and shouts of 'Asian money, Asian money' (ABC 2006). The events that followed remain unclear. According to some eyewitness accounts, the crowd had started to calm down after addresses made by a number of leaders, including Job Dudley Tausinga, Sir Peter Kenilorea and Bartholomew Ulufa'alu. It is claimed that PPF officers then decided to use tear-gas to disperse the crowd against the advice of Solomon Islander police officers (Confidential sources, Honiara). According to other sources, tear-gas was used after stones had been thrown at the police and a police vehicle had been sprayed with petrol and set alight. The use of tear-gas angered the crowd and seems to have immediately contributed to the riots, which resulted in the looting and burning of Chinese-owned retail stores in Chinatown and the Point Cruz and Ranandi areas, and the torching of several police vehicles.

The rioting and looting continued into the next day when the Pacific Casino Hotel (owned by businessman Patrick Leong) was burnt down and more police vehicles were destroyed. It was announced that military and police reinforcements were *en route* from Australia and New Zealand and that the governor-general had declared a curfew under the Preservation of Public Security Act. A petition was presented to the governor-general demanding the resignation of the prime minister. The petition was passed onto Rini, who promptly rejected it (SIBC 2006b). The situation had started to stabilise by Wednesday after the arrival of 120 soldiers and 30 police from Australia and a further 30 soldiers from New Zealand and 20 from Fiji. There were still, however, small pockets of unrest in the Kukum and Ranandi areas of Honiara (SIBC 2006c). During the two days of violence, 17 PPF officers and an unknown number of Chinese people, including children, sustained injuries. On Thursday, it was reported that 14 people had been arrested in the Malaitan township of Auki on suspicion of attempting to cause unrest there on the Tuesday evening (SIBC 2006c). Apart from this incident, the riots had been confined entirely to Honiara.

Rini was officially sworn in as prime minister on Thursday 20 April and, by the weekend, Sir Peter Kenilorea had been renominated, unopposed, for the position of Speaker of Parliament. On the Sunday night, Police Commissioner, Shane Castles, announced that the next day's parliamentary sitting to elect the deputy speaker—which was being contested by Sir Allan Kemakeza as the government's candidate and Patteson Oti for the opposition—was to be closed to the public. Sunday also saw the arrest of the Member for Central Honiara, Nelson Ne'e, on charges related to the riots. Another MP was arrested for breaking the curfew and was released on bail. Police were also seeking a third MP (Member for East Honiara, Charles Dausabea) for charges related to the riots, after they failed to capture him during a raid on his room at the Mendana Hotel on Sunday night (Solomon Star 2006g).

The political drama intensified as parliament resumed sitting on Monday under lock-down and a heavily armed police and military presence. Opposition spokesman and candidate for the deputy speaker's position, Patteson Oti, requested that the vote for the deputy speaker be postponed, arguing that the opposition was disadvantaged by the absence of one of its members, who was in police custody (Nelson Ne'e). Oti also challenged the closure of Parliament House as unconstitutional. There was also discussion in parliament of a vote of no confidence to be moved in the coming days. Immediately after the swearing in of MPs, members of the opposition absented themselves. Dausabea attended the parliamentary sitting but was arrested by plain-clothed detectives as he was leaving the house and charged with offences relating to the riots (SIBC 2006d; Solomon Star 2006h). Ne'e had his bail application rejected at the Magistrates Court.

Parliament resumed sitting the next morning under lock-down. Parliamentarians arrived under heavily armed police and military escorts. Overnight, the minister for police and national security, the police commissioner and the prime minister had all made statements rejecting claims by the parliamentary opposition that the arrest and continuing detention of two of its members were politically motivated (SIBC 2006h; Radio New Zealand 2006b). Oti once again objected to the lock-down of parliament, but the speaker upheld the situation, citing the separation of powers under the constitution. The speaker also insisted that parliament proceed with the election of the deputy speaker. Ulufa'alu then led an opposition walk-out from parliament, appealing to any MP 'with an ounce of Solomon Islands blood in him' to walk out with him (SIBC 2006e). Kemakeza was elected deputy speaker in the absence of the opposition. Dausabea had his bail application refused at the Magistrates Court under tight security.

The political situation reached a climax on Wednesday. Five members of the government (including four ministers), led by Sogavare, crossed the floor, giving the opposition a 28–20 majority. Before tabling the vote of no confidence, Oti demanded that the prime minister 'do the honourable thing' and resign. Parliament was adjourned for 15 minutes and, when it resumed about 10.15am, Rini announced his resignation. There was immediate jubilation on the streets of Honiara as taxis, buses and private vehicles sounded their horns and a large crowd made its way down to the Iron Bottom Sound Hotel to congratulate the opposition on its victory. There was a general feeling of relief in Honiara that eight days of intense political and social instability had come to an end, at least for the time being.

## What went wrong in Honiara?

Some of the causes of the rioting and looting that broke out after the election of the new prime minister remain obscure. The sequence of events that occurred at Parliament House on the afternoon of Black Tuesday is contested, as are some of the basic facts relating to those events. The extent to which the outbreak of violence was premeditated also remains unclear. It is possible, however, to identify some factors that arguably contributed to the social unrest. These are now considered.

### Frustration with the election outcome and the electorate's inability to influence electoral outcomes

The 2006 national election, and the subsequent formation of government and the second election for the new prime minister, clearly caused a great deal of frustration among the electorate. As in previous elections in Solomon Islands, and elsewhere in Melanesia, the final outcome was entirely unpredictable from the voter's perspective. In the context of an extremely weak party and policy environment, campaigns were fought on a parochial basis and had little or no bearing on the final composition of the government. There was no way for voters to know whether elected candidates would stay with their parties, who would form the government and who would be prime minister. Moreover, the electorate was particularly cynical about the circus-like dynamics of political camp formation and reformation. The alleged sponsoring of this process by prominent local businessmen of Asian origin fuelled a widespread belief that those vested interests had a strong influence on the final outcome of the election.

These underlying frustrations were exacerbated by the outcome of the parliamentary ballot for prime minister, which essentially returned to power the same coalition that had constituted the former Kemakeza government, with Kemakeza's deputy, Snyder Rini, the new prime minister. The Kemakeza government was extremely unpopular with the public from the moment it came to power after the 2001 election. Indeed, Kemakeza had been thrown out of the previous (caretaker) government of Sogavare (2000–01) for misleading cabinet and allegedly misappropriating funds in relation to the disbursement of a US$25 million loan from a Taiwanese bank, for which he assumed overall responsibility at the time as minister for national unity, reconciliation and peace (Dinnen 2002; Moore 2004).

Moreover, although the 2001 election had been declared free and fair by international observers, there is ample evidence to suggest otherwise. The country was still militarised with the 'joint operation' fighting Harold Keke on the Weather Coast. Honiara was controlled by ex-MEF militants and other parts of the country, such as North Malaita and Western Province, continued to experience violence and lawlessness. It was also reported that voters were intimidated at gunpoint in a number of constituencies in Malaita Province and in Rennell/Bellona. The public response to the announcement of Kemakeza's victory in the 2001 election was negative. 'There was a less than enthusiastic reaction from the crowd that had gathered outside the Parliament to hear the results. Nobody cheered when the governor-general made the announcement' (Radio Australia cited in Moore 2004:173).

Since the arrival of RAMSI in Solomon Islands in July 2003, there have been regular appeals in the letters to the editor and editorial sections of the local newspapers to arrest the big fish, including Kemakeza himself. These appeals intensified after the publication in late 2004 of an auditor-general's report into the disbursement of the loan mentioned above (Auditor-General 2004) and the subsequent arrest of Lucien Ki'i (Kemakeza's permanent secretary at the time) on corruption charges relating to the disbursement. The return to power of the same ruling coalition—headed by Kemakeza's heir apparent—was, for many people in Solomon Islands, the final fatal act in a process of mass political disempowerment.

## Lodging a claim against the government

Anthropologists David Akin (1999) and Roger Keesing (1992) have demonstrated that, since the early colonial period, Malaitan *kastom* ideologies have had a strong anti-government emphasis. Akin (1999:38) describes how compensation has 'long been a key symbol within Malaitan identity and resistance ideologies'. He locates the riots of 1989 and 1996 within this long-standing tradition of Malaitan, and particularly Kwaio, compensation claims against the government. Akin (1999:58) argues that while many factors were involved in the riots, including increasing urban unemployment and a growing 'rascal' subculture, all were underscored by 'enduring Malaitan discontent with government behaviour'. Drawing on Akin's work, Jolene Stritecky argued that the upshot of the 1989 and 1996 demonstrations in Honiara 'was that committing violence against persons not associated with the government, especially Chinese store owners, became par for the course in the Malaitan strategy for lodging a claim against the government' (2001:230).

Some former MEF militants whom I spoke to on Malaita about six weeks after the 2006 riots claimed that the riots were caused by Kemakeza's failure to pay 'rehabilitation to all the boys', as he had promised to (Confidential interviews). This sentiment is related to a broader and widely held belief among former MEF militants that the Sogavare and Kemakeza governments should have compensated them adequately for their role in securing Honiara, protecting the government and 'saving' the nation during the ethnic tension (Confidential interviews). They are also angry about never having received the rehabilitation provided for them under the provisions of the TPA of October 2000 and later promised to them by the Kemakeza government.[2] Seen in the historical context of Malaitan claims against the government, the involvement of disgruntled ex-MEF in the 2006 riots is highly plausible, particularly as the election effectively restored Kemakeza's coalition to power.

## Latent anti-Chinese sentiments

Honiara has a large underclass of disaffected unemployed young men, many of whom originate from the densely populated and historically underdeveloped island of Malaita. These men, known colloquially as *masta liu*, harbour latent resentment of the local Chinese business community, which to some extent is shared by the populace at large. During campaigning for the national election, candidates for seats in the East Honiara constituency, including Charles Dausabea, expressed concerns about the growth of the Chinese business community at a public forum held in Honiara, claiming that Chinese people were dominating local business and commerce and thereby disadvantaging indigenous Solomon Islanders (Solomon Star 2006a). A few months before the election, a Solomon Islander recounted to me a conversation he had recently had with an indigenous Fijian friend who was visiting from Fiji. His friend warned him that ethnic conflict could arise between Chinese migrants and indigenous people in Solomon Islands as it had in Fiji between indigenous Fijians and Indo-Fijians. His response to his friend's warning was that 'we already have an ethnic conflict with the *wakus* [Solomons Pijin for Chinese people]'.

Discussions with Solomon Islanders reveal that people distinguish between the long-standing Chinese families (many of whom have been in the country for several generations) and the newly arrived migrants, most of whom have come from Guangdong Province in southern China (see Moore this volume). The latter group, referred to frequently as the 'overnight passports', came into the country in increasing numbers during the social unrest of 1998–2003, allegedly under illegal or improper immigration arrangements. Indigenous Solomon Islanders regard them as being poorly integrated with local society, and they are often stereotyped as being money-hungry, rude and arrogant. It would appear that it was the newly arrived Chinese migrants who were particularly targeted during the riots and looting. Indeed, it is rumoured that the rioters were following a predetermined list of businesses that were to be targeted. The fact that some businesses owned by long-standing Chinese families such as the QQQ store in the middle of Chinatown were spared, indicates that some sort of selective targeting could indeed have taken place.

## Growing opposition to, and frustration with, RAMSI[3]

Since its inception in July 2003, RAMSI has been subject to increasing levels of criticism from certain sectors of Solomon Islands state and society, in particular the public service, parliamentarians and former associates of militant groups, especially the MEF. In late 2005, former MEF spokesman and prominent local lawyer Andrew Nori launched a High Court challenge to the legality of RAMSI, arguing that the legal instrument under which RAMSI operates—the Facilitation of International Assistance Act 2003 (the 'Facilitation Act')—was unconstitutional. The chief justice struck the case down in a lengthy judgement (High Court of Solomon Islands 2006).

Before his arrest, Dausabea, who also had close connections with the MEF, criticised aspects of RAMSI during an interview with Radio New Zealand (2006a). He stated that, as a newly elected MP, he was planning to scrutinise aspects of the Facilitation Act, particularly the immunity clauses, which granted RAMSI officers immunity from prosecution under the laws of Solomon Islands. It had been reported earlier in the local media that Dausabea wanted to 'get rid of RAMSI' (SIBC 2006a) and it was rumoured that he campaigned on an anti-RAMSI platform in the lead up to the 5 April national election.

An anthropologist who spent three months on North Malaita conducting research on the 'lost tribes of Israel' religious cult reports of pervasive anti-RAMSI sentiments among the local populace (see Jaap Timmer this volume). The deployment of RAMSI to North Malaita in 2003 was interpreted locally as an invasion of the island by foreign military forces. Moreover, in the teachings of the 'lost tribes' movement—currently enjoying considerable support in parts of North Malaita—RAMSI is described as the anti-Christ.

There is also evidence of growing disaffection with RAMSI among the public service, particularly within the Ministry of Finance, which is the focus of RAMSI's economic governance program. Before the national election, Ulufa'alu said that while there was still unanimous support for RAMSI among MPs, there was growing dissent in the public service (Ulufa'alu, personal communication, 26 February 2006). Concerns revolve around the fact that RAMSI advisers are perceived by local bureaucrats as contractors who are essentially working for private-sector interests, rather than for the public service. Furthermore, it would appear that the public-sector industrial dispute was fuelled by growing agitation among local Ministry of Finance employees concerning the great disparity between local and expatriate terms and conditions of employment. In his victory speech, Rini—who had been openly critical of the outgoing Minister for Finance, Peter Boyers, in meetings of the previous cabinet—criticised RAMSI for not doing enough to build the capacity of local staff within the Ministry of Finance (ABC 2006). Concerns about capacity building and counterparting in the Ministry of Finance were also highlighted in a Pacific Islands Forum Secretariat social impact assessment conducted in October 2003: '[a] repeating concern has been raised about the effectiveness of current counter-parting arrangements between RAMSI personnel and local DOF [Department of Finance] staff. Local staff members feel excluded and RAMSI personnel are not coaching/mentoring or transferring skills to national counterparts' (Pacific Islands Forum 2004:19).

Another factor that arguably contributed to the riots is the gradual erosion, over time, of RAMSI's authority. The 'shock and awe' generated by the initial deployment of RAMSI has well and truly worn off. People are keenly aware of challenges to RAMSI's infallibility, notably the fatal shooting of Adam Dunning in late 2004, which demonstrated that RAMSI did not, after all, have machines that would find all of the guns that hadn't been surrendered. According to an ex-militant and former follower of Harold Keke whom I spoke to on the Weather Coast of Guadalcanal, 'people are no longer afraid of RAMSI' (Confidential interview).

As mentioned above, the general public has voiced considerable frustration with RAMSI's inability or unwillingness to arrest the big fish in relation to crimes committed during the tension. While a number of high-profile parliamentarians have been arrested and charged with tension-related offences—notably Benjamin Una and Alex Bartlett—there are widespread feelings that RAMSI has not gone far enough. RAMSI has also been criticised locally for privileging a Western-style law and order approach at the expense of a Melanesian-style peace and reconciliation process (see Moore 2004:215–19). Calls for RAMSI to give greater support to Melanesian forms of peace building have come from elements of society as diverse as ex-combatants, chiefs, church leaders, public servants and judges, including the chief justice. The review of RAMSI conducted by the Pacific Islands Forum Eminent Persons' Group in June 2005 recommended that a policy paper be prepared to identify suitable models for a truth and reconciliation commission (Pacific Islands Forum 2005:paras 14, 63, 90[xii]).

The arrest of the two MPs and the lock-down of parliament attracted sustained criticism from MPs; while the allegations that the PPF failed to prevent (and even contributed to) the riots have been the subject of much public debate. There can be no doubt that the riots were disastrous for RAMSI's public image, with members of the public remarking cynically that the military and police reinforcements were too late, just as the original deployment of RAMSI came long after the open armed conflict in Solomon Islands was over. A further publicity nightmare for RAMSI was the leaking of a confidential email written by an Australian official working in the Solomon Islands Ministry of Finance and subsequently sent back to Canberra (Sydney Morning Herald 2006). The email claimed that on the eve of the parliamentary vote for the new prime minister, Australian High Commissioner, Patrick Cole, spoke with Sir Thomas Chan expressing his concern about the suitability of Rini as a candidate for prime minister. The email went on to criticise both candidates for the prime ministership, describing the next day's parliamentary poll as 'a depressing choice...either way things do not look good for the future of RAMSI or the future good governance of SI'.

Just as the riots of April 2006 could be seen partly in terms of the Malaitan tradition of 'lodging a claim' against the government, they can also be seen in the context of long-standing Malaitan resistance to alien authority. Viewed in this light, RAMSI is the latest 'alien' to attract the symbolic opposition of Malaitan *kastom*. In my discussions with Malaitan ex-militants, *kastom* was evoked frequently as a challenge to the mission, particularly its policing activities. They point to incidents such as trespassing on tribal lands, breaking into houses without permission and general cultural insensitivity in the way in which RAMSI police, and Australian police in particular, have conducted their operations on Malaita. Indeed, many people on Malaita regard the use of large numbers of armed soldiers and police in a number of failed attempts to capture fugitive Edmond Sae as excessive and tantamount to an invasion of Malaita.

The Malaita Ma'asina Forum also highlights these and other incidents in its denunciation of RAMSI.[4] The forum executive argues that Malaitans perceive the intervention as an exercise in recolonisation and Australian occupation in the context of broader 'Australian hegemony in the Pacific' (Malaita Ma'asina Forum Executive 2005:21–9). It is further argued that as well as perceptions, there have been some real issues (the types of incidents referred to above) that have given rise to growing Malaitan opposition to RAMSI. These issues are ultimately grouped under the rubric of culture: 'There are many cultural issues that for simplicity purposes could be labelled as insensitive to the culture of the people because of dissatisfaction with the Australian-led intervention' (Malaita Ma'asina Forum Executive 2005:21–9).

It is not my intention to engage here in a detailed discussion of local discourses surrounding RAMSI.[5] It is informative, however, to reflect on statements made by the Malaita Ma'asina Forum Executive (2005:27), which now appear somewhat prophetic. The forum executive warned that the 'long-term physical presence' of RAMSI in the Solomon Islands would 'create an environment for resentment and *subsequent resistance*' (my emphasis). It stated further that it was predominantly foreigners who were in favour of a long-term occupation and that '[t]his too will create resistance in due course and it is advisable that good intentions should not lead to *violence*' (my emphasis) (Malaita Ma'asina Forum Executive 2005:27).

### Mismanagement of the situation by the police, particularly the PPF

The extent to which PPF officers contributed to the riots by firing tear-gas at the crowd outside Parliament House on Black Tuesday is the subject of controversy. Former New Zealand parliamentarian and frequent visitor to Solomon Islands Richard Prebble claimed that AFP officers had erred by firing tear-gas at a peaceful demonstration, stating that the '[c]rowd was outraged and the riot spontaneous' (Solomon Star 2006j). The New Zealand Defence Minister, Phil Goff, rejected Prebble's comments during a press conference in Honiara. Goff stated that tear-gas was fired only after a police vehicle had been sprayed with petrol and set alight and stones had been thrown at police, some of whom sustained injuries (SIBC 2006f).

The public debate about the role of the PPF has raised broader issues concerning the cultural appropriateness of the RAMSI approach. For example, a Solomon Islander writing in the 'Private View' section of the *Solomon Star* stated

> I believe the situation could have been cool down [*sic*] if only RAMSI officers stopped using teargas and let Sir Peter Kenilorea [the speaker] address his own people [Solomon Islanders] on what he has according to the mediation process and restorative justice, which are deemed

appropriate to [the] Melanesian situation…Therefore let me advise the
RAMSI officers and military units, if…any disagreement arises between
the leaders and indigenous people of this country [Solomon Islands] please
allow Melanesians themselves to take the first approach to try and solve
their own internal matters and affairs (Solomon Star 2006j).

## The dynamics of the crowd in Melanesia: criminals or voyeurs?

The rioting and looting in Honiara demonstrated aspects of the particular
dynamics of crowd situations in Melanesia. In Papua New Guinea, for
example, organised events involving large numbers of people, such as cultural
shows and rugby league games, frequently end in violence and the use of
tear-gas. It would appear that Melanesian crowds can become agitated quickly
and without warning. Another element of this crowd dynamic is that after the
outbreak of any sort of disturbance, even something as apparently mundane
as a lone drunk passing out on the footpath, people will stop whatever they
are doing to observe the event. It would appear that many of the so-called
rioters and looters in Honiara were law-abiding citizens who had essentially
voyeuristic rather than criminal motives. According to people who witnessed
the events, these voyeurs—including many women and children—took the
opportunity, as everyone else did, of helping themselves to some of the goods
that were being looted from the Chinese-owned retail stores.

## The role of MPs in inciting the riot: the politics of disorder

Two MPs were arrested in relation to the riots: Charles Dausabea, Member
for Eastern Honiara, and Nelson Ne'e, Member for Central Honiara.
Both men were members of the Iron Bottom Sound Hotel camp in the
lead up to the parliamentary ballot for the new prime minister and, after
the ballot, became members of the parliamentary opposition. Dausabea
faced charges of inciting violence, threatening violence and intimidation,
while Ne'e was charged with two counts of intimidation and one count
of managing an unlawful society. Both suspects had their bail applications
rejected in the Magistrates Court and the High Court. During Ne'e's High
Court bail application, the government prosecutor alleged that he had
urged rioters to blow up Parliament House on Black Tuesday, calling out
'*dynamitim parliament*' (Solomon Star 2006j). Similarly, prosecutors alleged

that Dausabea had said to the crowd outside Parliament House, '[m]i fala lose nao, iu fala doim what nao iu fala likim [we have lost, you do what you want]' (Solomon Star 2006i). It is alleged further that Dausabea had driven through the streets of Chinatown on the evening of Black Tuesday urging rioters to continue looting. According to a witness statement, he told the crowd to 'Go ahead, go ahead, go ahead' (Solomon Star 2006j).

Rumours circulated in Honiara that on Easter Sunday, just days before the parliamentary vote for prime minister, Dausabea organised and sponsored a party at Ten Dollar Beach on the outskirts of town. It is alleged that he plied his guests, predominantly young men, with alcohol and told them that 'if things don't go our way on Tuesday, this is what you're going to do'. It certainly appears that the riots were a mix of premeditation, spontaneity, criminal opportunism and, as noted above, voyeurism. The fact that petrol spray devices were used to torch police vehicles at Parliament House points to premeditation, as do the reports that rioters had a predetermined list of businesses that were to be targeted.

It is not the first time that Solomon Islands MPs have been accused of stirring up social unrest for explicitly political purposes.[6] It has been argued by some that the outbreak of ethnic violence on Guadalcanal in late 1998 was precipitated deliberately by members of the parliamentary opposition (led at that time by Solomon Mamaloni) who were seeking to reassert control of the state, which had provided them with the lucrative proceeds of corruption in the logging industry during the late 1980s and 1990s. According to the so-called 'opposition conspiracy thesis', the reformist Solomon Islands Alliance for Change (SIAC) government, which came to power in 1997 and was led by Bartholomew Ulufa'alu, presented an unacceptable challenge to a powerful coalition of vested interests, including politicians, public servants and Asian logging companies. Unable to obtain numbers for a parliamentary vote of no confidence, these vested interests sought to stir up trouble on Guadalcanal in order to destabilise the government. According to Ulufa'alu, the 'militancy option' had been in place since the early 1990s, and would have been used to depose then prime minister Billy Hilly in 1994 had he not been forced to resign as a consequence of a number of defections from his cabinet.[7] From Ulufa'alu's perspective, militancy has for some time been regarded by some elements within Solomon Islands state and society as a 'reserve option when democratic processes fail'.[8]

There would appear to be some merit to this argument, at least as it relates to the coup. Greg Fry (2000:302), reflecting on similarities between the coups in Fiji and Solomon Islands, states: '[i]n both coups we note the importance of the middle class businessmen and politicians whose personal wealth and status are tied up with who controls the state…In the Solomon Islands, as in Fiji, the Ulufa'alu Government was introducing anti-corruption regulations which would upset established business connections.' Indeed, the SIAC government's Policy and Structural Reform Program—a mix of home-grown and donor-inspired initiatives—went much further than tackling corruption (Bennett 2000:360, 379–383). The government reduced the number of government ministries, down-sized the public service by 10 per cent and implemented significant reforms in the long-suffering forestry sector, including the drafting of a new Forestry Act and the establishment of a Forestry Board and a Forestry Trust. These reforms 'would have not only reduced the logging quota to a more sustainable level, but also would have seen much more regulation of the industry' (Bennett 2002:10). The 'oppositional conspiracy' theory holds credibility for some long-term observers of Solomon Islands politics (Herlihy 2003; Tony Jansen, personal communication, September 2004).

Although the military-style conflict ended after the TPA, banditry, corruption, intimidation and extortion continued to plague parts of the country—particularly Honiara, North Malaita and the Weather Coast of Guadalcanal—until the deployment of RAMSI in July 2003. Some ex-militants, particularly from the MEF, became indistinguishable from criminal gangs; and ex-militants and politicians benefitted from the abuse of the compensation and demobilisation processes and had vested interests in the prolongation of the lawlessness and disorder. Selected local business houses were awarded duty remissions and tax exemptions during this period (Dinnen 2002), and it was alleged that the backroom dealings also extended to the issuance of new logging concessions to Asian companies.[9]

Commentators have drawn on the work of Chabal and Daloz (1999) in Africa to describe the post-TPA situation in terms of the instrumentalisation of disorder: political élites were perpetuating lawlessness and disorder for their own economic and political benefit (Dinnen 2002; Fraenkel 2004). According to Dinnen (2002:289): '[t]he Sogavare government contributed significantly to the instrumentalisation of disorder over the past two years by using compensation as a key instrument in peacemaking.' The apparent involvement of two MPs in the riots could be understood best in the context of this process. There was a brief hiatus in the explicit incitement of violence by political élites after the deployment of RAMSI, it seems, followed by a return to business as usual.

Moreover, while attention has focused on the alleged involvement of local Asian businessmen and Taiwanese money in the recent national election and subsequent second election, the systemic corruption that has characterised the logging and fishing industries continues unabated and, if anything, has worsened since the arrival of RAMSI. Two auditor-general's reports were published in October 2005 cataloguing deepening corruption in the Department of Forestry, Environment and Conservation and the Department of Marine Resources (Auditor-General 2005a, 2005b). While local Asian businessmen and the Taiwanese government could have some influence on politics in Solomon Islands, we must not ignore the lucrative logging deals that have been the key driver of the politics of disorder in Solomon Islands for the past 20 years or so. There is no reason or evidence to suggest that the situation today is any better than it was almost 10 years ago, when Ian Frazer (1997b:67) wrote that popular opposition to the environmental, social and economic inequities of the logging industry 'is pitted against a ruling élite that is far less committed to democratic decision-making and more popular forms of rural development than it is [to] fostering, in its own interest and the interests of foreign capital, intensive exploitation of the last-remaining forests in the country'.

## Conclusion

The 2006 national election and subsequent formation of a government clearly contributed to the riots and looting that broke out in Honiara immediately after the announcement of Rini's victory in the parliamentary ballot for the prime ministership. The election exhibited all of the elements that have come to characterise national elections in post-colonial Melanesia: a large number of candidates and political parties, a high turn-over of MPs, gross under-representation of women, weak or non-existent policy platforms and a strong disjuncture between the politics of campaigning at the local level and the substance of the government that ultimately assumed power. There were also accusations of vote buying and the funding of electoral campaigns by local Asian businessmen and the Government of Taiwan. These interests were also widely believed to have been involved in the circus-like formation and reformation of political camps that occurred during the two weeks between the national election and the parliamentary vote for the new prime minister.

This latter process was the greatest single cause of the riots. The electorate felt entirely powerless to exert any influence over the formation of the government and the selection of the new prime minister. The people also felt that it was fundamentally unfair that powerful business interests, including foreign interests, should exert such a disproportionate influence on the political process. The return to power of the enormously unpopular coalition that had held the previous government of Sir Allan Kemakeza— with Kemakeza's former deputy as the new prime minister—was, for many people, the final exasperating episode in a political serial over which they had absolutely no control.

There were, however, clearly other factors at play, such as the large numbers of unemployed young men in Honiara who harbour resentment against an expanding Chinese business community, which is perceived as dominating business opportunities at the expense of Solomon Islanders. The recent history of conflict in Solomon Islands indicates that these men provide fertile ground for anyone who is seeking to stir up ethnic hatred and violence (see Fraenkel 2004).

The riots reflect growing frustration in various sectors of Solomon Islands society with RAMSI, particularly its inability or unwillingness to arrest the big fish. There have also been growing expressions of opposition to RAMSI, particularly from Malaitan quarters, and it would appear that the shock and awe that initially provided the intervention force with inviolable authority has eroded over time. The role of the PPF in contributing to the riots remains the subject of controversy and has clearly become politicised. Regardless of which version of the truth is the real one, RAMSI's reputation was damaged in the eyes of Solomon Islanders. Where was RAMSI? Why couldn't it stop the riots?

Former members of the MEF, disgruntled with the failure of successive governments to provide them with the rehabilitation provided under the TPA as well as compensation for their role in saving the nation during the ethnic tension, could also have played a key part in orchestrating the riots. This is consistent with the long-standing Malaitan tradition of employing compensation as a means of voicing dissatisfaction with the government. Moreover, it appears that RAMSI has become the latest alien to attract the symbolic opposition of Malaitan *kastom*.

The particular dynamics of the crowd in Melanesia were an important factor in the riots and looting. A significant proportion of the crowd, it seems, were voyeurs rather than criminals acting with malice aforethought. The spontaneity and speed of the events was characteristic of crowd dynamics in Melanesia.

The last and perhaps most unsettling factor contributing to the riots is the likely involvement of two MPs. The clock has been thrown back to a time before RAMSI, when political élites were able to instrumentalise disorder for their own aggrandisement. It would appear that while the presence of RAMSI could have put a temporary stop to the blatant sponsoring of violence by politicians, the politics of disorder has always been simmering away just under the surface. And while attention has been fixed on the role of local Chinese business and 'chopstick' diplomacy in recent events, let us not neglect the systemic corruption in the fisheries and logging sectors, the proceeds of which have, for many years now, provided the bulk of the spoils of the politics of disorder in Solomon Islands.

## Acknowledgments

I am grateful to Sinclair Dinnen, David Hegarty, Michael Morgan and Ben Reilly for comments on an earlier draft of this chapter, and to Stewart Firth for useful editorial suggestions. I take full responsibility for the content.

## Notes

1   Before the election, Member for Aoke/Langa Langa, Bartholomew Ulufa'alu, described this as a 'new type of politicking' in his constituency, which entailed candidates being paid to stand against him (Bartholomew Ulufa'alu, personal communication, 26 March 2006).

2   The section of the TPA titled 'Rehabilitation of militants' states that former members of the Isatabu Freedom Movement (IFM) and MEF will be repatriated to their home villages at the expense of the national government, and that the government will 'launch

public works programs' to employ ex-militants, and also provide counselling services for them (Solomon Islands Government 2000:PartTwo, Section 5). Former members of the MEF obviously have high and unrealistic expectations about these rehabilitation provisions.

3    During the riots, torched police vehicles and Chinese-owned businesses were graffitied with the words 'Fuck ramsi'. Other tags included 'Fuck *waku*', '2006 election corruption', 'Fuck Rini', 'We need a new PM' and 'Born to destroy'.

4    Evoking obvious connotations with the Maasina Rule Movement of the 1950s, the Malaita Ma'asina Forum is a non-governmental organisation that formed in September 2003 'as a voice to raise concerns and issues affecting Malaita and the people of Malaita' (Malaita Ma'asina Forum Executive 2005:3). Although the forum has a management council representing the 33 wards on Malaita, it is unclear how representative it really is. According to informants on Malaita, it has an ambivalent relationship with the provincial government. Kabutaulaka (2006:3) describes it as being 'pushed by a few élites in Honiara to serve their own political agendas'.

5    I have written about local perceptions of RAMSI in Allen (2006).

6    Note that a former minister in the national government, John Maetia Kaliuae, was found guilty of inciting the riots in 1989 (Fraenkel 2004:117).

7    Like the SIAC government, Francis Billy Hilly's National Coalition Partnership (NCP) was attempting to reform the forestry industry, which had become so corrupted under the governments of Solomon Mamaloni (for details of the reforms, see Frazer 1997a, 1997b; Dauvergne 1998–99; Bennett 2000). The NCP barely had a chance to implement the reform program before it was brought down by a series of cabinet resignations and defections in October 1994. It was proven later that five cabinet ministers of the NCP government had defected to join Mamaloni's Solomon Islands National Unity and Reconciliation Party (SINURP) after receiving bribes from Honiara businessman Robert Goh (Kabutaulaka 1997:488). Once in office, the SINURP government immediately set about dismantling the reform program and it was quickly back to business as usual for Mamaloni, who was the director of a logging company, and his ministers, most of whom were also involved in the logging industry (Frazer 1997a, 1997b).

8    Ulufa'alu 2004; taped interview with Bartholomew Ulufa'alu, 25 July 2004.

9    During the period of the conflict, the production and export of all primary export commodities declined; however, proportionately speaking, log exports declined the least and recovered the most rapidly (Central Bank of Solomon Islands 2005). In 2003, the value of log exports exceeded pre-conflict levels, which lends some weight to allegations that several new logging concessions were awarded after the coup in a number of back-door deals (Ulufa'alu 2004; taped interview with Bartholomew Ulufa'alu, 25 July 2004; Tony Jansen, personal communication, 10 September 2004). It has also been alleged that illegal logging activities increased during the period of the conflict (UNDP 2004).

# References

Akin, D., 1999. 'Compensation and the Melanesian state: why the *Kwaio* keep claiming', *The Contemporary Pacific*, 11(1):35–67.

Allen, M.G., 2006. 'Dissenting voices: local perspectives on the Regional Assistance Mission to Solomon Islands', *Pacific Economic Bulletin*, 21(2):194–201.

Auditor-General, 2004. *Report of the Auditor-General into: export import (EXIM) bank loan; other ethnic related disbursements*, November, Office of the Auditor-General, Government of Solomon Islands, Honiara.

——, 2005a. *Special Audit Report into the Financial Affairs of the Department of Fisheries and Marine Resources*, October, Office of the Auditor-General, Government of Solomon Islands, Honiara.

——, 2005b. *Special Audit Report into the Financial Affairs of the Department of Forestry, Environment and Conservation*, October, Office of the Auditor-General, Government of Solomon Islands, Honiara.

Australian Broadcasting Corporation (ABC), 2006. ABC Radio Australia, 18 April.

Bennett, J., 2000. *Pacific Forest: a history of resource control and contest in Solomon Islands, c. 1800–1997*, The White Horse Press and Brill Academic Publishers, Cambridge and Leiden.

——, 2002. *Roots of conflict in the Solomon Islands: though much is taken, much abides: legacies of tradition and colonialism*, Discussion Paper 2002/5, State, Society and Governance in Melanesia Program, Research School of Pacific and Asian Studies, The Australian National University, Canberra. Available from http://rspas.anu.edu/papers/melanesia/discussion_papers.

Central Bank of Solomon Islands, 2005. Various quarterly and annual reports. Available from http://cbsi.com.sb/index.php.

Chabal, P. and Daloz, J., 1999. *Africa Works: disorder as political instrument*, James Currey and Indiana University Press, London.

Dauvergne, P., 1998–99. 'Corporate power in the forests of the Solomon Islands', *Pacific Affairs*, 71(4):524–46.

Dinnen, S., 2002. 'Winners and losers: politics and disorder in the Solomon Islands 2000–2002', *The Journal of Pacific History*, 37(3):285–98.

Fraenkel, J., 2004. *The Manipulation of Custom: from uprising to intervention in the Solomon Islands*, Pandanus Books, The Australian National University, Canberra.

Frazer, I., 1997a. 'Resource extraction and the postcolonial state in Solomon Islands', in R.F. Watters and T.G. McGee (eds), *Asia-Pacific: new geographies of the Pacific Rim*, Hurst and Company, London.

——, 1997b. 'The struggle for control of Solomon Island forests', *The Contemporary Pacific*, 9(1):39–72.

Fry, G., 2000. 'Political legitimacy and the post-colonial state in the Pacific: reflections on some common threads in the Fiji and Solomon Islands coups', *Pacifica Review*, 12(3):295–304.

Herlihy, J.M., 2003. 'Marching rule revisited: when the cargo comes', *The New Pacific Review (La Nouvelle Revue Du Pacifique)*, 2(1):185–205.

High Court of Solomon Islands, 2006. *Andrew Gabriel Hanaipeo Nori v. Attorney-General, and Sandie Piesley (Commander of the Participating Police Force of the Visiting Contingent to Solomon Islands), and Alan James Morton, Graeme Leigh Marshall, Brett Darren Pattie, Paul William Tubman, Michael David Zschorn and Gavin Alan Campbell*, Civil Case No.172-05, 2006, High Court of Solomon Islands (Palmer, C.J.), Honiara.

Kabutaulaka, T.T., 1997. 'Melanesia in review: issues and events, 1996: Solomon Islands', *The Contemporary Pacific*, 9(2):487–97.

——, 2006. 'Melanesia in review: issues and events, 2005: Solomon Islands', *The Contemporary Pacific*, 18(2):423–30.

Keesing, R.M., 1992. *Custom and Confrontation: the Kwaio struggle for cultural autonomy*, University of Chicago Press, Chicago and London.

Malaita Ma'asina Forum Executive, 2005. *Building Peace and Political Stability in Solomon Islands: Malaita Ma'asina Forum perspective*, Solomon Islands Publications and Information Distribution Centre, Honiara.

Moore, C., 2004. *Happy Isles in Crisis*, Asia Pacific Press, The Australian National University, Canberra.

Morgan, M., 2005. *Cultures of dominance: institutional and cultural influences on parliamentary politics in Melanesia*, Discussion Paper 2005/2, State, Society and Governance in Melanesia Program, Research School of Pacific and Asian Studies, The Australian National University, Canberra.

Pacific Islands Forum (PIF), 2004. *Social Impact Assessment of Peace Restoration Initiatives in Solomon Islands*, March, Pacific Islands Forum Secretariat, Suva.

——, 2005. Mission *Helpem Fren*: a review of the Regional Assistance Mission to Solomon Islands, Report of the Pacific Islands Forum Eminent Persons' Group, May. Available from http://www.pmc.gov.sb/files/docs/epg_report_final.doc (accessed 5 May 2006).

Radio New Zealand, 2006a. Radio New Zealand, 25 April 2006.

——, 2006b. Radio New Zealand, 26 April 2006.

Reilly, B., 2004. 'State functioning and state failure in the South Pacific', *Australian Journal of International Affairs*, 58(43):479–93.

Solomon Islands Broadcasting Corporation (SIBC), 2006a. Solomon Islands Broadcasting Corporation, 10 April.

——, 2006b. Solomon Islands Broadcasting Corporation, 19 April.

——, 2006c. Solomon Islands Broadcasting Corporation, 20 April.

——, 2006d. Solomon Islands Broadcasting Corporation, 24 April.

——, 2006e. Solomon Islands Broadcasting Corporation, 25 April.

——, 2006f. Solomon Islands Broadcasting Corporation, 28 April.

Solomon Islands Government, 2000. *The Townsville Peace Agreement*, 15 October, Townsville.

Solomon Star, 2006a. *Solomon Star*, 3 April.

——, 2006b. *Solomon Star*, 6 April.

——, 2006c. *Solomon Star*, 7 April.

——, 2006d. *Solomon Star*, 10 April.

——, 2006e. *Solomon Star*, 13 April.

——, 2006f. *Solomon Star*, 18 April.

——, 2006g. *Solomon Star*, 24 April.

——, 2006h. *Solomon Star*, 25 April.

——, 2006i. *Solomon Star*, 26 April.

——, 2006j. *Solomon Star*, 27 April.

Sydney Morning Herald, 2006. 'Solomons a shambles: the email that got away', 1 May. Available at http://www.smh.com.au/news/world/solomons-a-shambles--the-email-that-got-away/2006/04/30/11463 35611877.html

Stritecky, J.M., 2001. Looking through a moral lens: morality, violence and empathy in Solomon Islands, PhD thesis, University of Iowa, Iowa City.

Ulufa'alu, B., 2004. Seminar presented at The Australian National University, Canberra, 15 July. Transcript available from http://rspas.anu.edu.au/papers/melanesia/seminars/04_07_15_sp_ulufaalu.pdf.

United Nations Development Programme (UNDP), 2004. *Solomon Islands Peace and Conflict Development Analysis: emerging priorities in preventing future conflict*, United Nations Development Programme, New York.

# Chapter 3

## No more walkabout long Chinatown: Asian involvement in the economic and political process

Clive Moore

In the 1960s, Solomon Islander Fred Maedola recorded a song with Viking Records that became a classic in the Pacific. Written by Edwin Sitori, it was called *Walkabout Long Chinatown*, and it described lyrically the delights of wandering through Honiara's Chinatown. Sadly, the old ramshackle Chinatown has disappeared, burnt to the ground during two days of rioting in April 2006 after the election of Snyder Rini as the eighth prime minister of the troubled nation. Chinatown was a short distance from the centre of modern Honiara. It was a homely place on the banks of Mataniko River, where rural Solomon Islanders felt less intimidated than in the air-conditioned specialist shops downtown; it was close to the main hospital, close to the central market and not far from the main wharves. Constructed when the capital shifted from bombed-out Tulagi to what became Honiara as the new town grew into a bustling city of more than 60,000 people, Chinatown remained the centre of *Waku* activities. *Waku* is the Solomon Islands Pijin name for the increasingly diverse local Asian community. It was used originally self-descriptively by Chinese residents (the only Asians in the early years) and derived from a Cantonese phrase '*wah kiu*', which translates literally as 'residing outside', but is better glossed as 'expatriate' or 'overseas Chinese'. In Mandarin, the phrase is '*wai jü*'. It was adopted by Solomon Islanders to describe the Chinese and now is used more widely for all Asians.[1]

Asians have played a large role in the economy for several decades and, more recently, some have become involved in politics. Some Asians participated in corruption that helped destabilise the government in the decades leading up to 1998, when the 'crisis years' began. During the crisis years (1998–2003), some *Waku* elements prospered through duty remissions and special deals. The fishery and forestry audit reports presented to parliament in October 2005 show clearly that Japanese, South Korean and Malaysian companies took advantage of the disturbed situation to increase their plunder of the nation's natural resources. The Regional Assistance Mission to Solomon Islands (RAMSI), which arrived in mid 2003, is intent on exposing corruption and enforcing accountability, but so far the emphasis is on seeking out corrupt indigenous officials. RAMSI has not tackled the illegal operations of the largely Asian-controlled foreign companies. The April 2006 devastation that destroyed one-quarter of the commercial premises in Honiara was targeted at the Chinese. The underlying dynamic tensions are, however, much wider, and include large-scale corrupt business practices by Japanese, Korean, Taiwanese, Malaysian and Philippine companies as well as by the diverse local Chinese community.

This chapter is not meant to be critical of the Chinese or wider Asian communities. As I will indicate below, many Chinese have been good Solomon Islands citizens for decades. Even the rioters recognised this when they specifically targeted individual Chinese stores and businesses while pointedly sparing others. Some analysis will be tempted to use an easy, broad bush to condemn 'the Chinese' or 'the *Waku*' as a whole. This is not only counterproductive, it is an over-simplification and distortion of the situation on the ground. What this chapter does discuss is corruption and the groups and companies most involved. There is no doubt that some elements of the *Waku* community are heavily involved in corruption, but so are political leaders and ordinary rural people—even if, in the main, the latter are unhappy, silent bystanders watching a cancerous growth that they know is wrong and is damaging their nation. The April 2006 upwelling of violence was a manifestation of trauma lurking just below the surface. There was no real attempt at cultural reconciliation after the end of the crisis years, which left many old wounds barely covered and open to infection.

The crisis years were not directly about corruption; however, everyone knew that certain politicians and public servants were 'on the take', although they felt helpless to do anything about it. The violence that surfaced between 1998 and 2003 was related mainly to antagonisms between two ethnic groups, the people of Guadalcanal and Malaita Provinces, and involved some, certainly not all, of the people from these provinces. Many of the participants were young, disenchanted males who could see no future for themselves and who reacted aggressively, aided and abetted by some of their leaders who should have known better. At the base of the tension was economic inequality, which included corruption but was much wider and covered overdevelopment without adequate compensation or consultation, and underdevelopment with little thought to the consequences (Moore 2004; Fraenkel 2004).

Although there are long-term smouldering resentments against the economic hold of the 'old' Chinese citizens, indigenous Solomon Islanders regard them very differently from the more recent Chinese residents and citizens, who are mostly from mainland China. The old Chinese families see with different eyes from the 'new' Chinese and ordinary Solomon Islanders know this. They belong in a way that the Gilbertese immigrant community also belongs—both are relics of British colonialism and are now part of the modern nation.

Politicians have blamed the Republic of China for its dollar diplomacy and the media has made much of the Taiwanese connection to the Solomon Islands. It would be a mistake to suggest that there is a large Taiwanese element in the local *Waku* community or that the *Waku* have benefitted from this corrupt diplomacy. A rogue *Waku* element certainly exists, but it stretches across the various Asian communities. The real beneficiaries of Taiwanese largess have been indigenous Solomon Islands politicians, who should shoulder the blame for the disgraceful burning and looting that took place in Chinatown. The underlying question is whether any one indigenous ethnic group orchestrated the unrest, and whether the remnants of the Malaita Eagle Force (MEF) are behind the burning and looting of Chinatown and other Chinese business ventures. The arrest of Charles Dausabea, Nelson Ne'e and Alex Bartlett for their involvement in the riots suggests some link to elements from Malaita, although not to the defunct MEF.[2]

The April 2006 riots were partly premeditated. The attacks were strategically targeted and clues existed before the outbreak that should have alerted the police to possible trouble. The police commissioner's lack of prior intelligence and seeming lack of an emergency plan to deal with what was always going to be a potentially explosive day added to the poor performance of the RAMSI police, and their lack of coordination with the local police indicates that long-term changes will be necessary if the RAMSI operation is to retain credibility. This chapter argues that *Waku* business interests and their corrupt influence on the political process are at the heart of the troubles in Solomon Islands. Although Chinese citizens and residents are not entirely innocent of involvement, they are not central to the corruption. Solomon Islanders watched helplessly for 20 years as corruption and government mismanagement increased; they were forced to live through the 1998–2003 crisis years, and then the indignity of an imported administrative and police apparatus. Their discontent boiled over after the post-election parliamentary vote for the prime ministership and the poorly handled situation in parliament. There was something very 'Solomon' about their reaction: despite the massive destruction, no one was killed; the disturbance was focused almost totally on Honiara; and, in a strange way, the riot and the related looting unified all ethnic groups. This chapter looks first at the history of the Chinese in the Solomon Islands, then at wider Asian business interests and connections with corruption. The final section tries to understand the riots and draw conclusions.

## *Waku*, business and corruption

The British Solomon Islands Protectorate was declared in 1893 and a small administration established in 1897. In 1908, Resident Commissioner, Charles Woodford, reported that although there were none in the protectorate at that time, during the 1890s and earlier in the 1900s there had been about 10 Japanese and Filipinos employed in the Solomons pearl-fishing industry. Single Chinese had been introduced via German New Guinea as cooks and gardeners, but most stayed for only six or 12 months. Woodford's explanation of their transitory behaviour was that they 'become discontented as they find no opportunity here of satisfying their desire for sexual intercourse', and that they were also looking for a back door into Australia (Woodford 1908).

More concerted moves to bring Chinese into the territory of the Western Pacific High Commission in 1908 came to nothing. This was due to antagonism from Boers and the British public to Chinese labourers taken to the mines of the Transvaal between 1904 and 1907, which led to the destruction of the unionist government in Britain in the 1906 general election. The anti-Chinese ripple flowed through into the British Pacific. The new Australian government also expressed an aversion to Asian migrants and did not want any in neighbouring colonies. Australia did its best to ensure that there were none in British New Guinea (Australian Papua from 1906). Then in 1910, the Colonial Office declined to allow Indian labour to be imported into the Solomon Islands and, two years later, also said no to similar plans to import Javanese. Lever's Pacific Plantations Limited also failed when it advocated the use of Chinese labourers during the 1910s and 1920s. There were exceptions in the Pacific: Chinese worked phosphate deposits on Nauru and Ocean Islands and plantations in Samoa; and New Zealand, short of labour, allowed Chinese immigrants entry after the 1918 influenza epidemic (Laracy 1974; Wilson et al. 1990; Meeke 1910).

The first Chinese tradesmen seem to have reached the protectorate in 1910. By 1913, Ah Choi had applied for a land lease on Kokona Island in the Gela Group, and, in 1914, Kwong Cheong had a trading business at Tulagi, the colonial capital. They probably came south from Rabaul, where the Germans had allowed Chinese immigration. In 1914, there were about 1,000 Chinese living in or near Rabaul.

The protectorate's Chinese community slowly increased, from 55 in 1920 to 90 in 1925, and to 164 in 1931 and 193 in 1933 (Laracy 1974; Woodford 1911; Bell 1927). Most stayed only for the duration of their contracts, but some used their savings and connections in Rabaul, Hong Kong and Sydney to import trade goods and establish stores. By 1918, there were 67 Chinese in Tulagi, where the protectorate's largest Chinatown was well established by the 1920s and 1930s, replete with trade stores and restaurants. They were allowed to set up stores on Isabel, at Gizo and in the Shortlands in the north, and at Auki on Malaita. Chinese also operated ships on trading circuits around the protectorate. Numbers had dropped to 180 by 1941, probably because the administration attempted to tighten entry requirements in the 1920s and early 1930s; the Hong Kong government did not issue passports and they were difficult to obtain in China. The resident commissioner had total control of all entries without passports and, in 1928, a new regulation levied a bond of not less than £20 on jobless immigrants. Restrictions were made even stricter the next year, but during the early 1930s a new high commissioner arrived, who had previously worked in Hong Kong and had higher regard for Chinese. All restraints on Chinese were lifted in 1933, although they were still not allowed to obtain freehold land. The major merchant companies—W.R. Carpenters, Burns Philp and Lever's Pacific Plantations—did not want competition from Chinese merchants and raised the usual complaints about their corrupting influence on the natives through gambling, alcohol and vice. The British attitude to the Chinese was made fairly clear during World War II when foreign nationals were evacuated but the Chinese were left behind. Some joined the Coastwatchers, others managed to take ship to Sydney or Noumea and the rest hid in villages for the duration of the war (Wilson et al. 1990; Laracy 1974; Bennett 1987).

The Chinese community increased after the war and began to integrate into colonial society in the late 1940s, 1950s and 1960s, adopting Christianity, establishing a Chinese-language school, taking out British citizenship and deliberately becoming part of Solomon Islands society. They grew to control much of the retail trade in the country and became dominant in Honiara and in the main provincial towns. One of the first signs of this change to permanent-residence status was the establishment of Honiara's Chinese Chung Wah School, organised and financed by Chinese residents and opened officially by Acting Resident Commissioner, J.D.A. Germond, on 15 October 1949. In the mornings, teaching was in English and, in the afternoons, in Cantonese. The first professional teacher was Fung Shiu Kat from Hong Kong, who arrived in July 1952 through arrangements between the Anglican Melanesia Mission and the Bishop of Hong Kong. The school went from strength to strength and today is one of the major schools in Honiara (PIM 1949, 1952).

In the early 1950s there were about 300 Chinese living in the protectorate, all involved in technical and commercial services. The president of the Chinese community in Honiara in the 1950s, and until his return to Hong Kong in 1962, was Chan Chee, general manager of Kwan How Yuan Pty Ltd, who was fluent in English. Lai Yuen Wo succeeded him. In the 1950s and 1960s, many Chinese residents applied for British citizenship. This was easier if they were Christian, and many became Roman Catholics, encouraged by Fathers van Mechlin and Leemans. In October 1961, 43 Chinese from Chinatown were christened, watched by another 60 Chinese Catholics in the congregation. A formal British Solomon Islands Chinese Association was formed in November 1965, with Peter Lai as president, James Wang as chairman, C.K. Ching as vice-chairman, Henry Quan and K.H. Ip as secretaries and Chow Leong as treasurer. Stephen Yee, Leong Fat and Paul Sze-tu took responsibility for social and educational activities.[3]

In the 1959 census, there were 366 Chinese in the Solomon Islands and another 100 or so in the 'mixed' category. In 1970, there were 577 Chinese and a growing number in the mixed category. The Chinese numbers sank to 452 in 1976, because some families left before independence, and had declined again by the time of the 1986 census to 342 (Solomon Islands Government 2002:32). Honiara's Chinatown of the 1960s and 1970s was the classic two-sided street of wooden red, green and blue trade stores with tin roofs and crossed-frame railing verandahs. Business was conducted behind counters in a central room and there were living quarters at the back (Laracy 1974). The same style of Chinatown existed at Gizo and Auki, with business links to the Honiara shops. The children of the first generation began to branch out into other economic ventures: they supplied logging camps, marketed trochus shell and *bêche-de-mer* and began specialist shops in the central business district along Mendana Avenue. There were always tensions because Solomon Islanders resented the Chinese stranglehold on retail and wholesale business, but they worked hard and served the nation and themselves reasonably well. These old Chinese prospered under the later decades of the British administration, which operated in a fairly non-corrupt and straightforward manner. The years around independence were a period of uncertainty about their future welcome, but many families stuck it out and prospered, becoming leading hoteliers and owning a wide range of businesses.

During the late 1980s and 1990s, a significant number of 'new' Chinese settled in the Solomon Islands, adding to the already established Chinese community. Many of this new generation are from mainland China and Malaysia. Far from espousing communism, many were refugees from the ideology who wanted to begin business ventures, become citizens and, in the long term, move on to Australia and New Zealand. They have worked hard, been able to send their children overseas for education and many have become good citizens. Some of the new Chinese, however, do not try to become part of local society: they do not learn Pijin, their shops are hot and lack comfort and they seem not to realise that donating to charities and so on is part of their obligations and useful grease to make the local social wheels go round. There is an element of disrespect for their customers, which is exacerbated when they sell cheap stock and refuse to honour warranty and basic quality obligations. Many Chinese are involved in small-scale corruption, bribing their way through customs procedures and generally greasing their paths with 'small' money just as the old Chinese learnt to do since independence. The new Chinese often run small businesses with indigenous Solomon Islanders as 'sleeping partners', and have begun moving (illegally) into bus and taxi businesses. Some Chinese businesses also commit minor abuses of commercial and health regulations, ignoring import regulations by bringing in food items with the signage only in Chinese and Bahasa Indonesia, leaving Solomon Islanders to scratch their heads about the content of the items they are buying. Many new Chinese wanted to become citizens before the statutory 10-year period (for the local advantages and as a gateway into Australia and New Zealand) and fostered a lucrative market in quick passports by paying bribes to members of the Citizenship Committee. They stayed during the crisis years, became richer and in truth were generous to the government and the people during the hard times, even if ultimately for their own purposes. By dint of hard work and subterfuge, the new Chinese were incorporated rapidly into the economy and grafted themselves onto the old *Waku* community.

The old and now the new Chinese families are well established and integrated into urban society. Some of the men have married indigenous Solomon Islanders while maintaining their cultural core and networks. Generally, they stay away from politics. Only two old *Waku* families have gone into politics: the Chan family, of Chinese descent, and the Sato family, of Japanese origin. Accountant and long-term resident Robert Goh also had considerable influence as an adviser to the government of Sir Allan Kemakeza (2001–06).

The Chinese families were the only *Waku* targeted in the burning and looting of April 2006. There was indigenous resentment against the Chinese for controlling the retail outlets, but they sold the right products at low prices and provided about 2,000 jobs in Honiara and more in other urban centres. One image gained from a stroll through Chinatown or along Mendana Avenue was of the bored Chinese *Misis* on her high chair near the cash register, surveying the scene like a tennis umpire while Solomon Islanders did the serving. The Chinese controlled a huge proportion of the retail trade (probably about 70–80 per cent) and the economy could not function without them. How much they have blocked indigenous entrepreneurs from emerging is difficult to calculate, but when I have asked Solomon Islanders why they shop in Chinese stores rather than supporting indigenous business, the usual answer is that the stock is cheaper and more varied.

## Other Asian business groups

How many Asians live in Honiara is hard to estimate. The 1999 census recorded 464 Chinese in the whole country, plus 2,870 individuals of 'mixed' ancestry, many of whom would have been part-Chinese. The 1999 census cloaked the remaining Asian groups, numbering 1,131, under 'other' (Solomon Islands Government 2002:32). I was present at Chinese New Year celebrations at the Pacific Casino Hotel in 2005 along with about 1,000 Asians, and there were celebrations at other hotels; however, this special day would have attracted visitors from other provinces.

The real hard-core corruption has come not from the old or new Chinese, but from Malaysian companies (many of which are connected to ethnic Chinese) and South Korean and Japanese interests. The accounts of Solomon Islands provinces and the national government have not been audited properly since the late 1980s. One of RAMSI's tasks has been to employ a large posse of auditors working from the Office of the Auditor-General. The findings for the Department of Forestry, Environment and Conservation and the Department of Fisheries and Marine Resources were presented to the national parliament in October 2005. They make interesting reading and provide a useful means for assessing more general patterns in the troubled nation.

## Logging

Solomon Islands' abundant hardwood forests began to be exploited commercially in the 1920s (Bennett 2000). The demand for the protectorate's timbers picked up in the 1960s and, by the late 1970s, timber was a major component of gross national product (GNP); however, less than 230,000 cubic metres was cut each year, well below the sustainable level, considered to be 325,000 cubic metres per annum. Most of the logging was carried out in Western Province and 90 per cent was exported, the majority as unprocessed logs. The early phase of timber exploitation was on government land or customary land leased by the government. The logging industry in the 1960s was dominated by Levers Pacific Timbers Ltd, which was a subsidiary of the United Africa Company (Timber) Ltd; an Australian company Allardyce Lumber Co., which also operated in Sarawak; and Kalena Timber Co. Ltd from the United States. Levers, the largest of the early companies, responsible for two-thirds to three-quarters of the logging, withdrew from the Solomon Islands in 1986 because of protests about its operations on New Georgia.

After independence in 1978, and particularly under the first Mamaloni government (1981–84), the logging focus changed to Asian companies, mainly from Malaysia, and the use of customary lands, which made up about 87 per cent of the total land area of the country. No longer able to obtain whole hardwood logs at home, Asian loggers moved into Solomon Islands (and Papua New Guinea), cutting down trees at an unbelievable rate. The Forestry Division, provincial governments and area councils did

**Figure 3.1    Solomon Islands: log production, 1963–94** ('000 cubic metres)

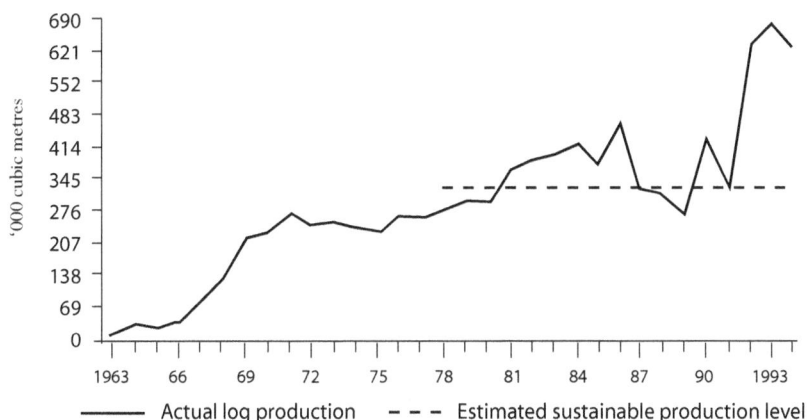

**Source:** Frazer, I., 1997a. 'Resource extraction and the postcolonial state in Solomon Islands', in R.F. Watters and T.G. McGee (eds), *Asia-Pacific New Geographies of the Pacific Rim*, Hurst and Co., London:328.

not have the resources to monitor and police logging. Loggers moved into Guadalcanal, Malaita and Makira-Ulawa provinces. The huge South Korean Hyundai Group set up the Hyundai Timber Company and began logging on Guadalcanal in 1983. Eagon Resources Development Ltd, another large South Korean company, set up on Choiseul Island in 1989. Malaysian companies moved in from 1991. Ian Frazer's figures suggest that 75 per cent of the log export industry in the 1990s was controlled by eight foreign companies, mainly from Malaysia, while Hyundai and Eagon controlled about 14 per cent. Other new, smaller companies also arrived, but many were undercapitalised and their output was comparatively slight. These Asian companies often operated corruptly, putting pressure on and providing monetary incentives for local officials. They developed close relationships with politicians and forged lucrative agreements with local companies to use their licence entitlements. Golden Springs International was one of these, buying local companies and using their licence concessions. In 1988, the ombudsman investigated Hyundai's Guadalcanal operations and Kayuken Pacific Ltd's Malaita operations, reporting most unfavourably. Asian companies continued to move to new areas, for instance Hyundai transferred to Vella Lavella (along with Allardyce), undertaking the first large-scale logging of the island. Licences for 1990 allowed 924,000 cubic metres to be harvested, which increased to 1.2 million cubic metres in 1992 and 3.3 million cubic metres in 1994 (Frazer 1997b; Dauvergne 1998:135–57).

By 1993–94, timber was providing 56 per cent of the value of exports from Solomon Islands, and about 35 per cent of gross domestic product (GDP). World prices reached US$386 per cubic metre in 1993, which encouraged an increase in the volume of logs exported to 624,000 cubic metres in 1994 and to 850,000 cubic metres in 1995. In 1990, timber exports were worth SI$60 million, but by 1996 they were almost six times higher at SI$349 million. In the years just before the crisis began in 1998, the Solomon Islands government depended on logging for 20 per cent of its revenue and 50 per cent of its export earnings. The Forestry Department estimated that of a total land area of 2.8 million hectares, 2,201,100 hectares (78.6 per cent) was forest, but about only 300,000 hectares (7.3 per cent) was easily available for commercial exploitation; the rest was too steep, inaccessible or in some way protected.[4] Eighty per cent of this available forest was customary owned. The rate of logging is clearly unsustainable and predictions are that, by 2010–15, all commercially exploitable land will have been cleared of forest. So far, only limited reforestation has occurred, and the long-term prognosis is bleak. Opposition from rural people to large-scale logging began in the 1970s, but the easy money continues to lure many customary landowners. Small local milling operations are now common, but they can never generate the huge revenues of whole-log exports. A few governments, particularly those of Francis Billy Hilly (1993–94) and Bartholomew Ulufa'alu (1997–2000), attempted to halt the rape of the forests, but they failed miserably against the combined power of the logging interests and their political cronies. Calculations of the revenue leakage in 1993 suggested that US$41 million was forgone (Moore 2004:75–7; Frazer 1997a:329 and Table 20.2).

Logging exports dropped slightly during the crisis years, continuing in areas away from the conflict. Afterwards, logging was the only growth industry, beginning to increase in 2003 with exports reaching 1,043,150 cubic metres in 2004, a 46.1 per cent increase in 12 months. Of that production, 68.3 per cent was in Western Province, 22.8 per cent in Isabel Province, 5.5 per cent in Choiseul Province and 3.5 per cent in other provinces (Hou 2002; Central Bank of Solomon Islands 2004:17). The same Korean and Malaysian companies are involved. The government remains

Figure 3.2    Solomon Islands: log volume and export prices, 1995–2004
('000 cubic metres, US$)

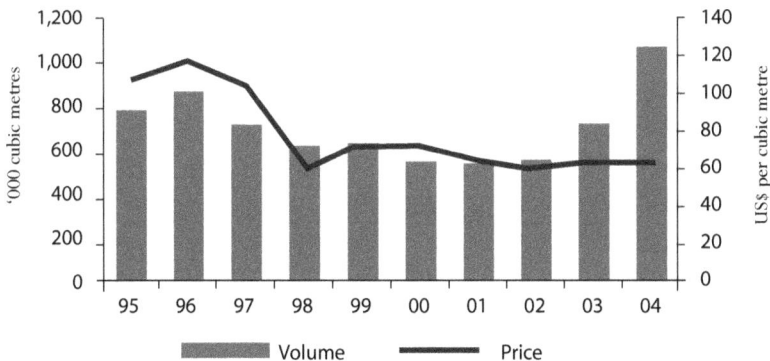

Source: Central Bank of Solomon Islands, 2005. *Annual Report, 2005*, Central Bank of Solomon Islands, Honiara:15.

desperate for money. The customary owners see the logs as their major asset and they are willing to risk the environmental consequences and continue to sell the wealth of future generations for a quite small proportion of the profits. The current act, introduced in 1969 as the Forest and Timber Act, has been amended several times and was renamed the Forest Resources and Timber Utilisation Act in 1984. A new Forest Act was passed in 1999 by the Ulufa'alu government but was not gazetted (hence, it never became law) although some of its clauses were implemented. One significant change was the substitution of provincial governments for area councils in negotiations. Another version was presented to cabinet in 2004 but has not been enacted by parliament, deferred for further consultations with resource holders. This has left the department with outdated regulations that enable the rorting to continue.

The main fees imposed are log export taxes, royalties to landowners, provincial government fees and corporate taxes on royalty payments and profits. The agency responsible for regulating the nation's forests is the Forestry Division of the Ministry of Forests, Environment and Conservation. Log export licences and exemptions from export taxes are issued by the Ministry for Finance, the Foreign Investment Board is responsible for approving applications and setting conditions and the Division of Inland Revenue collects the taxes (Dauvergne 1998). The path is convoluted and hard to follow, which advantages foreign companies or officials trying to exploit the system. The audit report found that procedures were blatantly breached, records were poorly maintained and there was more than a suspicion that some records had been destroyed deliberately to cover fraudulent or corrupt activities (Auditor-General 2005a:46, 63). The 2005 audit report shows that SI$99,863,335 of timber was exported during 2003–04, and SI$39,908,862 in revenue was forgone through exemptions, which escalated by 200 per cent between 2003 and 2004. It found that SI$4,173,910 worth of royalties from logging companies had not been collected, another SI$654,306 were classified incorrectly in the consolidated fund and SI$1,458,000 were diverted fraudulently as unauthorised allowances. In many cases, auditing was impossible and millions of dollars were unaccounted for. Unlawful *ex gratia* payments by the ministry were estimated at SI$1.5 million, and there seemed to be a genuine lack of clarity about which section of the government was responsible for collecting which form of revenue (Auditor-General 2005a).

# Fishing

The fishing industry has not been established as long as logging, but Solomon Islands' tuna stocks are one of the nation's most important assets, and the industry is now the largest domestic tuna-fishing industry in the southwest Pacific. A joint-venture arrangement began between Japanese company Taiyo Gyogyo and the national government, which formed Solomon Taiyo Ltd in 1972. A cannery at Noro in Western Province soon superseded the first, at Tulagi. The initial 25–75 split was gradually altered with different joint-venture agreements until, in the 1980s, Maruha Corporation (formerly Taiyo Gyogyo) of Japan held 51 per cent and the Solomon Islands government held 49 per cent. Purse-seiners, pole-and-line and long-line boats were used, originally owned mainly by Okinawans and manned by Solomon Islanders. The Solomon Islands government, working towards local ownership of the industry, established National Fisheries Development Ltd, 25 per cent of which was owned by Solomon Taiyo Ltd, but sold the ageing fleet to Canadian company British Columbia Packers Ltd. In 1990, this company re-sold to TriContinental of Singapore, a subsidiary of US TriContinental and Solomon Taiyo, trading as Tri-Marine International (Moore 2004:79–81; Frazer 1997a:326–7).

Tuna exports reached their peak in 1986–88, when the catch was more than 40 per cent of the nation's exports, outstripping timber (Frazer 1997a: Table 20.2). In the 1990s, the government issued excessive numbers of fishing licences and the industry peaked in 1995 when 56,135 tonnes of frozen, canned and smoked fish were exported. Solomon Taiyo Ltd always caused consternation in the Solomon Islands as the company recorded a profit only in two years out of 20; however, when a detailed report was commissioned into it in 1995, no evidence of transfer pricing was found. Kate Barclay, who has researched the industry, believes that the Japanese mother company used the Solomons company, representing only 5 per cent of its assets, as a pawn in much bigger moves in its relationship with the Japanese government. Contrary to this view, other evidence from inside the company suggests that the complex financial moves also cloaked transfer pricing.[5] The remainder of the industry consists of licences for about 30 foreign-owned fishing companies (almost all of which have connections with local politicians) to take 572,500 tonnes of tuna each year. Many of these are Taiwanese companies. During the 1990s, provincial governments began forming joint ventures with Asian fishing companies, allocating quotas within their provincial waters.

In 1997, the Ulufa'alu government's new Fisheries Act reduced the quota by 75 per cent to 120,000 tonnes per annum, intending to indigenise the industry. The plan was to sell the nation's holdings in Solomon Taiyo Ltd, but Maruhu was not cooperative and a buyer could not be found for such a seemingly unprofitable company. In 1998 the commercial fishing catch was 94,129 tonnes, worth an estimated SI$204 million or US$40.6 million, representing a significant sector of the economy. The total fish catch in 2004 was 28,235 tonnes, slightly down from 2003 and well within sustainable levels. When the tensions erupted, Maruhu withdrew from the whole venture, leaving the government with 100 per cent ownership of a new company, Soltai Fishing and Processing Co. Ltd. Western Province protested and was granted 45 per cent ownership, which was increased to 49 per cent in 2001 (Moore 2004:81–2).

The tuna industry has the same regulatory and revenue problems as the logging industry. The relevant act has too many loopholes and is poorly

---

**Figure 3.3     Solomon Islands: fish production and average prices, 1995–2004**
('000 tonnes, US$ '000 per mt)

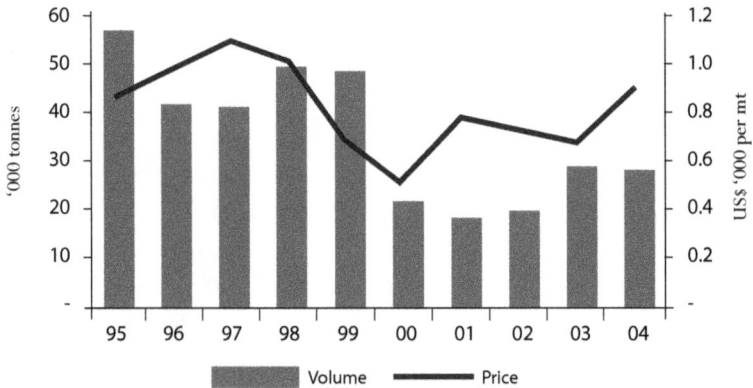

Source: Central Bank of Solomon Islands, 2004. *Annual Report, 2004*, Central Bank of Solomon Islands, Honiara:19.

enforced, the high price of licences leaves room for corrupt practices and the size of the catch is as imperfectly known as the volume of the timber exported. The relevant legislation is the Fisheries Act 1998 and the Fisheries (Tuna Fisheries) Regulations 1999. The audit report found that fishing licence fee revenues received into consolidated revenue were SI$4,948,923 in 2001, SI$4,089,052 in 2002 and SI$12,453,692 in 2003. The shortfall over the three years was SI$37.2 million, the diversions occurring in port sampling and training accounts (SI$3.85 million), in monies diverted from a foreign affairs account (SI$2.7 million), unpaid fishing licences (SI$9.3 million), under-collected fees (SI$8.86 million), a traceable SI$3–4 million misappropriated by staff of the ministry, plus an untraceable SI$10 million. While some allowance needs to be taken for the general breakdown in government services during these years, the audit suggests that the fraud was systematic, and much of the public money was easily traceable to the personal bank accounts of officers of the department or those of their spouses. Fees were often collected in cash, and unofficial receipts were issued. The deputy director of fisheries had verbally amended many licence and observer fees. Not unexpectedly, the public servants involved were quite uncooperative and reluctant to provide information. The audit concluded that there had been 'widespread misappropriation of public money' (Auditor-General 2005b:1–22).

During the previous 20 years, an unhealthy relationship had developed between the *Waku* and various governments, particularly those connected to Solomon Mamaloni. Bart Ulufa'alu, the prime minister evicted from office by a coup in 2000, has little doubt about the connection. Speaking at The Australian National University in 2004, he described the 'Solomon Islands underworld'

> I don't need to point fingers, those who are acquainted with Solomon Islands will already know what group it is. This particular group has been in office for some 20 years, off and on, and the aid community did not take a liking to them. And because of that, this group was isolated and therefore they moved more towards the business houses and the private sector for support. And hence they allowed the private sector, in terms of foreign investment, to come into the resource sectors of the economy, mining, forestry and fishing. So you find that the involvement of the private sector in forestry and fishing intensified, outside of the normal practice under

the colonial government and even immediately after Independence. In the 1980s the forestry sector was opened up and the fisheries sector was opened up to the private sector. And this moulded the relationship...That relationship placed the resources under threat of being exhausted, and the sustainability of the government became the bigger problem. I think this is the group that actually was working both in the political arena and the private sector arena as well as the underworld. And when the war broke out...these same groups took advantage of that, and they made a lot of money out of it (Ulufa'alu 2004).

Total domestic revenue in 2004 was SI$497 million—36.3 per cent higher than in 2003, largely because of greater taxation compliance (ADB 2005). The two audit reports estimated that, at the very least, more than SI$80 million that should have ended up in consolidated revenue during the early 2000s had been skimmed off by corrupt Solomon Islanders or was not paid by the foreign companies concerned. The reports are not comprehensive and it seems likely that even more money is involved. The two departments are important, but there are many more, plus the provinces, yet to be audited. Corruption also occurred through the lucrative exemptions to excise duty, and with aid money (particularly from Taiwan) skimmed off in the past five years (Moore 2004). The real dollar value of the corrupt practices since 2000 is hundreds of millions of dollars, and similar practices have gone on, to a lesser extent, since the late 1980s. The extent of illegal *Waku* practices beyond formal business dealings is unclear. In Papua New Guinea, a similar 'Asianisation' has led to the same pattern of corruption in business. It is also well known that in Papua New Guinea some recent Asian migrants are involved in illegal activities such as drug and gun running and prostitution. Presumably, the same pattern exists on a lesser scale in Solomon Islands. Leading Solomon Islands politicians have often hinted that Asian interests have interfered in the political process and the 2006 elections and the subsequent riots leave no doubt of this.

RAMSI has the unenviable task of guiding a suitable reform process for a nation of half a million people spread through nine island provinces and 190 islands. RAMSI has restored law and order and is now dealing with prosecutions of the 'big fish', while strengthening the public service and the economy (Moore 2006; DFAT 2004). The necessary legal processes to achieve convictions are so protracted that it is unlikely that the 'small fish' will ever face the courts. In any case, Rove Prison is full and who would be left to run the public service? Much of what is necessary to fix the problem goes under the title of 'institutional strengthening', not prosecution. The ombudsman's office must be strengthened and the parliament and public service have to be made accountable. The general public also has to be educated on the consequences of accepting corrupt practices as normal procedure. The reform process is under way. The re-established Institute of Public Administration and Management, assisted by AusAID advisers, has put almost 1,000 public servants through new training programs since it began in 2004, and RAMSI has instituted many community-level education programs.

## The April 2006 riots

There is not much doubt that there was an attempt at organisation of the riots. There seems to have been a core of about 30–40 agitators who led the crowd, and identifiable individuals were also responsible for setting most buildings alight. There was prior knowledge of the riot among some Solomon Islanders; the real success of the riots was, however, owed to the incompetence of the RAMSI police. There was no particular dominant ethnic element, except that Malaitans were proportionally the dominant group in Honiara. If anything, the looters were a cross-section of the urban poor across all provinces.

The crowd gathered at Parliament House turned into a riot just after 3pm on Tuesday 18 April. The announcement that Snyder Rini was the new prime minister occurred soon after midday and the trouble built up over three hours, during which various senior politicians tried to talk the mob down, to no avail. Despite the pleas of the Speaker of the House, Sir Peter Kenilorea, for the police not to use tear-gas, an attempt was made to disperse the mob with gas after stones were thrown and police vehicles were set alight. A three-hour video film exists of the scene at parliament that afternoon. Early on, the crowd was rowdy but unthreatening until the riot gear was handed out (only to RAMSI officers) and tear-gas was fired, which, according to the police, was at 3.22pm.[6] There are several remarkable things about the video footage, clarified by my later discussion of the events with members of the crowd. The local police were totally unprotected and understandably frightened, while the RAMSI officers wore protective jackets and eventually used clear protective shields. The resultant injuries were to the protected foreign police, which indicates what the mob thought of the relationship between the two police groups. The most telling sign of the lack of RAMSI preparedness was the absence of a megaphone, which made communications difficult. The other absence was that of the police commissioner, which the crowd took as a sign of arrogance. Had senior political figures and senior police been allowed to talk the crowd down, Solomon Islanders feel sure the riots would not have occurred. Some early reports said that the crowd used petrol in squeeze bottles to set the RAMSI vehicles alight, which would indicate prior planning. In reality, the fuel was cigarette-lighter refill fuel, which is available readily at any Solomon Islands sporting event or crowd scene, hawked about with cigarettes and betel-nut.

The crowd at Parliament House became a violent mob and managed to destroy several RAMSI vehicles. They continued to stone the police, who never managed to regain control. On 19 May, Police Commissioner, Shane Castles, attempted a defence of his police in the *Solomon Star*. He said that several malevolent groups were purposely gathered at key spots: around Central Market and King George VI Market, in Chinatown and at the City Centre Building. His interpretation was that these groups were organised, however all of these places were shopping and recreation areas and they were always full of loiterers. Central Market positively seethes with people six days each week. Castles claimed that 'large crowds' had gathered in Chinatown by 2pm, which is not borne out by evidence from shopkeepers there, who received warnings relayed from shopkeepers in central Honiara at 2pm. These warnings alerted them that trouble was brewing; there were no large crowds yet for them to see. When the riot spread to the central business district, it was swelled by some of the crowd from Parliament House, but this downtown riot seems to have acted fairly independently. Opportunist looters increased the ranks of the aggrieved protesters. The actions of some elements of the downtown mob were quite premeditated, although this does not seem to apply to the initial mob at Parliament House. There are reports of men in red T-shirts who seem to have been organising proceedings in the central business district. This second mob gathered over several hours and was 1,000 strong when looting began between 3.30 and 4pm. Acor's small shop in the City Centre Building, Wing's and Sunrise supermarkets and other shops along Hibiscus and Mendana Avenues were looted, but very little of the main commercial centre was affected. Prominent old Chinese-owned stores, such as Acor's Bookshop and Sweetie Kwan's shop, were untouched, and the government offices, banks and embassies escaped unscathed. Local police mingled with the mob but could only watch helplessly as the crowd surged around them.

The third phase began when elements of the mob headed down Mendana Avenue to Chinatown, joined by others along the way, and began quite targeted looting and burning. Only one building (old Chinese owned but operated by new Chinese) was destroyed opposite Central Market, leaving half a kilometre of shops untouched. Interestingly, Dettke's huge hardware store, which was close by, escaped attack, in part, because it had increased security for the day. Almost all of the destruction in Chinatown was targeted at the new Chinese, and many of the old Chinese stores survived. Sir Tommy Chan's Honiara Hotel and his son's video shop in Chinatown escaped attack, as did the businesses of a number of Chinese who were married to Solomon Islanders or were old Chinese: H.M. Long, J.B. Leong, Quan Chee, Solo Tai, QQQ and Aba. QQQ and Aba had their own security forces. Aba was well known during the crisis years for employing up to 100 men in his security force and had done so again. QQQ had a sizeable number of Reef Islanders armed with bows and arrows at the ready, and understandably was spared. The mob wanted to target Chan's Honiara Hotel, because of the family's involvement in politics, but was held off by the increased, mainly Malaitan security and the Christian authority of a force of *Tasesiu*—the Anglican Melanesian Brothers, who exercise strong *mana*. Chinese escaped by swimming or rafting across the Mataniko River, helped by Solomon Islander friends and police (Guadalcanal Network Forum 2006).

The eyewitness reports are quite extraordinary.

As we got closer to Chinatown the sky really started to light up with a big blaze. We took the shortcut through the Fiji settlement, and as we rounded the corner, we could see that Chinatown was ablaze. REALLY REALLY ABLAZE. As we popped up onto the road that leads up to the old Mataniko River Bridge I was confronted by RAMSI guys in riot gear who were holding the crowd back. You would not believe this unless you saw it. From the old Mataniko River bridge end (Vuvula Poultry end) both sides of the main street of Chinatown were fully ablaze, with explosions going off at random. At least 20 buildings were completely engulfed in flames. There was also a decent wind blowing down the river that was feeding the fire, and blowing it further down the street. A new building was being engulfed every five minutes, and the flames went at least 30 metres into [the] air. From the looks of it, the whole of Chinatown is going to burn down to nothing.

After a few more large explosions, we decided to walk up Skyline Road to get a more on top view of what was happening to Chinatown. As we got to the Tehamorina turn-off, we could see that at least one third of Chinatown was ablaze, and the fire was heading down towards the Chun Wah end. I don't even think ten fire engines would have made a dent in the fire, considering how old the buildings are, and that they are all wooden, close together, and I'm sure have no fire control gear inside (Guadalcanal Network Forum 2006).

Not all the looted or burnt businesses were Chinese owned—indigenous Solomon Islanders owned some. In the end, proximity went against some, as once fires began, they spread out of control. Nearby New Chinatown was left safe, probably because of a police presence at the eastern end of the old Mataniko River Bridge.

Late Tuesday afternoon, the Pacific Casino Hotel was stoned, but the complex was too well guarded, so the mob dispersed. They returned on Wednesday, and the entire 800 metre-long complex with casino, sports facilities, restaurants, bars and accommodation was looted, torched and reduced to rubble. The destruction of the hotel complex, which contained multiple business interests, requires several points of explanation. It has long been rumoured that the 'old' Chinese owner, Patrick Leong, obtained the land by bribery, alienating what should have been public domain on the sea-shore for the poorer suburbs of Vura and Kukum. There was also anger at the existence of the casino and rumours of prostitution operating from the hotel. Leong also made two mistakes: first, he relied almost solely on RAMSI for his protection, rather than bringing in Malaitan security. The men from the neighbouring Malaitan Fishing Village area offered to guard the hotel complex for half a million dollars ($5,000 a man), but Leong refused, foolishly trusting RAMSI to keep him safe. His other error was that his hotel housed the offices of Robert Goh, Prime Minister Kemakeza's much disliked 'one-dollar' advisor. Goh's house was also the only private residence that was deliberately destroyed. The hotel was seen as the major RAMSI social base in Honiara through accommodation and its restaurants and bars, which also earned the establishment the resentment of many Solomon Islanders. Despite RAMSI recounting constantly how loved it is by the people, RAMSI staff and the other aid-funded expatriates are a new élite, driving around in air-conditioned four-wheel drive cars and living high. They are in Honiara only for the extra money in allowances and socialise mainly with each other. This combination of factors led to the demise of the Pacific Casino Hotel.

Despite the police commissioner's protestations to the contrary, the Tuesday mob was aggravated by the initial tear-gas attack. The mob was soon made braver by alcohol taken from the looted shops. The looters were men, women and children—a mixed bunch from all provinces, although Malaitans predominated (they make up the majority in Honiara). Goods were stockpiled at nearby work places and houses and then transported to the suburbs. Even patients from the nearby hospital participated, and took goods back to the wards. The *Solomon Star* (2006a) reported: '[t]he protestors, a plethora of races, from Solomon Islands provinces, who little over a year ago were at war with one another, were now united against the government…The looters grabbed what [they] could including bicycles, mattresses and whatever they could carry back home.'

Greed united Solomon Islanders, but in the main the burning and looting was well controlled, blatant and methodical.

On the Wednesday, a mob went to the governor-general's residence via the Kukum–East Kola Road up from Kukum Highway, where they delivered a petition demanding that Rini resign. They then returned peacefully to Kukum, stopping only to burn the house of Robert Goh. At Kukum Market, shops on one side of the street were burnt, while those on the opposite side survived. A number of Chinese shops at Ranadi were also burnt: Tongs big complex next to the King George VI School farm, some of the Chinese stores opposite the school and adjacent industrial properties. The Solbrew factory was surrounded by the mob late on Wednesday and was under attack, but the alcohol supply remained untouched.[7] Curfews were imposed and RAMSI and the local police set up road-blocks. The fire brigade and the local police performed admirably in difficult circumstances. About 50 emergency services personnel were injured during the riots, but there were no deaths, which is remarkable considering the scale of the riots. Australia and New

Zealand flew in extra troops and police. Solomon Islanders recount the puzzlement on the faces of the troops, who arrived ready for action, Timor-Leste-style, but found themselves welcomed by smiling locals, who just a day before had trashed, burnt and looted. Gradually, the situation came back under control. Rain helped put the fires out.

Once the flames died down, people began to take stock of what had happened and searched for answers. There were calls for a commission of inquiry. The police commissioner said that his forces had no prior intelligence of the riots, and were not prepared for the level of violence that occurred (Wate 2006c). This fails to recognise that the announcement of the result of the vote for prime minister was the most important political announcement since Manasseh Sogavare became prime minister in June 2000 after the coup. Even a football game at the sports ground near Chinatown can lead to riots there, and the political climate in Honiara was tinder-dry on 18 April, which was reason enough for concern.

There had been three serious youth riots in Honiara before: in 1989, 1993 and 1996. The largest was in October 1989, when 3,000 Malaitans, mainly youths and young men, insulted by scurrilous words written on the wall of Central Market, went in pursuit of Rennell and Bellona people and attempted to march on White River settlement west of Honiara. Over several days, shops were ransacked and people were injured. The police managed to diffuse the situation, 45 arrests were made, the national government paid Malaita Province SI$200,000 in compensation and one prominent Malaitan ex-cabinet minister went to jail for two months for his botched attempts at achieving conciliation (Moore 2004:52). There was also a major riot at Lawson Tama Oval in 1998, when then Police Commissioner, Frank Short, ordered his riot police not to use tear-gas, even when they were being pelted with rocks. As Short commented in relation to the 2006 riots: 'I knew that an overreaction could have provoked large-scale violence' (Short 2006). A former assistant commissioner Mike Wheatley supported him.

> Even if there was a lack of intelligence available, [and] something did really happen as a surprise, there are well-established procedures. [If] you go back through [the] history of the police force, there are well-established procedures to call out, to muster people, to call out including headquarters staff, and one of the first places you respond to, is Chinatown (Solomon Star 2006g).

The size of the April 2006 riots was hard to predict, but violence was always a possible outcome of the vote for the prime ministership.

The riots gathered momentum over 24 hours and were poorly handled by RAMSI. There was also clearly prior knowledge of what was about to occur. For instance, local police went door to door along the central Mendana Avenue shops fully two hours before the riot at Parliament House, telling the Chinese shopkeepers to close their doors because they had intelligence of the coming attack. Whether they were following established local procedures, or reacting to local intelligence, is not clear. John Roughan (2006), writing in the *Solomon Star*, challenged the RAMSI version that police were caught by surprise.

> That 'story' doesn't stack up! At least two hours before the first smoke whispers rose in Chinatown's buildings and well after the troubles around Parliament House had ceased to worry, senior citizens were telephoning the proper authorities—Police Headquarters, Governor General. They informed them what was going to happen. The message was sent loudly and clearly: Chinatown was the mob's next target. Sir Henry Quan of QQQ, having been warned by a long time storeowner in the middle of Honiara's business sector, spoke directly to police authorities and warned them in no uncertain terms that a mob was moving towards Chinatown, it would be looted and even worse, could be burnt to the ground.
>
> The Police response was curious! Sir Henry was informed that the police force was already overstretched and it was going to station its forces to protect Honiara's centre. Had such a decision been made with civilian concurrence? Who had made such a decision and under what authority? [These] are only a few of the questions that a properly set up Commission of Inquiry must study.

What was the level of RAMSI intelligence gathering? What was their relationship with the local police, whom they had been working alongside for almost three years? Why were RAMSI officers wearing riot gear while the local police were not? Why weren't extra police or troops flown in by Wednesday morning, which would have saved the Pacific Casino Hotel complex? At 9.40pm on Tuesday 18 April, the Australian foreign minister agreed to extra military forces being put on standby. An official request for military reinforcements was made at 1.15am on Wednesday 19 April, but the extra forces did not arrive until late afternoon and into the evening of that day (Wate 2006c). After the crisis abated in 2003, RAMSI promised that extra troops could be flown in from Townsville very quickly. Australian Army sources suggest that three days are needed to move a large force of this nature, and the 16–24 hour gap between the decision and troops reaching Honiara is very fast by their standards. It seems that Australia moved its disciplined forces as fast as it could. But it was not fast enough. Why was there no rapid-deployment force available? Could more police have been sent more quickly? If there was a fault, it was that RAMSI did not prepare for the possibility of violence, or was not willing to be seen bringing in more forces before the announcement of the election of Rini as prime minister. Even on Wednesday night, Australian authorities were indecisive. A foreign affairs official faced by furious Australians at the Airport Hotel, some of whom had been injured, tried to tell them to fend for themselves, until they blocked his exit and demanded immediate action. An Australian Air Force Hercules evacuated them a few hours later.

Why is Taiwan being blamed for everything? On Wednesday 3 May, the Republic of China Embassy in Honiara issued a pathetic press release, pleading with Solomon Islands not to sever diplomatic ties, which is what Sogavare had announced he would do when he became prime minister, with a shift to recognition of mainland China (Chen 2006). For Taiwan, the stakes are diplomatic not economic. There are very few Taiwanese citizens involved in business in the Solomon Islands, except in the fishing industry. The Solomon Islands government has remained a constant supporter of Taiwan since independence in 1978, despite a few flirtations with mainland China designed to make Taiwan jealous, not to ruin the diplomatic marriage. Taiwan has poured many millions of dollars into the Solomon Islands, but local Chinese have little time for the Taiwanese government and certainly have not benefitted financially. The nation has benefitted from legitimate development projects, but there is no proof that old or new Chinese have been used as a conduit to launder Taiwanese government funds, although there remains a strong suspicion that illegal money is laundered through the casinos. There is no doubt, however, that the 2001–06 government of Sir Allan Kemakeza did very well out of the relationship.

The Chinese community is too diverse to describe as being united. One interesting sidelight to this sorry tale is the cash deposits made into the banks after the riots. On Friday 21 April, when the banks reopened, the ANZ Bank in downtown Honiara at Point Cruz received SI$ 24 million

(US$3 million) in cash deposits, while the NBSI received SI$10 million in cash deposits, mostly from Chinese. If we presume a similar amount was suddenly deposited in Westpac accounts, something like SI$50 million (US$6 million) came out of hiding (Brown 2006). The Chinese have never entirely trusted the banks, and prefer to hide some of their money away from the prying eyes of the taxman and the central bank. It is no wonder that Solomon Islanders are suspicious of Chinese business operations.

The main Chinese political players are Sir Thomas and Laurie Chan of the Honiara Hotel and Alex Wong of Iron Bottom Sound Hotel. The wealthy Chans backed the previous government of Sir Alan Kemakaza and the new but short-lived government of Snyder Rini, providing a base for the Rini group. Their main motivation, apart from the tax breaks they have received over many years, was to get hold of Honiara's third casino licence. The first licence went to the Honiara Casino, which is owned by the Chen family of Singapore and other Chinese interests, and managed locally by Hayden Fargas. Honiara Casino has never been attached to a hotel, but plans are proceeding to build on land near the Town Ground. The second licence went to Patrick Leong's Club Supreme casino at the Pacific Casino Hotel. The Chans wanted the third licence for their hotel and had almost achieved their desire, even building suitable premises, but they were refused a licence. Alex Wong, who housed Job Dudley Tausinga's group at his Iron Bottom Sound Hotel, fell out with the Taiwanese a few years ago and more recently has backed the recognition of mainland China. The bills for the politicians camped at Iron Bottom Sound Hotel were rumoured to have been paid by Honiara Casino sources, via Charles Dausabea, but were eventually paid by companies connected to the politicians. Sogavare's political group was holed up at the Pacific Casino Hotel (until it burnt down). Sogavare has links to other Asian figures and to large business interests. One of these is Filipino logging businessman Roman Quitales, said to be the inspiration for Sogavare's 'social credit' philosophy, enunciated during the run up to the election, which includes printing more money to eliminate poverty and abolishing all banks, including the central bank. The Dettke family (of German and Guale origin) who own ITA Hardware and many other business interests, also supports Sogavare. Despite his public denial, Bobo Dettke is rumoured to have paid all the bills for Sogavare's group at the Pacific Casino Hotel.

The wild card that no one could control was Charles Dausabea, Member
for East Honiara, who originally sided with Tausinga's political camp. Along
with another Honiara MP, Nelson Ne'e, Dausabea was arrested on suspicion
of orchestrating and encouraging the rioters (Solomon Star 2006b).[8] Alex
Bartlett, a former Malaitan politician and ex-MEF leader from Small Malaita,
was also arrested on similar charges. Dausabea's actions followed a pattern
set over many years: he was an ex-MEF leader from the Fataleka district in
Malaita, who was banned from entering Australia. The extent of Malaitan
control of the riots is still unclear. Sogavare, thankful for Dausabea's support
in his election as prime minister on 4 May, and no doubt making a point to
RAMSI about who controlled Solomon Islands, named Dausabea as his new
police minister, while he was in jail. Ne'e was offered the tourism portfolio.
The govenor-general, however, refused to swear the men in while they were
in jail, causing Sogavare to appoint acting ministers. In the end, they were
dropped from the cabinet altogether (O'Callaghan 2006; Wate 2006d).

It will be a long time before the Solomon Islands recovers from this blow.
Some of the Chinese families will never return and business confidence will
not be restored for many years. Many of the businesses that were destroyed
were not insured or had policies that did not cover riot. At least 2,000
people lost their jobs (600 at the Pacific Casino Hotel alone) and thousands
of Solomon Islander families (estimates suggested 15,000 individuals) in
Honiara suffered extreme poverty as a consequence of the events of April
2006. Food shortages began immediately after the riot and the price of basic
consumer goods soared even for rice, of which there was plenty in reserve;
this smacked of profiteering. Without its Chinese business, Telekom forecast
a large loss. The Solomon Islands National Provident Fund expects to lose
SI$500,000 a year in contributions. The 6,000 tourists who visit Solomon
Islands each year will be slow to return. Inflation (running about 10 per
cent) is expected to increase to more than 15 per cent (Solomon Star 2006b,
2006c, 2006d, 2006e, 2006f).

The *Solomon Star* has carried many heartfelt apologies from Solomon
Islanders to the Chinese community, expressing shame for the terror and loss
they have suffered. Solomon Islanders are trying to come to terms with what
happened. The high level of support for RAMSI has been damaged and its
officials must try to deepen the very shallow level of cultural understanding
they have of Solomon Islanders. The recent events show that a large

number of Solomon Islanders are no longer willing to tolerate corrupt government, nor what they see as double standards in the way RAMSI has selected individuals for prosecution for crimes committed during the crisis years. In his contribution to this volume, Transform Aqorau suggests that the deep cause of the destructive riots is the cancerous corruption that has affected the timber industry since the 1980s, which has spread through the entire body of the nation.[9] I would add the fishing industry to his argument. There is no doubt that this corruption is linked to Asian business interests, but it has been encouraged by leaders in local communities and politicians who have benefited along the way. The problem is now how to halt the cancer without losing the patient: the innocent people of Solomon Islands.

While they were quite obviously antithetical to modern democratic practices and should be discouraged from ever occurring again, the disruptions of what is now known as Black Tuesday made many politicians reconsider their arrogant disregard of the electors who voted them into power. The nation cannot be ruled by a 1,000-strong Honiara mob; but there was an element of people power involved in it all, which forced an elected prime minister to resign. Future Solomon Islands governments and other nations in the Pacific region would be wise to take note.

## Acknowledgments

I acknowledge the assistance of the Australian Research Council and the comments and guidance of various individuals, most of whom prefer to remain anonymous.

## Notes

1   I am indebted to Garth Wong, Chi-Kong Lai, Tarcisius Tara Kabutaulaka and David Akin for their help with the meaning of the word.
2   Bartlett, an ex-parliamentarian, was secretary-general of the MEF Supreme Council. Dausabea was also involved intimately in the MEF.
3   The association also had advisors from the wider community: Michael Rapasia (Legislative Council Member for Guadalcanal), Maiano Kelesi (Member for North Malaita), Father Wall (a nominated member), Silas Sitai and Dr Gideon Zoloveke (PIM 1950; British Solomon Islands Protectorate News Sheet 1961, 1962, 1965).

4   Dauvergne (1998:145) suggested that 480,000 hectares were suitable for commercial logging, while other sources went as low as 280,000 hectares.
5   Interview with Augustine Manekako, White River, Honiara, November 2004.
6   Information from Paul Roughan, 18 April 2006.
7   Information from Paul Roughan, 18–19 April 2006.
8   They were allowed to vote in the Thursday 4 April election in which Sogavare became prime minister.
9   See also Aqorau 2006.
10  The high commissioner had already been in trouble with the short-lived Rini government in May, when he was summoned to explain an email sent by a senior RAMSI official, which contained allegations that Cole was dissatisfied with the 18 April candidacies of Rini and Sogavare for the position of prime minister. Cole's reply was not acceptable and Rini wrote to Australia's Prime Minister, John Howard, to complain, recommending that Cole be recalled. Prime Minister Sogavare did not pursue Rini's call, but kept watch and was unwilling to let Cole overstep his mark again (see Honimae 2006; Eremae 2006; Wate 2006a, 2006b). For a biography of Patrick Cole, refer to http://www.dfat.gov.au/homs/sb.html. Robert Hooton replaced Cole in March 2007.
11  See also Solomon Star 2006h.

# References

Andrusiak, K. and Merritt, C., 2006. 'Fear for Einfeld as new résumé flaws revealed', *The Australian*, 31 August.

Aqorau, T., 2006. 'Corruption no secret in Solomon Islands', Pacific Islands Report, 9 May, Pacific Islands Development Program/East–West Center, University of Hawai'i. Available from http://pidp.eastwestcenter.org/pireport/2006/May/05-09-com2.htm (accessed 16 May 2006).

Asian Development Bank (ADB), 2005. 'Economic trends and prospects in developing Asia: Solomon Islands', in *Asian Development Bank Outlook 2005:II*, Asian Development Bank, Manila. Available from http//www.adb.org/Documents/Books/AFO/2005/sol.asp (accessed 2 January 2006).

Auditor-General, 2005a. *Special Audit Report into the Financial Affairs of the Department of Forestry, Environment and Conservation*, October, Office of the Auditor-General, Honiara.

——, 2005b. *Special Audit Report into the Financial Affairs of the Department of Fisheries and Marine Resources*, October, Office of the Auditor-General, Honiara.

Bell, W.R., 1927. District Officer W.R. Bell to Resident Commissioner, 12 June 1927, SINA BSIP 14/60.

Bennett, J.A., 1987. *Wealth of the Solomons: a history of a Pacific archipelago, 1800–1978*, University of Hawai'i Press, Honolulu.

——, 2000. *Pacific Forest: a history of resource control and contest in Solomon Islands, c. 1800–1997*, White Horse Press and Brill, Cambridge and Leiden.

British Solomon Islands Protectorate News Sheet, 1961. *British Solomon Islands Protectorate News Sheet*, October.

——, 1962. *British Solomon Islands Protectorate News Sheet*, February.

——, 1965. *British Solomon Islands Protectorate News Sheet*, 15 November.

Brown, T., 2006. *Solomons Update*, Bishop Terry Brown, 27 April.

Central Bank of Solomon Islands, 2004. *Annual Report, 2004*, Central Bank of Solomon Islands, Honiara.

——, 2005. *Annual Report, 2005*, Central Bank of Solomon Islands, Honiara.

Chen, A.C.S., 2006. ROC (Taiwan) is Solomon Islands' Most Reliable Partner, Press release from Ambassador Antonia C.S. Chen, Embassy of the Republic of China (Taiwan), Honiara, 3 May.

Dauvergne, P., 1998. 'Weak states and the environment in Indonesia and the Solomon Islands', in P. Dauvergne (ed.), *Weak and Strong States in Asia-Pacific Societies*, Department of International Relations, Research School of Pacific and Asian Studies, The Australian National University, Canberra: 135–57.

Department of Foreign Affairs and Trade (DFAT), 2004. *Solomon Islands: rebuilding an island economy*, Australian Government, Canberra.

Eremae, O., 2006. 'Rini hits at Australia', *Solomon Star*, 3 May.

Fraenkel, J., 2004. *The Manipulation of Custom: from uprising to intervention in the Solomon Islands*, Victoria University Press, Wellington.

Frazer, I., 1997a. 'Resource extraction and the postcolonial state in Solomon Islands', in R.F. Watters and T.G. McGee (eds), *Asia-Pacific New Geographies of the Pacific Rim*, Hurst and Co., London.

——, 1997b. 'The struggle for control of Solomon Island forests', *The Contemporary Pacific*, 9(1):46–53.

Guadalcanal Network Forum, 2006. *Ripota*, Guadalcanal Network Forum, 18 April. Available from http://tutuvatu.com.

Honimae, J., 2006. Rini Recommends Cole's Recall, Press release, 3 May, Solomon Islands Government Communications Unit, Honiara.

Hou, R.N., 2002. 'The Solomon Islands economy: recent developments and the impact of ethnic tensions', *Pacific Economic Bulletin*, 17(2):15–32.

Iroga, R., 2007. 'Sir Amet doubtful for inquiry', *Solomon Star*, 26 February.

Laracy, H.M., 1974. 'Unwelcome guests: the Solomons' Chinese', *New Guinea and Australia, the Pacific and Southeast Asia*, 8(4):27–37.

Laurere, N., 2006. Registrar of the High Court, *Solomon Star*, 18 September.

Manu, M., 2006. 'Fono scorns PM's action', *Solomon Star*, 25 August.

Meeke, J., 1910. J. Meeke, Chairman, Lever's Pacific Plantations Ltd. to Secretary to High Commissioner, 8 November, Microfilm 2916 CO225/92, Western Pacific No.3141 10/11:Labour in the Solomons.

Merritt, C., 2006. 'Einfeld grants in spotlight', *The Australian*, 29 August.

——— and Andrusiak, K., 2006. 'Two more groups deny that Einfeld holds posts', *The Australian*, 13 September.

Moore, C., 2004. *Happy Isles in Crisis: the historical causes for a failing state in Solomon Islands, 1998–2004*, Asia Pacific Press, The Australian National University, Canberra.

———, 2006. 'Beyond RAMSI: the future of the Solomon Islands', in A. Brown (ed.), *Development and Security in the SouthWest Pacific*, International Peace Academy, New York, and the Australian Centre for Peace and Conflict Studies, University of Queensland, Brisbane.

Nason, D., 2006. 'Uni can't find any record of Einfeld', *The Australian*, 28 August.

O'Callaghan, M.L., 2006. 'Solomon ministers sacked before Downer lands', *The Australian*, 19 May.

Ong, T., 2006. 'Einfeld cut from Honiara inquiry', *The Australian*, 18 September.

Pacific Islands Monthly (PIM), 1949. *Pacific Islands Monthly*, November.

———, 1950. *Pacific Islands Monthly*, June.

———, 1952. *Pacific Islands Monthly*, November.

Roughan, J., 2006. 'More questions than answers!', *Solomon Star*, 1 May.

Short, F., 2006. 'Letter to the editor', *Solomon Star*, 24 May.

Solomon Islands Government, 2002. *Report on the 1999 Population and Housing Census: analysis*, Solomon Islands Government, Honiara.

———, 2007. First Interim Report of the April Riot Commission of Inquiry, 12 July 2007. Available from http://www.pmc.gov.sb (accessed 25 July 2007).

Solomon Star, 2006a. *Solomon Star*, 19 April.

———, 2006b. *Solomon Star*, 25 April.

———, 2006c. *Solomon Star*, 26 April.

———, 2006d. *Solomon Star*, 27 April.

———, 2006e. *Solomon Star*, 6 May.

———, 2006f. *Solomon Star*, 19 May.

———, 2006g. 'Riot inexplicable says Wheatley', *Solomon Star*, 7 June.

———, 2006h. *Solomon Star*, 27 October.

———, 2007. 'Commission of inquiry on April riot near completion', *Solomon Star*, 19 January.

Ulufa'alu, B., 2004. Current issues of politics and development in Solomon Islands, Transcript of seminar presented at The Australian National University, Canberra, 15 July.

Wate, A., 2006a. 'RAMSI adviser sent home over leaked email', *Solomon Star*, 3 May.

———, 2006b. 'Govt will not pursue recalling Cole', *Solomon Star*, 9 May.

———, 2006c. 'Police chief replies to criticisms', *Solomon Star*, 19 May.

———, 2006d. 'A step further PM' , *Solomon Star*, 19 May.

Wilson, M., Moore, C. and Munro, D., 1990. 'Asian workers in the Pacific', in C. Moore, J. Leckie and D. Munro (eds), *Labour in the South Pacific*, Department of History and Politics and the Centre for Melanesian Studies, James Cook University, Townsville: 78–107.

Woodford, C.M., 1908. Resident Commissioner Charles M. Woodford to High Commissioner Sir Everard Im Thurn , 13 February 1908, Western Pacific No.13758 CO225/83 (1908).

———, 1911. Resident Commissioner C.M. Woodford to District Officer T.W. Edge-Partington, 24 December 1911, SINA BSIP 14/6.

# Chapter 4
## Westminster meets Solomons in the Honiara riots

Tarcisius Tara Kabutaulaka

On Wednesday 19 April 2006, the Solomon Islands national capital, Honiara, woke up to the smouldering remains of the previous day's rioting, which had left much of Chinatown burned to the ground, shops looted, vehicles torched, a number of police officers injured and a newly elected prime minister in hiding.

That morning, the sky opened and sprinkled rain as though to cool the anger that had led to the mayhem. In some places, the flames flared on in defiance, eating away the old wooden structures that were once part of a bustling shopping district. In other parts of town, such as the Ranadi industrial area and the Kukum sea front, the looting and destruction continued. For example, the Pacific Casino Hotel, owned by Patrick Leong, was attacked and set on fire on Wednesday 19 April.

This was the first mass destruction of its kind ever seen in Honiara. During the social unrest of 1998–2003, the capital city had not been attacked or damaged in this manner. Even the riot of 1989 was nothing compared with what happened on what is now referred to commonly as 'Black Tuesday'.

Like the defiant flames in Chinatown, the memories of what happened in April 2006 will not go away easily. People will remember it for many years to come and many want an explanation—not only why it happened, but why, despite the presence and might of the Australian-led Regional Assistance Mission to Solomon Islands (RAMSI), it was not stopped. Further, many people want to know how such an event could be prevented from happening again. In search of an explanation, the Manasseh Sogavare-led government, which took office after the riots, set up a commission of inquiry to look into the riot.[1]

Even before the fires on the streets of Honiara were put out, commentators and spin-doctors were quick to draw connections between the events of Black Tuesday and the civil unrest of 1998–2003, which led to the deployment of RAMSI. What happened in Honiara on 18 and 19 April cannot, however, be explained in terms of those events alone. In fact, it had less to do with civil unrest and more to do with what people perceived as the corruption of the democratic process. In particular, the protest (which led to rioting and looting) highlighted concerns about the process of selecting a prime minister, and allegations that domestic and international business interests had influenced the formation of government. Further, it raises broader questions about the representation that forms the foundation of the Westminster parliamentary system. It also raises questions about the appropriateness of the Westminster system for Solomon Islands.

My interest here is not to point a finger at those who might have had a hand in organising the rioting and destruction of property; that is a matter for the courts to deal with. Rather, I am interested in examining some of the underlying assumptions of the Westminster system and the challenges of implementing it in Melanesian countries such as Solomon Islands. Here, I discuss how Solomon Islander politicians used (and abused) the Westminster system, especially in the lead up to the April 2006 election of the prime minister, to produce an outcome that contributed to the riots, looting and destruction of parts of Honiara. I also explore how the Westminster parliamentary system, by virtue of its institutional design, exacerbated the situation. I suggest that there is a need to include some 'Solomon Islands flavour' in the Westminster system that we adopt.

I assert that there were two ways in which the Westminster system contributed to the April 2006 riots. First, the system is designed to be adversarial: it sets groups up against each other and assumes that 'better' decisions are made through political antagonism. Second, the first-past-the-post electoral system adopted by Solomon Islands often fails to produce candidates that receive a majority of the votes cast in an election, raising the question of whether the government that is ultimately elected by parliament reflects the choice of a majority of the public. Ordinary citizens have no direct control over the formation of government and the choice of prime minister. It is assumed that members of parliament will have the interests of their electorates at heart and form governments that represent those interests. Consequently, there is frustration when such choices do not reflect popular support. In April 2006, that frustration spilled over into the streets of Honiara.

## Westminster meets Solomons: issues and challenges

Discussions about how British colonial rule could be best administered in Solomon Islands took place in official circles long before the country gained independence in 1978. After the 1927 murders of District Officer W.R. Bell and a cadet on Malaita, for example, the Secretary of State for the Colonies appointed Sir H.C. Moorhouse to conduct an official inquiry into the circumstances surrounding the murders (Keesing and Corris 1980). Moorhouse's report, among other things, highlighted the need to put in place an appropriate and locally acceptable administrative system that reflected local systems of governance and was informed by Solomon Islanders' viewpoints. He also recommended that traditional leadership systems and leaders be recognised and utilised in the administration of the colony, especially in choosing headmen who represented the administration and enforced its rules at the local level. Moorhouse stressed the importance of ensuring that they were men with genuine authority and following in the community (Healy 1966:194–204). This led to the establishment of native councils and courts (Healy 1966). Solomon Islanders were, however, kept at the lower levels of the administrative ranks, as headmen and district constables, or 'ples men' as they were referred to in Pijin. The term ples man was in reference to the fact that these men enforced the colonial government's laws at the local level, the ples (place).

The push to improve the colonial administration and involve Solomon Islanders was disrupted by World War II. After the war, however, the colonial government continued to advocate local-level administration through the introduction of the Native Administration Regulation 1947, which provided for statutory sub-district councils. These were regarded as a preparation for larger councils that were introduced later. The establishment of larger councils was hastened by the demands of the Ma'asina Rule Movement, which led to the establishment of the Malaita Council in 1953 (Laracy 1983). Other councils were later established for other districts, giving Solomon Islanders greater participation in administration at the local level (Healy 1966; Bennett 1987).

By the 1960s, Solomon Islanders were beginning to participate, not only as headmen, *ples men* and local council leaders, but as members of the Legislative Council, which was established in 1960. One of the issues discussed in the Legislative Council was the need for an appropriate system of government. A Legislative Council paper of 1968 (BSIP 1968), for example, observed that the 'Westminster pattern of government has either failed, or had to be substantially modified to meet the political needs of some developing countries in the Commonwealth'. It went on to state that 'increasing doubt has been expressed whether in our [Solomon Islands] circumstance and for the foreseeable future political progress, following the Westminster model, is suitable or desirable' (BSIP 1968). In response to this paper, the Legislative Council, in December 1968, appointed a select committee to look into a proposal for an alternative to the Westminster system. This led to the British Solomon Islands Order 1974, which introduced a system of government by committee, in which a single council, known as the Governing Council, replaced the legislative and executive councils. Legislative functions were vested in the Governing Council, while executive functions were shared among committees set up to look after specific areas: finance, natural resources, social services, works and communications and internal affairs. The committees were responsible to the council, which acted as an executive body when meeting in private, and as a legislature when holding public meetings (Saemala 1983).

According to Francis Saemala (1983:4), the committee system was favoured over the conventional Westminster system because 'it had unifying features which were needed in our diverse situation; it was like a one-party system, and would prevent potentially divisive political parties emerging; it was wiser to have inexperienced elected representatives working closely with their senior civil servants; and the system was more in line with Melanesian traditions of consensus'.

The conventional Westminster system, with its emphasis on government and opposition, had the potential, in a culturally diverse Solomon Islands, of creating divisions along island, district or linguistic lines (see Paia 1975; Russell 1970).

After only three years, however, the committee system was rejected. In late 1972, the Governing Council set up a committee that undertook widespread consultations within the country and overseas. The committee recommended against the Governing Council and its committee system, opting for a more conventional Westminster system of ministerial government. The British Solomon Islands Order 1974 consequently provided for separate legislative and executive bodies, it established for the first time the office of the chief minister and provided for a largely elected legislature and an executive with a majority of elected members (Saemala 1983; Ghai 1983).

The decision to adopt a Westminster system was made despite the fact that, at the community level, there was widespread demand for alternative forms of governance and for recognition of community leaders and traditional structures and systems of governance. The Constitutional Committee set up in August 1975 and tasked with the responsibility of consulting citizens on the independence constitution recommended, for example, that local government be strengthened and a 'large degree of autonomy' be given to local councils, and that 'a place be found for traditional leaders in an advisory or second-house capacity' (Ghai 1983:14).

At the local level, community movements and personalities emerged, providing alternatives to the colonial administration, or working in parallel with it. The most well known example of this was the emergence of 'resistance movements' such as the Ma'asina Rule Movement, which started on Malaita (Laracy 1983), the Moro Movement on Guadalcanal (Davenport and Coker 1967; O'Connor 1973) and Silas Eto's Christian Fellowship Church (CFC) in North New Georgia (Tuza 1977). Although these were sometimes described as millenarian or cargo-cult movements, they represented Solomon Islanders' attempts to establish alternative institutions based on local communities and drew their inspiration from kastom[2] and introduced norms and values. Although they borrowed some ideas and administrative structures from the colonial government and Christianity, their constituency was predominantly local and they recognised and used the cultures and political entities that existed before European contact. While the Ma'asina Rule Movement was disbanded by the colonial administration in the 1950s, the Moro Movement and CFC continue to provide alternative ideas and structures of governance, as well as alternative world-views and approaches to development.

Solomon Islanders recognised the challenges of adopting a system of government that had no resemblance to the systems that existed in their societies before colonisation and that continued to exist long after it. Further, in opting for the Westminster system, the government not only marginalised traditional mechanisms of governance, it ruled out other options. On the eve of independence, there were discussions about the need to adopt a system of government that would suit a country such as Solomon Islands, which is culturally and linguistically diverse and geographically dispersed, a system that recognised and enabled local communities to govern themselves while being part of a central government. In this discussion some people, especially those from the Western[3] and Guadalcanal provinces, demanded a federal system, or what was commonly known locally as the state government system. Central to the argument of proponents for federalism was the belief that it would decentralise and devolve power, and allow communities to exercise control over and benefit from the development of their natural resources. The Western and Guadalcanal provinces were quite aggressive in their push for federalism. In 1978, on the eve of independence, Western Province threatened to break away if the state government system (federalism) was not adopted (Premdas et al. 1983).

Despite this, federalism was dropped in favour of a provincial system of government, similar to that adopted in neighbouring Papua New Guinea (Premdas and Steeves 1984; Larmour and Qalo 1985). The desire for federalism, however, continued and was expressed publicly on various occasions in the post-independence period. It re-emerged as one of the central demands of the Guadalcanal militants during the recent period of civil unrest, it was taken on by Guadalcanal Province (Guadalcanal Province 1999) and was adopted as a central resolution of the Townsville Peace Agreement (TPA) signed between the conflicting parties on 15 October 2000. The government of Sir Allan Kemakeza then put in motion a process aimed at introducing a federal system. The United Nations Development Programme (UNDP) assisted with nation-wide consultation, which led to the drawing up of a draft federal constitution. At the time of writing, however, the draft constitution has not been put through parliament, although the Sogavare government (like its predecessor) lists this as a priority.

Let me now outline some of the issues and challenges that influence how the Westminster system functions in Solomon Islands. First, the Westminster system—as it was adopted in Solomon Islands—has little institutional and emotional connection to people in local communities. The disconnect between local communities and *gaumane* (government) is compounded by the government's weak capacity to manage the economy, enforce the law and deliver goods and services. This limits the government's presence in and impact on the lives of the majority of people. In colonial days, administrators were assigned to each district in the form of district officers, headmen and *ples men*, who were the foot soldiers of the administration, executing its instructions and enforcing its laws. Although many of these roles were relatively rudimentary, the fact that these government agents—especially the headmen and *ples men*—lived among the people and toured their districts regularly ensured that the *gaumane* was present in people's lives. For example the *ples man,* who was the constable and law enforcement officer at the community level, had a uniform that he wore during his tours. After independence, field and extension officers responsible to the provincial and central governments replaced the *ples men*. Over the years, however, because of the weakness of support mechanisms, many of these officers no longer performed their duties effectively or efficiently. Many substations were closed, resulting in a decline in the visibility of government and its impact on the lives of people in communities, especially those far from Honiara. This made the disconnect between government and communities more pronounced.

Solomon Islands is unlike places such as Samoa, Fiji and Vanuatu, where the *matai, Bose Levu Vakaturaga* (the Great Council of Chiefs) and the *Malvatumauri* (National Council of Chiefs) respectively link local communities to the national government and give people a sense of connection to the government. This is important; even if the traditional leaders have limited powers, their roles are only symbolic and the connection to local communities is nominal. The draft federal constitution for the Solomons, while proposing the inclusion of traditional leaders, does not incorporate them in the same way as the *matai* in Samoa.[4] It does not provide the kind of recognition or confer the powers accorded to the *Bose Levu Vakaturaga* in Fiji and the *Malvatumauri* in Vanuatu.

In Solomon Islands (as in other Pacific island countries), the Westminster system exists and functions, often uncomfortably, within a society in which people's relationship with leaders and their reactions to issues of public interest are determined by cultural norms and values and political structures different from those in countries such as Australia, New Zealand and the United Kingdom. Consequently, the institutional structures of the

Westminster system and the values and norms it espouses have been difficult to impose in nations such as the Solomon Islands. This is complicated by the fact that the British colonial administration never attempted to blend the Westminster system with local cultures and traditions. This is different from countries such as Samoa and Fiji[5] where, as mentioned above, the colonial administration recognised and included traditional leadership systems in the formal institutional structures of government, a practice that ensured the formal government was linked to local communities.

As stated in the introduction, the Westminster system is, by design, adversarial and can contribute to local and group antagonisms beyond parliament. It pits groups against each other—opposition and government—and assumes that improved decisions are made through these adversarial relationships. The parliament is like a stage where the drama focuses on debates, in which people with differing ideas and opinions confront and often shout at each other across the floor. Indeed, parliamentary debates are sometimes like a stage play, where politicians are the performers and the constituents are the audience. The physical design of the parliament—with MPs in a circular space below and the audience in a gallery overlooking them—often reminds me of the auditoriums of ancient Rome, where gladiators fought for entertainment. Here, politicians are like gladiators providing entertainment for their constituents, who expect them to perform on the floor of parliament. Those who are quiet, do not stand up, raise their voice and perform in dramatic ways are often referred to as '*nogud*' (not good) MPs. This confrontational nature of the Westminster system is fundamentally different from the way in which discussions are conducted in traditional Solomon Islands contexts, where differences are worked through until consensus is reached, and shouting is generally shunned.

Further, in countries such as the United Kingdom and Australia, there are institutions and rules that regulate and mediate the adversarial contest to ensure it does not degenerate into violence. Much of the contest is channelled through political parties that have been built up over many years, and which play an important role in organising ideas, choosing candidates and wooing voters. The party becomes the avenue through which people express their different political opinions. In countries such as Solomon Islands, however, where parties are weak, other entities are sometimes mobilised and used to play out these differences. These include *wantok* groups, tribes, political supporters, businesses and individuals. Further, in the absence of ideological platforms that have society-wide acceptance, people mobilise around local issues and personalities about which they feel passionate. Consequently, outward expression can at times become emotionally charged and potentially violent. As we saw in the case of Honiara in April 2006, the rivalry that is supposed to be contained in parliament spilled into the streets. As will be discussed below, certain politicians allegedly encouraged their supporters to cause violence if they lost on the floor of parliament. These politicians—if the allegations are true—knew that they could not appeal to their parties because they were weak or because they didn't belong to one, so they appealed to their supporters outside parliament.

Strong political parties are vital for the proper functioning of the Westminster system. Parties in Solomon Islands, however, tend to be weak and loosely organised (Kabutaulaka 2006; Alasia 1997; Fugui 1988). In his address during celebrations for the country's tenth independence anniversary, Sir Baddeley Devesi, the country's first governor-general, highlighted the difficulties of adopting the Westminster system in a situation in which there were no developed political parties: '[a]fter ten years, Solomon Islands has not been able to meet the demands of the Westminster model for a solid majority in Parliament by one party to allow it to govern effectively. While political rivalry is the essence of the Westminster Parliamentary system, Solomon Islands after ten years has not been able to get that established' (Devesi 1992).

More importantly, the weakness of parties results in loosely formed governments and political alliances, or what Steeves (1996) refers to as 'unbounded politics'. Further, party weakness has had an adverse impact on the process of selecting governments and on people's relationship with government. Because of the weakness of parties, when voters cast their votes in national elections they are concerned more with electing individual MPs rather than the party to which the candidates belong, and which they hope will subsequently form government. Parliament forms the government, and the voters have little (if any) control over it. It starts after the national election, as the potential prime ministerial candidates lobby and woo members for support—what Mary-Louise O'Callaghan (this volume) appropriately refers to as the 'auctioning' of MPs. Therefore, when voters cast their vote at a national election, they are not really voting for a government. Rather, they are voting only for an individual MP. In the choice for prime minister (and hence, government) they become spectators, like those people who gathered outside Parliament House on 18 April 2006 and the thousands of other Solomon Islanders who listened on the radio. In this process, it is assumed that an MP's choices when in parliament will represent those of his/her constituents. This is often not the case, as politicians choose which party they will join and who they will align themselves with after the election and without consulting their constituents.

This is unlike the system in a place such as Australia, where a voter votes for a party to form government and therefore has a hand in choosing the government. The voter, in other words, votes for an individual because of his or her membership of a party that the voter wants to be in government.

The question of whether or not the electoral system produces majority representation is important to consider in this discussion because the Westminster system (and other forms of representative democracy) are built on the principle of majority rule. In Solomon Islands, one needs to examine the first-past-the-post electoral system that the country adopted, and the outcomes it produces. Experience shows that because of the design of the first-past-the-post system, most MPs receive less than half of the votes cast in their constituency. This means that the MPs are not the choice of a majority of voters.[6]

It follows that the prime minister and the government he selects also do not represent the choice of the majority. This, therefore, undermines the principle of representation through majority rule, which is fundamental to the liberal democracy from which the Westminster system draws its norms and values. The Westminster system is built and functions best on the assumptions of representation—that citizens are represented in decision making by the people that a majority of them have chosen. This, in turn, gives legitimacy to the MPs and the government that they, in turn, select. Let me now explore the events of April 2006 and see how they illustrate some of these broader issues.

Election, rioting, and looting

When Solomon Islanders turned up in large numbers to cast their votes in the national election of 5 April 2006, there was widespread hope that parliament would elect a new government to steer the country away from the path followed in the previous 27 years of independence. That hope slipped away through the cracks in the parliamentary process when, on 18 April 2006, it was announced that MPs had elected Snyder Rini as prime minister.

Rini received a cold reception when the Governor-General, Sir Nathaniel Waena, declared him the new prime minister and presented him to the hundreds of people gathered at Vavaya Ridge, outside the national parliament building. For these people, Rini represented the 'old guard', the same group that his predecessor, Sir Allan Kemakeza, led in the previous parliament and who, in the eyes of many Solomon Islanders, failed miserably in the credibility stakes. Rini was Kemakeza's deputy in that government.

So, how did Rini manage to win the election for prime minister and bring the old guard back into power? To answer this question, one needs to examine the process of selecting a prime minister in Solomon Islands, the weakness of party systems, the fluidity of political alliances and the nature of Solomon Islanders' participation in and reaction to parliamentary politics. This provides an insight into how Solomon Islanders use the Westminster system and the outcomes it produces.

After the national election (which international and local observers declared as being generally clean and fair) the newly elected MPs gathered in Honiara to elect the prime minister. As usual, in the period between the announcement of the election results and the vote for prime minister, the various coalitions (referred to commonly in Solomon Islands as 'camps') lobbied intensely and tussled to win the support of MPs, especially the new ones who had not yet been attracted to a particular camp. There were allegations that lobbyists, especially businessmen—mostly Chinese, or *Waku*, as they are known in Solomon Islands[7]—paid large sums of money to individual MPs to ensure that any government that was formed served their interests.

After the national election, two major camps were formed and they gathered at different hotels in Honiara. The first camp comprised the Association of Independent Members of Parliament (AIMP), the People's Alliance Party (PAP) and the Lafari Party. Many of the MPs who had been in the previous government were present, including Kemakeza (the parliamentary leader of PAP) and Rini (the parliamentary leader of the AIMP and deputy prime minister in the previous Kemakeza government). This group stayed at the Honiara Hotel, owned by local ethnic Chinese businessman and national president of the AIMP, Thomas Chan (known commonly as Tommy Chan). He was also allegedly the financial sponsor of the group, enticing MPs to join this camp.

The other camp, which assumed the name 'the Grand Coalition', was a coalition of a number of parties: the Nasnol Pati, the Rural Advancement Party, the Liberal Party, the Democratic Party, the Social Credit Party (SoCredit) and some independents. They camped at the Iron Bottom Sound Hotel, owned by Alex Wong, an ethnic Chinese (Taiwanese) businessman and naturalised Solomon Islander. This camp included veteran politicians such as Job Dudley Tausinga and three former prime ministers: Bartholomew Ulufa'alu, Francis Billy Hilly and Manasseh Sogavare. The group also included two other important figures: Charles Dausabea, the MP for East Honiara (who is a colourful character with a shady reputation), and Nelson Ne'e, the newly elected MP for Central Honiara. Both allegedly had connections with Malaitan militants during the height of the civil unrest and both emerged as important players in the period after the election of the prime minister. The two drew much support from the squatter settlements behind Honiara that are populated predominantly by people from Malaita, who harboured a certain degree of antagonism towards RAMSI, which was invited into the country by the Kemakeza government. In their political campaigns, Dausabea and Ne'e expressed anti-RAMSI sentiments. Further, during a campaign debate at the Panatina campus of the Solomon Islands College of Higher Education (SICHE), Dausabea and other candidates for the East Honiara constituency raised concerns about the influence of *Waku* in the country's political and economic affairs (Solomon Star 2006a).

After the national election, those MPs who were undecided about their political affiliation were ushered to join either of the two camps. In one incident, two newly elected MPs from Temotu Province arrived in Honiara on a flight from the provincial capital of Lata and were whisked off to the Iron Bottom Sound Hotel, while their luggage was taken to the Honiara Hotel. Dausabea was reportedly the Grand Coalition member who went to the Honiara Hotel to retrieve the two MPs' luggage and moved them to the Iron Bottom Sound Hotel. In the days that followed, the two camps engaged in an intense competition to gain the numbers necessary to form government in what is sometimes referred to as the 'body-count' competition.[8]

As this political drama unfolded, one of the key protagonists (although sometimes an elusive player) was Manasseh Sogavare, the MP for East

Choiseul. His SoCredit Party had won only two seats in the election despite its intensive political campaign and controversial policies promoted by its Filipino secretary, Roman Quitales. From the beginning, Sogavare wanted to become prime minister but knew that he did not have the numbers to form a government, and could not join the AIMP/PAP/Lafari coalition because of his past differences with Kemakeza. In 2000, as prime minister, Sogavare sacked Kemakeza, who was then his deputy, over allegations of the misuse of funds allocated for compensation payments for properties damaged during the civil unrest. This soured relationships between the two. Sogavare, therefore, teamed up with the Grand Coalition camp, hoping to be nominated as its candidate for prime minister; however, he lost the nomination to Tausinga, a veteran politician and MP for North New Georgia. After his loss to Tausinga, Sogavare withdrew his support for the Grand Coalition and created a third camp, pulling with him a number of MPs. They camped at the Pacific Casino Hotel, owned by yet another ethnic Chinese businessman, Patrick Leong. It was also alleged that he had the support of businessman Bobo Dettke, whose mother is from Guadalcanal and whose father is Chinese.

Three names were subsequently put forward as contestants for prime minister: Rini for the AIMP/PAP/Lafari coalition; Tausinga for the Grand Coalition; and Sogavare. On 16 April, the Solomon Islands Broadcasting Corporation (SIBC), the national radio station, reported intense lobbying, with the AIMP/PAP/Lafari coalition claiming to have 28 MPs, while the Grand Coalition claimed 27 MPs (which totalled 55 MPs in a 50-member parliament). Meanwhile, Sogavare's group also claimed to have a majority. The SIBC reported that 'the three groups are tossing around the same people in the 50-member parliament' and 'where an MP does not make up his mind on which group to join, the dollar will make the decision for him' (SIBC 2006). On 18 April, in the first round of voting, Tausinga received 22 votes, Rini 17 and Sogavare 11. Sogavare was subsequently eliminated. He and all but one[9] of his supporters threw their lot in with the AIMP/PAP/Lafari camp, which meant that Rini won with 27 votes against Tausinga's 23 votes.

After Rini's victory, there was a protest outside the national parliament. Many of those who gathered there were from eastern and central Honiara constituencies and were supporters of Dausabea and Ne'e, who had hoped that their camp would form government and that they would be given ministerial portfolios. Rini's victory, however, meant that their MPs not only failed to capture government, more importantly, they lost the competition between the two camps. For Dausabea's supporters, this was humiliating for a man who had a reputation as a tough guy, and who was regarded as a linchpin and kingmaker in the election of the prime minister.[10] There were widespread allegations, therefore, that Dausabea and Ne'e had a hand in orchestrating the mob's activities. At the time of writing, they had been charged with inciting the riots and were awaiting court hearings (SIBC 2006). If the allegations are true, one could interpret the actions of the two MPs and their supporters as an example of the adversarial character of the Westminster parliamentary democracy spilling into the streets. Conscious of the weakness of parties and the inability of their political camp to form government, the men found it convenient to mobilise supporters outside parliament. Many of these supporters took the competition to form a government seriously. When their side did not win, those supporting Dausabea and Ne'e took matters (and their anger) onto the streets of Honiara. Consequently, a competition that, according to the Westminster system, was supposed to be contained to parliament unravelled into rioting, looting and the destruction of commercial and residential property.

It is unclear whether or not Sogavare anticipated the violent public reaction to Rini's election. It is evident, however, that he eyed the situation with interest and manoeuvred his way to capture the prime ministership. Right after Rini's election, Sogavare was outside parliament with other MPs and the Speaker of Parliament, Sir Peter Kenilorea, asking the crowd to be calm. Rini was in power for only eight days before being forced to resign on 26 April 2006, after four of his supporters crossed the floor (Solomon Star 2006b).

After the violence and Rini's resignation, Sogavare withdrew his support for the AIMP/PAP/Lafari coalition and made a deal with the Grand Coalition, earning himself its nomination for prime minister and pulling his supporters along with him. The other camp nominated the MP for Central Kwara'ae, Fred Fono. In the second prime ministerial election on 4 May 2006 (conducted in the shadows of the violence that had followed the first election) Sogavare emerged victorious, with 28 votes to Fono's 22 votes (Solomon Star 2006c).

## Reflections

The events leading up to the election of the prime minister and the violence that ensued raise important issues about how the Westminster system works in Solomon Islands and the political outcomes it produces.

First, those events highlight the need for post-colonial societies such as Solomon Islands and other Melanesian countries to think seriously about the appropriateness (or otherwise) of the system of government they inherited from their former colonial powers. There is a need to reform the Westminster system to ensure its relevance to and appropriateness for their societies. This was highlighted by Sir Arnold Amet from Papua New Guinea, who chaired the Pacific Islands Forum Observer Team at the April 2006 national election in Solomon Islands. Discussing the Honiara violence, he noted that the challenges faced by countries in the South Pacific were

> ...legacies of colonial democracies that have imposed these political structures upon culturally different peoples of the Pacific. These institutional structures and processes are not necessarily compatible with our traditional cultural ways of governing our people...After these 20 to 30 years of independence in our small island nations, we must ask the question, are these structures and processes really working? (Amet 2006).

The crucial questions, however, are: how is this done in a country such as Solomon Islands, where there are diverse traditional systems of governance? How are traditional structures, norms and values incorporated into the Westminster system when the two are often incompatible? In cases where traditional forms of governance exist, they are often marginalised, shunned or described as cult movements because they do not fit with Western-introduced governance, religious beliefs and ways of thinking. In Solomon Islands, classic examples include the Moro Movement on Guadalcanal and the CFC in North New Georgia. For nearly five decades from the late 1950s until his death on 21 November 2006, Pelise Moro instituted an alternative governance system drawing inspiration from Guadalcanal *kastom*, or what he often referred to in the local language as '*ghoro ghoro ni ghita* [our way of living]' (Davenport and Coker 1967). He and his Gaena'alu Movement (formerly called the Moro Movement) were often dismissed as 'backward' and cultic. The movement was never brought into discussions about governance and development as a legitimate local entity that could provide alternative forms of governance and the means for mobilising villagers and communities. In fact, when the Moro Movement began, part of its objective was to establish *bisinis* (business) in an attempt to become self-sufficient and not remain dependent on the colonial administration, which Moro saw as having failed to meet the needs of the people of the remote Weather Coast, in particular, and Guadalcanal more generally. The movement, therefore, started coconut plantations, bought outboard motors and fibreglass canoes and taxis, which it operated in Honiara. It also collected 'taxes' from its members. These attempts to enter the business world failed largely because of poor management. They demonstrated, however, the ability of a local leader to mobilise support and govern at the local level (see O'Connor 1973; Davenport and Coker 1967; Kabutaulaka 1990).

The CFC was shunned somewhat less because it assumed an identity as a Christian church and was therefore seen as 'modern', unlike the Gaena'alu Movement which was often viewed as an impractical attempt to return to *kastom*. The CFC was sometimes described initially as a cult and was shunned by the mainstream Methodist Church, from which it broke away. As Jutta Bruenger (1988:5) notes, however, the CFC leader, Holy Mama Silas Eto, 'showed amazing abilities for organizing and leading peoples, young and old. He developed quickly into the religious as well as the secular leader of the village.' By the 1930s, he had developed a model village and over the years organised his followers into an economically productive unit, which financed its own schools and health care centres. By the 1960s, the colonial administration was appreciative of the CFC's commitment to finance its own projects and provide social services for its followers (Bruenger 1988; Harwood 1974; Tuza 1997).

Today, the CFC is included in mainstream discussions about development. This is partly because one of the late Eto's sons, Job Dudley Tausinga, is a prominent and long-serving politician and deputy prime minister at the time of writing. Further, the church organises its followers around the local *butubutu* (clans), mobilises them for economic productivity around the establishment of forest (teak) plantations (Fa'anunu n.d.) and continues to fund social services such as schools and health care for its followers. The CFC is therefore recognised for its active participation in the Solomon Islands cash economy through the establishment of forest plantations and the exportation of timber. The government's recognition of the CFC was epitomised by the knighthood, in October 2005, of Reverend Ikan Rove, the spiritual authority of the CFC and Eto's elder son. He was awarded a Knight Commander of the Civil Division of the Most Excellent Order of the British Empire (KBE) in recognition of his 'long and committed service to community development and dedicated leadership to the Christian Fellowship Church (CFC) in Solomon Islands' (People First 2006a). Despite this recognition, the CFC is rarely discussed as providing an alternative governance structure, especially in the post-conflict era, when such alternatives are needed. The goals and experience of the Gaena'alu Movement and the CFC are often viewed as being not applicable to current political issues and are, in fact, marginalised in governance discussions. They need to be brought into mainstream discussion and put forward as alternative ways of exercising local-level governance and of mobilising people for development.

Similar suggestions about the potential for local communities to take on roles often played by government are found in discussions of law and order—as in the case of Sinclair Dinnen's (1997, 2002, 2004) discussions about Papua New Guinea. While there is validity in the argument for greater local involvement in addressing law and order problems, there is often the challenge of ensuring that local communities do not act outside the law. This is illustrated in the recent case of Wagina, in Choiseul Province, where community leaders imposed corporal punishment (whipping) for anyone found to have broken community rules. They were subsequently visited by a high-level delegation from the Ministry of Police and Justice, who told them to stop such punishment because it was unlawful (People First 2006b). In Papua New Guinea, such action has been mitigated by instituting a piece of legislation—the Village Courts Act of 1973—which regulates and standardises the administration of justice at the village level.

## Conclusion

Despite the challenges, it is possible to incorporate traditional or local-level entities into the governance process alongside the Westminster system, and entities such as the CFC and the Gaena'alu Movement could become central to discussions of systems of governance. Such entities are important for connecting the central government with local communities and making people feel part of government—a vital perception for creating a sense of belonging in countries such as Solomon Islands, which are culturally and ethno-linguistically diverse.

In the draft federal constitution currently being examined by the Constitutional Review Committee, chiefs (or community leaders) are recognised and included in the institutional structure of government through a provision that allows them to participate in decision-making processes. It is envisaged that this will help connect local communities with the central government and mitigate some of the problems associated with the inappropriateness and irrelevance of the Westminster system.

The Honiara experience also indicates that it might be worthwhile to put in place legislation to regulate how politics is played out—outside and within parliament. Two of the most important issues are the electoral system and political parties. Institutional strengthening alone, however, will not change political outcomes, as there is also a need to change the political culture. That will take a long time to achieve. For now, it is obvious that the first-past-the-post system is not producing representative governments; therefore, it is important to review the electoral system with the objective of introducing one that produces representative government.

Related to this is the need to regulate political parties to ensure that competition for power is kept within parliament and between parties, rather than spilling onto the streets in public violence. Solomon Islands could learn from the experiences of Papua New Guinea and the impacts of its Organic Law on the Integrity of Political Parties and Candidates. This legislation is yet to be implemented in a national election; however, experiences from by-elections have highlighted some of the challenges this law will encounter.[11]

The violent events in Honiara on 18 and 19 April 2006 were manifestations of long-standing issues that were inherent in the institutional structures, norms and values of the Westminster system of government. They highlight the need for reform in Solomon Islands—reforms that recognise the importance of traditional systems of governance and of changes to the political process to ensure that it produces representative government. Failure to do this will risk politics pouring out into the streets in violent ways such as those we saw in April 2006.

## Acknowledgments

Thank you to Professor Robert Kiste, Dr Jerry Finin, Dr Terence Wesley-Smith and Professor Murray Chapman for commenting on an earlier draft of this paper. While I am grateful for their comments and suggestions, the paper is mine and I take full responsibility for its content and any errors or misinterpretation.

## Notes

1    At the time of writing (September 2006), there was intense debate surrounding the terms of reference for the inquiry and the appointment of 'disgraced' former Australian Federal Court judge Marcus Einfeld. This led to the dismissal of the Attorney-General, Primo Afeau, and the appointment of controversial Australian lawyer Julian Moti as his replacement. This raised concerns about political interference in the judiciary. It culminated in the expulsion of the Australian High Commissioner to Solomon Islands, Patrick Cole, resulting in a diplomatic row between Canberra and Honiara. At the time of writing, this had not been resolved and Australia had not yet appointed a replacement for Cole. On 29 September 2006, Moti was arrested in Port Moresby by PNG authorities at the request of the Australian government. His arrest was in relation to child sex offences in Vanuatu in 1997 (see Sydney Morning Herald 2006). He later boarded a PNG military aircraft and flew to Munda in the Western Province, where he was arrested and charged with travelling to Solomon Islands illegally. The diplomatic stand-off between Canberra and Honiara continues.

2    Here, the term '*kastom*' is used loosely to refer to what are generally regarded as traditional customs, or those from *taem bifo* (the past) and connected to ancestors. The term 'tradition' is also used loosely throughout this paper to refer to past beliefs and practices, although I acknowledge that some of these have relatively recent origins, or have changed over time.

3    At that time, the Western Province included what is present-day Choiseul Province.

4    In Samoa, only *matai* can contest and hold seats in parliament. The draft federal constitution in Solomon Islands provides for chiefs (community leaders) to participate in governance at the local community level.

5    It should be noted that the situations in Fiji and Samoa are complicated and that *matai* and *ratu* do not always represent the interests of the community. Hence, the authority of the *matai* and *ratu* is often challenged and there have been allegations that these traditional leaders are corrupt and fail to redistribute wealth, as required of them by tradition. In the 2006 Fiji coup, for example, one of the issues emerging from the initial stand-off between the military and the Great Council of Chiefs, and the overt defiance of chiefly authority, was accusations that chiefs misused their power. Morgan

Tuimaleali'ifano (2006) discusses not only the expenses required for installing a *matai* title, but the corruption that weaves through it.

6    For more on the electoral system, and in particular the 2006 national election, see Jon Fraenkel's chapter in this volume.

7    For discussions on Asians (Chinese) in Solomon Islands, see the chapter by Clive Moore in this volume. Also see Laracy 1974 and Willmott 2005.

8    For details on the events after the national election, see Jon Fraenkel's chapter in this volume. Also see Mary-Louise O'Callaghan's chapter in this volume.

9    It was later rumored, although never confirmed, that although Sogavare encouraged his supporters to vote for Rini, he voted for Tausinga.

10   An alternative view is held by Dr Transform Aqorau, who insists that Dausabea no longer had the clout he enjoyed when he was in parliament and when the late Solomon Mamaloni was prime minister. Aqorau argues that Dausabea was not the linchpin or kingmaker in the selection of prime minister. Rather, he asserts, the real linchpins were 'some fairly well known power broker[s] lurking in the background somewhere, seemingly oblivious to the situation, but certainly strenuously working in the background to influence…[the prime ministerial] election results'. See http://www.solomonstarnews.com/?q=node/8011 (accessed 26 October 2006).

11   See, for example, Gelu 2005.

# References

Alasia, S., 1997. *Party politics and government in Solomon Islands*, Discussion Paper No.97/7, State, Society and Governance in Melanesia Program, Research School of Pacific and Asian Studies, The Australian National University, Canberra.

Amet, A., 2006. 'Lessons to learn from SI poll', *The National*, 1 May. Available from http://www.thenational.com.pg/050106/column6.html (accessed 17 October 2006).

Bennett, J.A., 1987. *Wealth of the Solomons: a history of a Pacific archipelago, 1800–1978*, University of Hawai'i Press, Honolulu.

British Solomon Islands Protectorate (BSIP), 1968. *Interim proposals on constitutional development*, Legislative Council Paper, No.119 of 1968, Honiara.

Bruenger, J.R., 1988. Holy Mama: the bigman of paradise, Unpublished paper.

Davenport, W.H. and Coker, G., 1967. 'The Moro Movement of Guadalcanal, British Solomon Islands Protectorate', *Journal of the Polynesian Society*, 76:123–75.

Devesi, B., 1992. 'Independence or dependence', in R. Crocombe and E. Tuza (eds), *Independence, Dependence, Interdependence: the first 10 years of Solomon Islands independence*, Institute of Pacific Studies, University of the South Pacific and Solomon Islands College of Higher Education, Suva and Honiara.

Dinnen, S., 1997. *Law, order and state in Papua New Guinea*, Discussion Paper 97/1, State, Society and Governance in Melanesia Program, Research School of Pacific and Asian Studies, The Australian National University, Canberra.

——, 2002. *Building bridges: law and justice reform in Papua New Guinea*, Discussion Paper 02/2, State, Society and Governance in Melanesia Program, Research School of Pacific and Asian Studies, The Australian National University, Canberra.

——, 2004. *Lending a fist? Australia's new interventionism in the southwest Pacific*, Discussion Paper No.2004/5, State, Society and Governance in Melanesia Program, Research School of Pacific and Asian Studies, The Australian National University, Canberra.

Fa'anunu, K., n.d. Christian Fellowship Church reforestation: a change in customary land tenure in the Solomon Islands?, unpublished manuscript.

Fugui, J.M., 1988. Politics and political parties in the Solomon Islands: an assessment, MA thesis, University of Canterbury, Christchurch.

Gelu, A., 2005. *The failures of the Organic Law on the Integrity of the Political Parties and Candidates*, Working Paper, No.2005/03, State, Society and Governance in Melanesia Program, Research School of Pacific and Asian Studies, The Australian National University, Canberra.

Ghai, Y., 1983. 'The making of the independence constitution', in P. Larmour (ed.), *Solomon Islands Politics*, Institute of Pacific Studies, University of the South Pacific, Suva:9–52.

Guadalcanal Province, 1999. *Bona Fide* Demands of the Indigenous People of Guadalcanal, Document submitted to Solomon Islands Government, 2 February.

Harwood, F.H., 1974. The Christian Fellowship Church: a revitalization movement in Solomon Islands, PhD dissertation, University of Chicago.

Healy, A.M., 1966. 'Administration in the British Solomon Islands', *Journal of Administration Overseas*, July:194–204.

Kabutaulaka, T.T., 1990. 'A sociopolitical movement: the Moro Movement of Guadalcanal', *O'O Journal*, 2(15):19–24.

——, 2006. 'Parties, constitutional engineering and governance in Solomon Islands', in R. Rich with L. Hambly and M.G. Morgan (eds), *Political Parties in the Pacific Islands*, Pandanus Books, The Australian National University, Canberra:103–16.

Keesing, R.M. and Corris, P., 1980. *Lightning Meets theWestWind: the Malaita massacre*, Oxford University Press, Melbourne.

Laracy, H.M., 1974. 'Unwelcome guests: the Solomons' Chinese', *New Guinea and Australia, the Pacific and Southeast Asia*, 8(4):27–37.

——, 1983. *Pacific Protest: the Ma'asina Rule Movement, Solomon Islands, 1944–1952*, Institute of Pacific Studies, University of the South Pacific, Suva.

Larmour, P. and Qalo, R. (eds), 1985. *Decentralisation in the South Pacific: local, provincial and state government in twenty countries*, Institute of Pacific Studies, University of the South Pacific, Suva.

O'Connor, G., 1973. The Moro Movement of Guadalcanal, PhD thesis, University of Pennsylvania, Philadelphia.

Paia, W.A., 1975. 'Aspects of constitutional development in the Solomon Islands', *Journal of Pacific History*, 10(2):81–9.

People First, 2006a. 'Her Majesty Queen Elizabeth II knights Rev. Ikan Rove', PFNet. Available from http://www.peoplefirst.net.sb/news/News.asp?IDnews=6038 (accessed 27 October 2006).

——, 2006b. 'Elders of Wagina agree to stop corporal punishment', PFNet. Available from http://www.peoplefirst.net.sb/news/News.asp?IDnews=6620 (accessed 27 October 2006).

Premdas, R. and Steeves, J., 1984. *Decentralisation and political change in Melanesia: Papua New Guinea, the Solomon Islands andVanuatu*, South Pacific Forum Working Paper, No.3, University of the South Pacific, Suva.

Premdas, R., Steeves, J. and Larmour, P., 1983. 'The Western breakaway movement', in P. Larmour with S. Tarua (eds), *Solomon Islands Politics*, Institute of Pacific Studies, University of the South Pacific, Suva:164–95.

Russell,T., 1970. 'The 1970 constitution for the British Solomon Islands', in M.Ward (ed.), *The Politics of Melanesia*, University of Papua New Guinea and The Australian National University, Port Moresby and Canberra.

Saemala, F., 1983. 'Constitutional development', in P. Larmour (ed.), *Solomon Islands Politics*, Institute of Pacific Studies, University of the South Pacific, Suva:1–8.

Solomon Islands Broadcasting Corporation (SIBC), 2006. SIBC News. Available from http://www.sibconline.com.sb/story.asp?IDThread=62&IDNews=15049 (accessed 17 October 2006).

Solomon Star, 2006a. 'Candidates highlight concern over Asians', *Solomon Star*, 3 April 2006. Available from http://www.solomonstarnews. com/?q=node/7830 (accessed 26 October 2006).

———, 2006b. 'PM Snyder Rini resigns!', *Solomon Star*, 26 April. Available from http://www.solomonstarnews.com/?q=node/8214 (accessed 23 October 2006).

———, 2006c. 'SI new prime minister elected', *Solomon Star*, 4 May. Available from http://www.solomonstarnews.com/?q=node/8326 (accessed 23 October 2006).

Steeves, J.S., 1996. 'Unbounded politics in the Solomon Islands: leadership and party alignments', *Pacific Studies*, 19(1):115–38.

Sydney Morning Herald, 2006. 'New Solomons attorney-general arrested', *Sydney Morning Herald*, 29 September. Available from http://www.smh.com.au/news/World/New-Solomons-attorneygeneral-arrested/2006/09/29/1159337330111.html.

Tuimaleali'ifano, M., 2006. 'Matai titles and modern corruption in Samoa: costs, expectations and consequences for families and society', in S. Firth (ed.), *Globalisation and Governance in the Pacific Islands*, ANU E Press, The Australian National University, Canberra. Available from http://epress.anu.edu.au/ssgm/global_gov/pdf_instructions.html.

Tuza, E., 1977. 'Silas Eto of New Georgia', in G. Trompf (ed.), *Prophets of Melanesia: six essays*, Institute of Papua New Guinea Studies, University of Papua New Guinea, Port Moresby:65–87.

Willmott, W., 2005. *A history of the Chinese communities in eastern Melanesia, Solomon Islands,Vanuatu, New Caledonia*, Working Paper No.12, Macmillan Brown Centre, Christchurch.

# Chapter 5

## Rainbows across the mountains: the first post-RAMSI general election

Sam Alasia

The social crisis that ravaged Solomon Islands from 1998 to 2003 has taught us many lessons. 'Rainbows across the mountains' symbolises a genuine wish by Solomon Islanders to rebuild their country with new insights and understanding. Some improvements, such as a vigorous campaign for a clean election, were seen in the 2006 national election, the first since RAMSI arrived in Solomon Islands in 2003. The Sogavare government, which assumed power in May 2006, has made a priority issues of good governance, quality leadership, the weeding out of corruption, national healing, decentralisation and equitable distribution of development and wealth. Though we face many challenges and difficulties, we hope that with political stability, a renewed wave of commitment and dedication by Solomon Islanders and the support of RAMSI, friendly nations and donor partners, we will achieve some of our goals.

When I was a small boy on Malaita Island in the early 1960s, whenever a rainbow appeared in the sky we were reminded by the elderly not to point our fingers at it. They told us that our fingers would be burnt or cooked. This created a tradition of fear and no one dared point at rainbows when they appeared. In the Bible, however, we are told that the rainbow is God's promise to us that He will not destroy the Earth again with floods. This represents commitment and hope. Solomon Islands has experienced seasons of joy and sadness but perhaps no real progress in its 30 years of political independence. During the flood represented by the social crisis between 1998 and 2003, Solomon Islands nearly collapsed and disintegrated (Moore 2004; Fraenkel 2004; Bennett 2002; Kabutaulaka 1999; Dinnen 2002).

Fortunately, we saw a rainbow in the sky in July 2003, which represented not fear but hope. That rainbow was the Regional Assistance Mission to Solomon Islands (RAMSI) (Moore 2005; Kabutaulaka 2005; Wainwright 2005; Brown 2005; Fullilove 2006). Then we saw another rainbow across our mountains, illuminating the tops of Tatuve on Guadalcanal and Alasa'a on Malaita, representing a genuine wish for a new and better Solomon Islands. This second rainbow was the 2006 general election. It was the vehicle to facilitate this wish and hope. Much has been said about arcs of instability in the Pacific; these rainbows represent arcs of stability and unity, reaching out to the different islands, cultures and people in Solomon Islands.

This chapter highlights some aspects of national and electoral politics in Solomon Islands, discusses the 2006 national elections (the first after RAMSI arrived) and touches on the policies of the second Sogavare government, which came to office in May 2006. Right at the beginning, I need to state my background and rationale. I have an academic interest in the politics and contemporary history of Solomon Islands (Alasia 1988, 1989, 1997), but I am also a participant in Solomon Islands politics. I was involved in the 2006 election as an adviser to Job Dudley Tausinga (one of the candidates for prime minister) and at the time of writing was a political advisor to Prime Minister Manasseh Sogavare. During the 1980s, I served a term as Minister for Education and I was, for a time, an adviser to Sogavare during his first term as prime minister in 2000. For more than 20 years, I have been involved in the affairs of my nation. I am not a dispassionate outside observer; I am a knowledgeable insider who has been able to talk openly and privately with many Solomon Islands leaders, and in my own small way have been able to shape government policy. There are some drawbacks to this, as I am bound by an oath of secrecy and obviously it is not in my interest to make public information that should remain private. The reader must accept this declaration and read on with it in mind. I believe that I have enough academic integrity to be able to separate political rhetoric from the truth. At heart, I am a Solomon Islands nationalist and, in the conclusion, I wear my nationalist heart on my sleeve, stating my thoughts as an indigenous Solomon Islander, not an academic. If Pacific islanders are to be involved in writing about the history and politics of our islands, we must be part of a reconceptualisation of the way we write. Total academic detachment and distance is not necessarily the way to decolonise Pacific studies or provide an indigenous perspective. One final point—this chapter was finalised in October 2006 and therefore does not reflect developments since that time.[1]

The 2006 general election was the seventh national election since the country achieved independence in 1978 (Moore 2004; Larmour with Tara 1983). RAMSI was deployed to the Solomon Islands in July 2003 at the invitation of the Solomon Islands Parliament—primarily to assist in the restoration of law and order and security. In mid 2003, the nation was sliding further into lawlessness, which forced the economy and state apparatus into near collapse. The social crisis from 1998 to 2000—which in many ways extended until the middle of 2003—was the culmination of a range of negative factors such as poor planning by previous administrations, mismanagement of the country's resources, corruption and land-tenure problems.

Decisions on land tenure are crucial to the future development of the nation. There are three types of land ownership in Solomon Islands: Crown, alienated and customary land. Eighty-five per cent of land is customary owned and this is where the majority of the population resides (Larmour 1979:Appendix II, 249). Solomon Islands is a nation of villages and villagers existing mainly through subsistence agriculture. As such, it is villagers who hold the principal key to development and progress, and who are the real power-brokers in terms of politics. It is their votes that decide the political future. Ordinary villagers have, however, been left out of political and development processes for far too long, and they feel that the parliament is not representative of their views. Part of the rehabilitation that is required is effective participation by rural Solomon Islanders in the electoral process—whether for local, provincial or national leadership. The Sogavare government elected in 2006 has promised to give emphasis to village-level development in a belief that this is the key to prosperity in Solomon Islands.

## The lead up to the 2006 general elections

Parliament had its final meeting in December 2005 and was dissolved on 20 December, and all members went home to prepare themselves for Christmas and the general election. The April 2006 general elections differed from previous elections in at least three ways. First, a larger number of political parties and groupings competed than ever before. For example, 10 political parties or groupings contested the 1997 elections and nine the 2001 election. In the 2006 elections, the number surged to 16. The party led by Sogavare— the Solomon Islands Social Credit (Socred) Party—fielded a large number of candidates. Three other parties were also led by former prime ministers: Bart Ulufa'alu's Liberal Party (which fielded a similar number of candidates to Socred); the People's Alliance Party (PAP), led by Sir Allan Kemakeza; and the Nasnol Pati (National Party), headed by Francis Billy Hilly. Three of the political party leaders were citizens of non-indigenous origin: Chinese hotelier Sir Tommy Chan led the Association of Independent Members of Parliament (AIMP), David Kwan led the Solomons First Party and Bobo Dettke (of German and Guadalcanal descent) headed the One Nation Party. Several other party leaders were long-term politicians. Job Dudley Tausinga, son of Ikan Rove—the Holy Mama or Supreme Authority of the Christian Fellowship Church (Tuza 1977)—led the Solomon Islands Party for Rural Advancement (SIPRA). The Democratic Party was led by lawyer Gabriel Suri. Malaitan John Garo headed the new Lafari Party, and Bellona trade unionist Joses Tuhanuku led the Labour Party. Long-time political hopeful Malaitan John Maetia Kaliuae led the United Party. Kemuel Laete led the Solomon Islands Youth for Change Group, and Edward Ronia headed the Christian Alliance Party. Candidates grouped loosely with the National Council of Women which, in a sense, became another party, and other independent candidates supplemented these formal political parties.

A few of these parties and groupings were well organised and well prepared for the election, while others were heard of first only a few weeks before the election. PAP, the longest surviving political party, was well organised, but it suffered under its own weight and age. The previous PAP-led government of Sir Allan Kemakeza had paid little or no attention to supporting the party. Consequently, some PAP officials became disgruntled and joined other political parties or groupings. In Solomon Islands, the government does not provide funding to support party officials, but this could change, as the new Sogavare government intends to introduce regulations to support party officials and secretariats.

The second factor that made the 2006 general election different from previous polls was that it generated a lot of interest and a greater number of individual candidates contested it. There were 328 candidates in the 2001 general elections; in 2006, there were 453 candidates, an increase of 125. The 2006 election saw, for the first time, a large number of women candidates (26). Interestingly, the province providing the highest number of women candidates (12, including three in Honiara) was Malaita, which is predominantly a patrilineal society. The next largest number came from Guadalcanal and Isabel provinces. The National Council of Women backed 15 of these candidates.

Some patterns remain the same in each election. There is no provision for absentee voting. Many Solomon Islanders returned to their villages all over the country to cast their votes, their trips home often paid for by aspiring political candidates (Wate 2006b). And, as usual, early in the run up to the election, individual candidates and the government attempted to clear the air on a number of issues. Some candidates manoeuvered to boost their image. For example, Joses Tuhanuku, the president of the Labour Party, called on voters to rid politics of Kemakeza.

> The whole country knows that Allan Kemakeza was involved in a lot of very bad things during the ethnic tension. When he became Prime Minister in 2001, he appointed the ex-militants with guns to be his body guards, now most of them are in Rove prison and it is the RAMSI that is guarding him…Because of his lack of vision, Kemakeza has become a puppet for foreign interests, serving not the nation but his own and his cronies' vested interests (Solomon Star 2006b).

This call, however, fell on deaf ears. Even the fact that police had begun investigations into Kemakeza's alleged corruption in relation to huge pay-outs he made to himself when he was Minister of National Unity, Peace and Reconciliation in 2000—and allegations about his relationship with Geoffrey Moss, an Australian businessman banned from Solomon Islands (Mamu 2006b; Keilor 2006)—did not affect his re-election as MP for the Savo/Russells electorate. His re-election could demonstrate that local allegiances mean more than allegations of malpractice against a minister of the Crown.[2] There was also a certain kudos attached to Kemakeza as a former prime minister and the man who had invited RAMSI to Solomon Islands (Mamu 2006g).

On the other hand, one of Kemakeza's ministers, Alfred Sasako, was not as fortunate. Sasako, a seasoned journalist, created controversy with at least two diplomatic missions in Honiara—the Taiwanese Embassy and the Australian High Commission. In his media exchanges with the Taiwanese

Embassy, Sasako claimed that he had spent SI$315,000—given to him by Taiwan to build a police house at Ato'ifi in his constituency—but the Taiwanese ambassador, Antonia C.S. Chen, disputed this claim.

> There were many withdrawals of cash from the project account, but no specific explanation was given as to how the cash were [sic] spent…From their initial costing, the materials will cost $140,000. But in the course of construction, they claimed that they ran out of materials so they came back and asked for some more finance…then they ran out of materials and came back a third time (Solomon Star 2006a).

Ambassador Chen pointed out that the cost of the police house should have been much less than SI$315,000. Sasako also accused Australia of interfering in Solomon Islands' internal affairs. The Australian High Commissioner, Patrick Cole, described Sasako's accusations as baseless: '[g]iven the corruption and good governance problem[s] faced in the region by some seeking to run offshore international shipping registers, Australia made no secret of its strong support for the [Solomon Islands government's] decision not to proceed with establishing a register of its own' (Solomon Star 2006b).

A few days later, Prime Minister Kemakeza sacked Sasako from the cabinet for unnecessarily causing a stir with two of Solomon Islands' diplomatic friends. Sasako's outbursts and his widely publicised marital infidelity—highlighted on the front page of the *Solomon Star*—were adequate grounds for his constituents in East Kwaio to give him a 'thumbs down' and he lost his seat.

Many other accusations and exchanges of views on various issues, national and local, occurred during the run up to the elections and on the campaign trail. Candidates and parties campaigned for good governance and quality leadership, the eradication of corruption, fair distribution of development, unity and peace, law and order, economic recovery, the provision of adequate education and health services and women's issues. Most of all, however, they jockeyed for position in what was the most highly contested race in the nation's history.

The newspapers carried campaigns for fair and honest elections and advice on the roles of MPs. Individuals such as Dr Kabini Sanga, a New Zealand-based Solomon Islander academic, wrote newspaper articles explaining the role of Mps as lawmakers and leaders. School students, clergy and one former governor-general also had their say (Sanga 2006; Concerned Students, Woodford International School 2006; Wate 2006e). The editorial in the *Solomon Star* the day before the election urged people not to be bribed by small gifts and promises from candidates.

> Forget about what others may say to you, or any material goods that a candidate has already given you. When you go to the polls, it is you and your conscience alone. Forget about the candidates that gave you money or goods and asked you to vote for him or her. Forget about that relative candidate of yours who asked you to vote for him or her because he or she is your relative. Your future and that of your nation, is much more important than a bag of rice or $100. This election is an opportunity for all of us to get rid of former MPs who did nothing in the last House, and replace them with quality and capable ones. At the polling station tomorrow, let your conscience decide (Solomon Star 2006c).

Two civil society groups campaigned strongly in urban and rural areas. The first was the AusAID-funded Civic Education Project, which had teams in all provinces creating awareness to help citizens vote wisely. The second group was Winds of Change, which, through its Clean Election Campaign, did its best to inspire all citizens to vote honestly and wisely. It urged sitting MPs, candidates and voters alike to sign a 'Voter's Pledge' committing potential politicians not to accept bribes or make false promises, and for everyone to reject corrupt dealings and vote selling (Figure 5.1). Some 5,000 voters, MPs and candidates signed the pledge forms. Whether they committed themselves honestly to their pledges is another matter, but this at least reminded candidates that people were concerned about dirty politics and that voters should not be bought with money or false promises (Wate 2006a, 2006f; Mamu 2006c, 2006f, 2006h).

The third factor that made the 2006 general elections different from previous elections was the use of the single ballot box system. Initial criticisms of this system abated after the electoral office and a civic education team conducted a massive educational campaign among voters. The single ballot box system definitely prevented the practice of selling votes or ballot papers on election day, but what it might not have stopped was a range of last-minute and unwarranted activities during the night before election day. This became known as the 'devil's night' because many cases of vote buying took place. That this occurred is common knowledge, but no one has challenged it in the courts.

No one political party or group was able to field candidates for all 50 electorates. The Liberal and Socred parties sponsored more than 30 candidates each, while most parties managed to field between five and 20 candidates, with the Solomon Islands Youth for Change Group sponsoring only one candidate in East Honiara.

---

Figure 5.1    Advertisement for the Clean Election Campaign, by Winds of Change, promoting the voter's pledge

---

Clean Election Campaign

**Have you signed your pledge yet?**

CTION CAMPAIGN
...TE..S PLEDGE
I PLEDGE THAT I will not ...

Accept bribes
Accept any false promises
Sell my vote
Involve in any corrupt
activity before, during
or after the elections.

I PLEDGE THAT I will ...
Use my full conscience to
decide my vote
Listen to God to help me
decide my vote
Vote for an honest leader.

Signed
Name
Village
Constituency
Province
Date

Make A Personal Pledge to
Make this A Clean Election

YOU and YOUR VOTE
CAN make a DIFFERENCE

Winds of Change

# The 5 April 2006 national elections: results

Three observer groups with 44 foreign observers from the United Nations, the Commonwealth Secretariat and the Pacific Islands Forum, bolstered by local volunteers, were present during the election in Honiara and in the provinces. They managed to visit more than 150 of the 802 polling stations in 29 of the 50 electorates (Wate 2006c, 2006d; Mamu 2006d, 2006e). The 2006 election was an improvement on the 2001 election because of the absence of guns and intimidation. The observer teams were satisfied and reported that the elections were free, fair and conducted in an orderly manner. In spite of this, some voters still claimed the elections were biased and unfair.

Of the 342,119 registered voters, 192,775, about 56 per cent, cast their votes in a population estimated to be about 500,000. In 2001, there were 178,083 votes cast from among 280,790 registered voters, or 63 per cent (Mamu 2006a). The fact that one constituency did not go to the polls because the sitting member (Job Dudley Tausinga) was returned unopposed meant that the percentage of those who voted in 2006 was lower than in 2001. Approximately 1,500 spoilt votes were recorded throughout the nation, mainly because of uncertainties in relation to using the single ballot box, but also because of poor-quality printing (Solomon Islands Government 2006a).

It is interesting to look back at my own predictions made the day before the election. I said that no political party would win more than 15 seats, which was a very different situation from 1989, when Solomon Mamaloni won 26 seats and formed the only one-party government in the history of the nation. My prediction of a coalition government proved quite correct (Wate 2006g). Another typical pattern in Solomon Islands politics also continued: the 50-seat parliament had an equal share of old and new members. Unfortunately, none of the 26 female candidates won, once more making parliament a male-dominated affair. The main problem for female candidates was that although they drew strong support during campaigning, the mood changed just before and on election day because male relatives and husbands usually have the final say on how women vote. Male candidates also had more money to buy votes. The average female candidate had only SI$ 10,000–20,000 of personal funds available for campaigning, whereas male candidates often had access to SI$ 100,000–200,000 gained

from business connections. The legal maximum under the Electoral Act is
SI$50,000 a candidate, but it is very difficult to track how candidates spend
money during their campaigns. Families are inclined to block vote. A split
for voting purposes is frowned on and, once more, women follow the lead of
the family's male voters. After the election, the National Council of Women
called for the introduction of quotas for women members of parliament
(Mamu 2006i). Of the democratic governments in the world, about only
10 have no female representatives—five of these are in the Pacific.

The following seven political parties or groups failed to gain a seat in
the present parliament: the One Nation Party, the Solomons First Party,
Solomons Christian Alliance Party, the United Party, the Labour Party, the
National Women's Council and the Solomon Islands Youth for Change Group.
With the exception of the Labour Party and the United Party, these were
late contenders who appeared just a few weeks before the election and had
no real substance. Party fluidity and instability will remain a major problem
in Solomon Islands politics for some time. This problem could be eradicated
by the Sogavare government's plan to introduce legislation to strengthen
political parties and discard Clause 66(2) of the national constitution, which
provides for the existence of independent groups in parliament. The initial
division when the new parliament sat was that the Socred Party ended up
with two seats, AIMP had 11, PAP had four, SIPRA had five, the Nasnol Pati
had five, the Liberals had three, the Democratic Party had four, the Lafari
Party secured two seats and the rest were independents (Solomon Islands
Government 2006b). This scenario changed during 2006 as MPs moved
from one party to another, or from opposition to the government side,
and as cabinet ministers resigned or were sacked. In its initial months, the
Sogavare government gained strength.

## Formation of a new government: the election of Snyder Rini as prime minister

Soon after the election results were announced, new MPs made their way
to Honiara for the vote for the prime ministership and the formation of a
new government. Only five politicians signed the Winds of Change pledge
that they would not accept bribes in relation to the vote for prime minister
(Mamu 2006k). Unaligned politicians found themselves wooed, cajoled

and finessed by all groups; rumour has it that some MPs were bribed with
between SI$20,000 and SI$60,000 to change sides, but all groups denied this.
This scene described in the *Solomon Star* (Mamu 2006l) is typical: Martin Maga
(MP for Temotu Pele) and Japhet Waipora (MP for West Makira) arrived in
Honiara on a domestic flight on 12 April. Sir Tommy Chan beat Patteson Oti
to the airport and whisked them away to his Honiara Hotel. Oti marched in,
forcefully removed them and sped them off to the Iron Bottom Sound Hotel
(Mamu 2006l). The AIMP, PAP and Lafari members set up camp at Chan's
Honiara Hotel, immediately claiming 24 MPs (Mamu 2006j). People were
clearly irritated with the Kemakeza government and with this attempt by the
same group to hold power. Many Solomon Islanders wanted change, which
showed in the final alignment of members. All other political parties outside
the Honiara Hotel camp held a joint meeting, chaired by Job Tausinga, on 11
April and agreed that they would organise themselves with the aim of forming
an alternative government. On 12 April, all members of the Socred Party,
the Democratic Party, SIPRA, the Nasnol Parti, the Liberal Party and some
independents met at the Iron Bottom Sound Hotel to discuss the idea of signing
a memorandum of understanding (MOU) to guide and govern their working
relationship, and to commit to forming the next government.

During the meeting, 26 MPs signed the MOU and four more promised
to join. Even with those who signed up on 12 April, the coalition already
represented more than half the 50-member parliament (Mamu 2006m). The
Iron Bottom Sound group agreed to conduct an internal election and begin an
elimination process to confirm one candidate for the post of prime minister.
This vote took place on 13 April: the candidates were Tausinga, Patteson
Oti, Derek Sikua, Joses Sanga and Milner Tozaka. One notable absence was
Sogavare and the other Socred Party MPs. Because of a misunderstanding,
they did not participate in the internal election even though they had signed
the MOU the previous day. After the signing of the MOU, Sogavare and his
group (which then numbered about five MPs) decamped to the Pacific Casino
Hotel and prepared to consolidate their numbers for the internal elimination
process. When Sogavare and his group arrived at the Iron Bottom Sound Hotel
on 13 April to participate in the internal election, a commotion took place
during which they were accused of trying to destabilise this camp. As a result,
Sogavare's group withdrew and confirmed the formation of a third political
camp at the Pacific Casino Hotel.

Before the elimination process, all candidates who contested the leadership signed an important pledge. They promised that, even if they lost, they would remain part of the group and support the winning candidate, who would eventually be their nominee for the post of prime minister. After four rounds of voting, Tausinga was declared the group's candidate. After that elimination, only one candidate (Milner Tozaka) broke his pledge and left to join the Honiara Hotel Group, which had endorsed as its candidate Snyder Rini (the deputy prime minister and education minister in the previous government). By 13 April, it was obvious that three political groups would compete for the prime ministerial post at the first meeting of parliament on 18 April. On Friday 14 April, the governor-general announced the three candidates for the post of prime minister: Tausinga, Sogavare and Rini. Had Sogavare remained with the Iron Bottom Sound group, Tausinga would have become the new prime minister; however, with three groups at three different locations, a complex round of campaigning occurred during the several days before the vote. The many negotiations between the three political camps were also played out in the media. The Tausinga-led group claimed it had the numbers to form the next government, while Rini's group counter-claimed and assured the nation that it had the numbers to form government. Wild claims were made and, at one stage, basic arithmetic suggested that there were 72 MPs involved—in a 50-seat parliament.

Sogavare's camp held the balance of power because it had 10–11 members at any one time, and it seemed possible that Sogavare could pull support from Rini's and Tausinga's groups to form government. There was also the possibility that Sogavare—who had already served as prime minister—would back Tausinga because he was the longest serving MP and because of the nature of Tausinga's electorate, which was the most stable in the nation. In practice, other forces were at play; 17 April was the second 'devil's night', with continuous twists and turns. During the night, the Iron Bottom Sound group heard confidential reports that Sogavare was willing to back Tausinga. Tausinga's camp did manage to get Sogavare and his group's support, but it was later alleged that Rini offered a better deal in terms of portfolio arrangements and possible project financing. In spite of this, the Tausinga camp was still confident of winning, even though the number of MPs supporting him fluctuated between 22 and 23. The number of MPs in Rini's camp fluctuated between 17 and 18.

On the morning of the parliamentary vote, the Mps at the Iron Bottom Sound Hotel had breakfast and, after a short prayer, 20 of them boarded a bus while two others went in private vehicles. A large crowd had already gathered outside Parliament House. The governor-general, assisted by the clerk to the national parliament and the attorney-general, conducted the election. After the first round, Tausinga polled 22 votes, Rini 17 and Sogavare 11 (Mamu 2006n). In the final round after Sogavare had been eliminated, Rini polled 27 votes and Tausinga 23. When the Governor-General, Sir Nathaniel Waena, first appeared on the balcony of parliament and presented Rini as the new prime minister of Solomon Islands, there was a negative reaction from the waiting crowd. People began shouting 'Corruption', '*Waku* [Chinese] government', 'Same old government' and 'We want Tausinga'. The crowd was unhappy to see Kemakeza's former deputy as the new prime minister. They claimed that Rini's government would be the same as its predecessor—full of corruption and a puppet to Chinese businessmen such as Sir Tommy Chan and Robert Goh. The crowd at parliament definitely did not accept the decision and was horrified at the thought of another four years under 'Asian influence'.[3]

## The 'Black Tuesday' riots

From just after midday until 6pm, the crowd prevented the new prime minister and his supporters leaving parliament. Only the 22 MPs who had voted for Tausinga were allowed to pass. The situation was unprecedented. At one stage, the RAMSI Participating Police Force (PPF) and security tried to help Rini escape, but they were stoned; several PPF officers were injured. PPF reinforcements arrived with riot gear, ready to do battle. The Speaker of Parliament, Sir Peter Kenilorea, appealed to the crowd to go home and to respect the parliament's decision, but they would not listen to him. As the afternoon went on, the situation deteriorated. The crowd torched and burned several RAMSI vehicles and about 50 RAMSI/PPF personnel were hurt. Kenilorea also appealed to the PPF not to use tear-gas, but was ignored. The use of tear-gas certainly aggravated the situation. Luckily, no one was killed.

Another crowd had massed in Point Cruz, the centre of Honiara, and just after 3pm they began to loot nearby shops. Their numbers were swelled by the crowd from parliament (which is just above the Point Cruz area) and, after 6pm, the new crowd moved into Chinatown (a half-hour's walk away) selectively burning and looting Chinese-owned shops and businesses. About 600 Chinese fled to the Rove Police Club for safety. Some Chinese were airlifted out of the country during the next few days, but for those who stayed, Rove became a refugee camp for several weeks where the Solomon Islands Red Cross looked after them. While many returned to mainland China, most are now back in Honiara, although not in Chinatown, which has not yet been rebuilt.

After the crowd left parliament, the prime minister and members of the new government were moved to the Rove police headquarters under tight security and remained there for that night and the next day. Looting and burning continued around Chinatown until the next day. RAMSI and the PPF were ill prepared and could do little. RAMSI planning had cut the police force, removing most of the officers and temporarily weakening the force's capacity to deal with crises. The police chose, wisely, not to aggravate the crowd and looters, as they really could do nothing against the mob; consequently, however, local and PPF police stood helplessly by as millions of dollars worth of stock was looted and almost all buildings in Chinatown were destroyed. There was also some damage in surrounding suburbs, such as Kukum. I was with the Tausinga camp and the situation in Honiara was still very tense when we held meetings at the Iron Bottom Sound Hotel to assess and monitor developments. Later that day, two MPs who had voted for Rini—Patrick Vahoe and Trevor Olovae—crossed over to join Tausinga's camp. They had been under pressure from their constituents to switch sides.

The next day, 19 April, 1,000 people marched to Government House to present a petition to the governor-general to remove Rini. Waena thanked them and told them to go home, promising that he would seek legal advice before responding to their petition in a live broadcast on national radio in two hours. The crowd had been well behaved, until, on the way back down the hill, they stopped to burn Robert Goh's residence at East Kola Ridge and burned and looted the Pacific Casino Hotel, where Goh had his office. Goh always claimed that his involvement in government was limited to a one-dollar annual fee, but few believed him. The rioters claimed that Goh, a shareholder in the Pacific Casino Hotel, and his company, which audited government accounts, had siphoned off millions of dollars under Kemakeza's administration. Goh's was the only private house deliberately targeted by the mob. Patrick Leong, the main owner of the Pacific Casino Hotel, later accused RAMSI of not adequately protecting his property. Foolishly, he had relied on RAMSI police for protection and had refused an offer from members of the nearby Malaitan Fishing Village to protect his property (for a considerable price).

As promised, on the evening of 19 April, in a live address to the nation, the governor-general responded to the petitioners' demand and explained that, as the defender of the national constitution, he would not encourage Rini to resign. Rini stressed that he would not resign because this would set a bad precedent; he denied that he had bought votes and denied any Asian influence on his government. The next day, three important events occurred: under tight security, Rini was sworn in as prime minister; the governor-general imposed a curfew, from 6pm to 6am (Lamani 2006; Wasuka 2006a); and extra troops arrived from Townsville. The opposition then lodged a motion of no confidence in the prime minister as well as a motion to dissolve parliament, and called on the governor-general to convene parliament. These actions were primarily to ensure that the crisis would be solved only on the floor of parliament. The governor-general duly convened parliament on 26 April.

Over two days, one-quarter of the commercial centre of Honiara had been destroyed and a foreign racial group targeted. Church leaders and ordinary Solomon Islanders apologised to the Chinese for the destruction of their property. One of the first to do so was Archbishop Adrian Smith of the Catholic Church, and the Vatican was one of the first foreign governments to assist the Chinese refugees, with a small donation of SI$38,000. One long-time Chinese resident and leader, Sir Henry Quan, had forewarned in early 2006 that the new Chinese immigrants were causing problems for the established Chinese residents. Many of these 'new' Chinese had been involved in scandals and corrupt practices, such as the fraudulent issuing of passports for remuneration, which allowed them to receive Solomon Islands citizenship after only two years, instead of the normal 10. Indeed, the looters did not target businesses belonging to Quan, George Wu or Aba Corporation, the owners of which were long-time Chinese residents and Solomon Islands citizens. The Chan family of Honiara Hotel also survived with their assets intact, due to their substantial private defence force and the help of the Anglican Melanesian Brothers, who unleashed their religious *mana* (power) on behalf of Chan's hotel. After the riots, Quan was forthright in saying that some of the new Chinese were to blame for the unfortunate situation. He was also very critical of RAMSI's PPF for its lack of preparedness.

## The 26 April meeting of parliament: Prime Minister Rini resigns

The numbers game continued, but at least this time, there were only two political groups: Rini's and Tausinga's, each with 25 MPs. The political situation was still uncertain as no MP really wanted to switch sides. On 25 April, a day before the meeting of parliament, Steve Abana, the MP for Fataleka—sensing that no camp would give way to the other—made a breakthrough with the idea of inviting Sogavare and his colleague Clay Soalaoi (MP for Temotu Vatud) to join forces with Tausinga. This would increase that side's position to 27 MPs. To break the political deadlock, Tausinga acted for the betterment of the nation, relinquished his bid for the post of prime minister and offered to support Sogavare. I had been involved in Tausinga's political campaign and had the opportunity of discussing this very important matter. We agreed that it had to be done. This humble gesture by Tausinga will go down in the nation's political history as one of the greatest moments: an act that saved the nation from more turmoil.[4] On 26 April, just before parliament met, Sogavare and Soalaoi (who were still cabinet ministers in the Rini government) arrived at the Iron Bottom Sound Hotel and accompanied Tausinga to parliament.

There was a heavy RAMSI military and security presence around Parliament House. The motion of no confidence in Rini was scheduled to be moved during the meeting; however, before moving it, the outspoken MP for Temotu Nende, Patteson Oti, made a statement in parliament recommending that Prime Minister Rini resign rather than face the no-confidence vote, as he no longer had the necessary support. Rini was surprised to see two of his ministers sitting on the opposition bench and he asked the parliament for a brief adjournment for consultation purposes. When parliament resumed half an hour later, Rini acted honourably, in compliance with tradition and the national constitution: he resigned on the floor of parliament. After eight days in office, Rini became the shortest serving prime minister in Solomon Islands history (Wasuka 2006b, 2006c).

After Rini's resignation, there were shouts of jubilation in the streets of Honiara, as people felt that Rini had finally listened to them (Rusa 2006). The repercussions of the riots continued, however, with fears that essential food items, provided mainly by Chinese shops, would run out. This was only temporary and the economic effects of the riots were not serious except, of course, for the Chinese shop-owners. The final political fall-out was more devastating than the initial food shortage. Two Honiara MPs, Charles Dausabea and Nelson Ne'e, were arrested and placed in police custody, as they were alleged to have been involved in orchestrating the riots. The overall situation improved and the curfew was lifted on 27 April. People were free once again to move around the capital after dark (Wate 2006h).

## The election of Manasseh Sogavare as prime minister—4 May

When nominations for prime minister opened on 27 April, the political group at Iron Bottom Sound Hotel nominated Sogavare as its candidate, with Tausinga, Sikua, Oti and Ulufa'alu (whom Sogavare had replaced as prime minister in 2000) as his nominees. The Rini camp put forward Fred Fono, the MP for Central Kwara'ae, as their candidate (Wate 2006i). For the first time in Solomon Islands' political history, a second round of campaigning for the election of a prime minister was held within a month. The political situation was still tense and uncertain, because, after the arrests of Dausabea and Ne'e, the Sogavare camp decreased by two to 25 MPs, while Fono maintained 23 members. The Sogavare group consolidated its numbers by holding a series of daily meetings. There was tight security to prevent agents from the other group coming in to lure members away. The same was true of Fono's camp, backed by the AIMP, PAP, Lafari Party and the Independent Group (Wate 2006j).

The party leaders within the Sogavare group appointed a drafting committee to draw up new policy initiatives in the event of Sogavare's election as prime minister. I was appointed the chairman of the committee and our task was to harmonise the different views on a wide range of issues raised in the manifestos of the six political parties and groups, namely the Socred, Liberal, SIPRA, Democratic and Nasnol parties and a few independents. The priority at that stage, however, was to consolidate the group supporting Sogavare. The final meeting on the afternoon of 3 May was attended by 25 MPs, with the support of the two MPs in custody.

During the night of 3 May, security personnel at the Iron Bottom Sound Hotel confirmed that Fono's agents had tried all night to lure at least two Malaitan MPs from the Sogavare camp. Fono even gave a note to a senior security officer, Medley Kwalumanu, promising him SI$10,000 if he could persuade the MP for Lau/Mbalelea, Samuel Bentley Rogosimani, and the MP for East Kwaio, Stanley Sofu, to change sides. This note was kept as evidence. Several weeks later, when Fono claimed that Sogavare's camp used dirty tactics before the election, Kwalumanu spoke out against Fono in the media, calling him a hypocrite, and the note bearing Fono's signature and mobile phone number was published in the *Solomon Star* (Wate 2006l). This silenced Fono.

On 18 April, the crowd outside Parliament House had been noisy. On 4 May, it was silent, waiting nervously for the result of the contest between Sogavare and Fono. The governor-general had agreed that the two MPs who were in police custody could participate in the election. A bizarre scene ensued as parliament waited while two officials, accompanied by police, went to the police cells so Dausabea and Ne'e could cast their votes (Wasuka 2006d).[5] After only one round of voting, Sogavare polled 28 votes to Fono's 22.[6] Sogavare was duly elected prime minister for the second time. When the waiting crowd received this election result, there was shouting and cries of delight in the streets and vehicles blared their horns. At the Iron Bottom Sound Hotel, the MPs who had voted for Sogavare waited for the prime minister-elect singing hymns of praise. When Sogavare arrived, Bishop Leslie Boseto, the MP for South Choiseul, said prayers of thanksgiving. Tausinga was the last MP Sogavare embraced and they sat down together to enjoy the celebrations.

Manasseh Sogavare was born on 17 January 1955 in Papua New Guinea. A Seventh-day Adventist from eastern Choiseul, he left high school in 1974 to become a clerk in the Honiara Consumers Cooperative shop, but soon moved to another clerical position, in the Inland Revenue Division of the Ministry of Finance. Sogavare rose through the ranks to become the Commissioner for Inland Revenue in 1991 and permanent secretary in the Ministry of Finance in 1993. He resigned in 1994 because of a disagreement with the Mamaloni government, and went to study accounting and economics at the University of the South Pacific in Suva, Fiji. He won the East Choiseul seat in the 1997 elections and became minister for finance in the Ulufa'alu government. Sacked in 1999, Sogavare became leader of the opposition and completed a flexible-delivery Masters degree in management studies from

Waikato University. When Sogavare took over from Ulufa'alu in late June 2000, large forces were positioned against him. His first prime ministership was a balancing act, as he had to placate the Malaita Eagle Force (MEF) and the Isatabu Freedom Movement (IFM). After the general election in December 2001, he became leader of the opposition for a period.

By the time he was voted in as prime minister for the second time, he was a much wiser man, and well blooded in the political arena. A powerfully built martial arts expert with the distinctive jet-black skin typical of the western Solomons, Sogavare is physically impressive. He dresses well and has piercing eyes. A day after his election, Sogavare announced his new cabinet line-up, but two appointments did not go down well with the public or overseas observers: Dausabea and Ne'e were offered portfolios, with the justification that they had been charged but should be presumed innocent until convicted. The situation was made worse when Sogavare offered Dausabea the police and national security portfolio. National and international commentators ridiculed Sogavare, spoiling what had until then been support from all sides. Australia's Foreign Minister, Alexander Downer, was scathing, but, as Sogavare said at the time, Australia and members of RAMSI had no right 'to interfere in matters concerning the appointment or removal of ministers within the Government of Solomon Islands' (Wasuka 2006e). After local pressure was applied, however, caretaker ministers were appointed and, a little later, Dausabea's and Ne'e's appointments were withdrawn (O'Callaghan 2006; Wate 2006k; Wasuka 2006f).

Two weeks later, the Grand Coalition for Change policy framework document was released. In the foreword, Prime Minster Sogavare wrote

[t]he Grand Coalition for Change Government is very serious about leading this country in the direction that will benefit and uplift the people of Solomon Islands. To this end, it has to be reform minded, people focused and rules based. It will remove barriers that impede 'development with a human face' to occur at the grassroots level and will carry out policies through government structures that will deliver results. The GCC government's vision is to give this country hope, prosperity and peace in a secure environment (Grand Coalition for Change Government 2006).

The document focused principally on a bottom-up approach to rural development, which was to be implemented once funds were allocated in the February 2007 national budget.

Of the many pressing issues the government faced, the main ones were: understanding the causes of the Honiara riots; determining the future relationship with RAMSI; federalism; the need to restore ethical leadership; establishing a commission of inquiry into land dealings on Guadalcanal before the crisis; and the need for a truth and reconciliation commission relating to the 1998–2000 crisis period.

With regard to the April 2006 Honiara riots, a commission of inquiry was established to look into its causes; unfortunately, however, attempts were made to derail it. The appointed chairman, former Australian judge Marcus Einfeld, came under scrutiny in the Australian and Solomon Islands press for exaggerating his qualifications and anomalies in other legal matters (Mamu 2006o, 2006q; Wate 2006s; Nason 2006; Merritt 2006; Andrusiak and Merritt 2006; Merritt and Andrusiak 2006). In the Solomon Islands, Attorney-General, Primo Afeau, challenged Sogavare in court over two of the inquiry's terms of reference concerning Ne'e and Dausabea. He argued that they should not be included in the commission's brief as this would constitute contempt of court (Mamu 2006p, 2006q; Afeau 2006; Wate 2006n, 2006o; Sogavare 2006) because Dausabea's and Ne'e's cases were already being tried. In his deliberations on 6 September, however, Justice John Brown of the High Court ruled that the two terms did not constitute contempt as the commission had not begun. The two terms were, first, for the commission to investigate the role of any MP (including Dausabea and Ne'e) in the execution of the April civil unrest; and second, to review the circumstances relating to the arrest, charging and detention of those accused, as well as to investigate and evaluate the basis on which their continued detention in custody was reasonably justified and not politically motivated. The commission was set to proceed with its work. Sogavare initially stood by Einfeld and the terms of the commission, but he eventually gave in—replacing Einfeld as head of the commission with a retired Papua New Guinea judge. He also eventually backed down over the two contentious terms of reference.

There were allegations that RAMSI and the Australian High Commission played a part in attempts to derail the commission of inquiry because it might find fault with the RAMSI police and the Australian police commissioner for not doing enough to contain the riots.[7] On 12 September, the Australian High Commissioner, Patrick Cole, was expelled—a severe move that no government would take without great provocation. Unwilling to

countenance the continued bullying and criticism by Australia and Cole—
who was accused of trying to stop external funding of the commission—and
given Cole's previous behaviour, which had led Rini to ask for his recall,
Sogavare ordered that Cole be removed (Wate 2006t; Walters 2006).
Australia's Foreign Minister, Alexander Downer, countered by saying that
he believed the expulsion was 'a personalised attack for no good reason'
(ABC 2006) and that the Sogavare government was using the commission
of inquiry to cloak the nefarious activities of Dausabea and Ne'e, as well as
to attack RAMSI. Others have suggested that Sogavare has been beholden
to Dausabea since 2000, when he and other Malaitans supported Sogavare's
nomination as prime minister (Manimu 2006). There has also been criticism
of the relationship between Sogavare and Julian Moti, an Australian lawyer
of Indo-Fijian descent, who has become mixed up in the legal wrangling
over the commission. Aspects of Moti's past have led to questions about
his suitability for office (Downer has also been scathing about Moti).
Nevertheless, Moti was made a QC and was appointed to replace Afeau as
attorney-general (Wate 2006q, 2006r; Eremae 2006; Kenilorea 2006; Moti
2006). During this difficult time, Australia's media behaved disgracefully
in its unwarranted attacks on the Solomon Islands government (Sydney
Morning Herald 2006; Skehan 2006; Sheridan 2006; Walters 2006; The
Australian 2006).

The second pressing issue for the new government was to arrive at
some understanding with RAMSI to strengthen the partnership, taking into
account areas in which RAMSI should start training Solomon Islanders to
take over from it, even if this takes another five or so years. The government
agreed that RAMSI has a role to play in rehabilitating Solomon Islands and
it renewed its tenure in 2006, but a thorough reassessment was considered
necessary. The Sogavare government was reasserting national sovereignty and
RAMSI seemed uneasy about this. RAMSI and particularly Australia as the
major partner were largely able to have their own way with the Kemakeza
government between 2003 and early 2006. The ease with which they could
'handle' the Solomon Islands government no longer exists and RAMSI and
Australia are smarting under the strain of dealing with the independent
Sogavare government.

The third leading issue was the long-standing wish by the majority of
Solomon Islanders to implement federalism. The costs involved in establishing

federalism and the shape it will take have not yet been confirmed—the matter was to be finalised in 2007 through a national independent constitutional congress. A few provinces have already prepared themselves for federalism. For example, Makira/Ulawa Province has passed an ordinance known as the Community Governance Regime, which involves setting up ward councils of chiefs and ward development authorities. Interestingly, they do not want new elections or a state parliament (see Scales, this volume).

The fourth major issue was to ensure that ethical leadership is practised; this involves weeding out corruption and bad governance. The government commenced preparing several pieces of legislation, including an anti-corruption bill, a political parties integrity bill and a code of conduct for all MPs. It is galling to have the Australian prime minister and foreign minister accuse the Sogavare government of corruption when it is trying hard to introduce mechanisms that will place limits on corruption.

The fifth matter was the institution of a commission of inquiry into land-tenure issues on Guadalcanal before the social crisis that began in 1998. This is the basis of Guale concerns, which will not be quieted until there is a thorough investigation of the events that led to the crisis years. The sixth urgent matter was the establishment of a truth and reconciliation commission to uncover the root causes of the social crisis of 1998–2000 and to provide an opportunity for real healing to take place. There have been calls for such a commission from many quarters and it is necessary to achieve national reconciliation and unity. Once again, however, RAMSI and the Australian High Commission have not been supportive.

Since independence in 1978, the Solomon Islands government has always supported the Republic of China (Taiwan) while often also flirting with the People's Republic of China (Moore 2004:163–4). Although Sogavare made certain statements that seemed ambivalent and Taiwan's ambassador issued a plaintive plea for continued support (Chen 2006), Sogavare finally came out strongly in support of Taiwan. Before taking a trip to Taiwan in July 2006, he gave assurances that he was not displaying a double standard and requested that the Nasnol Pati dishonour a memorandum of understanding it had signed with the government of mainland China in late 2005 (Wate 2006m). Francis Billy Hilly and his party rejected the request, saying that the issue was never raised at joint party meetings. This led Sogavare to sack Hilly from his cabinet and replace him with Ped Shannel from the opposition, although it has also been suggested that Sogavare was protecting the general secretary of his political party, Filipino Siri Ramon Quitales (Mamu 2006r). For Sogavare, this was an issue about the integrity of his government, but no doubt it will also reap benefits in strengthening the relationship with Taiwan.

In October 2006, the opposition moved a motion of no confidence against the Sogavare government; however, Sogavare's diplomatic fracas with Australia only strengthened his domestic standing and the motion was defeated.

The 2006 general election brought with it much hope and a wish for clean and honest government. The three different observer teams agreed that the elections were free, fair and honest. When Rini was voted in as prime minister on 18 April, the people's hopes for a better Solomon Islands were short-circuited and the Honiara crowd reacted negatively, causing the April riots. One could argue that Honiara is not representative of the nation—and certainly the nation cannot be ruled by a Honiara mob—but I would argue that the crowd captured the mood of the majority of Solomon Islanders, who wanted change and were devastated to see Rini elected. The destructive actions of the mob, however regrettable, in their own way resembled the people's power that swept Corazon Aquino to office in the Philippines in 1986. The people spoke and the politicians had to listen.

The April riots were also a symptom of something bigger and deeper. The targets were Chinese business houses because they had been controlling the country's economy for so long. People resented the fact that some Chinese had become involved in politics and corruptly influenced politicians. The Chinese faced the brunt of the rage of indigenous Solomon Islanders, but they were the obvious face of a much larger Asian community and extensive corruption. For example, Koreans, Malaysians and Filipinos represent corrupt forces in the logging industry and the new Chinese (as distinct from the 'old', pre-World War II Chinese families) became involved in scandals such as the fraudulent issuing of passports. These new Chinese are notorious for the poor treatment of their workers. As well, foreigners (mainly Chinese) own a large amount of property in Honiara. These matters do not go down well with the populace, whose anger welled over in April 2006.

When RAMSI first came to the Solomon Islands, there were high hopes that the nation's problems would be tackled. Slowly, this is occurring, but too slowly, and much more still needs to be done. Sogavare's Grand Coalition for Change government was setting priorities intended to improve people's lives. Political stability is crucial to ensure a conducive environment for economic progress and, after the experiences of April 2006 which saw factions of MPs camped in three hotels (at great expense), it was clear that ways must be found to improve political stability. Legislation is to be introduced so that the governor-general could approach the MP who commands the most support after an election to form government. The intention was to get rid of the corrupt politics and the political horse-trading that presently mars our parliamentary system.

The second Sogavare government intended to embark on a program of land reform to deal with the convolutions of Solomon Islands' traditional land-tenure systems. A tribes and customary land titles bill was to be drafted with the intention of encouraging people to work on their land, open it up for development and make customary land a transferable commodity. Cultural mapping of land also continued under the Customary Land and Recording Act (Wate 2006p). The decentralisation of power and development are crucial issues and the government intended to work in this area to ensure that rural people benefit from their hard work and resources.

The people know that, ultimately, they are the owners of the resources and the development process. They must become full participants in this bottom-up approach to rural development, knowing that they have contributed to the overall development and progress of Solomon Islands. It is only then that we will realise that a rainbow across the mountains is part of this development and we should not fear pointing our finger at it. By pointing our finger at the rainbow in the sky, we are aiming to build a sound, united, peaceful and progressive Solomon Islands for us and our children.

## Acknowledgments

This chapter was completed in late 2006. It contains the author's own opinions and is in no way representative of the views of the then Solomon Islands government.

# Notes

1  I take as my text here Hereniko and Wesley-Smith 2003.
2  Kemakeza was arrested in October 2006 (Wate 2006u).
3  A video recording exists of the lead up to the riot outside parliament, recorded for use by a new TV station in Honiara.
4  Tausinga became deputy prime minister, until his resignation in December 2006.
5  There was a precedent for this: another MP had been allowed to vote while in hospital.
6  It was alleged that Rini voted for Sogavare.
7  See Moore, this volume. Moore concluded that the police commissioner was unprepared to handle the situation and that the RAMSI police performed poorly. The Australian government reaction to the commission of inquiry seems to indicate that they fear a similar conclusion.

# References

Afeau, P., 2006. 'Letter from Attorney-General to Prime Minister', *Solomon Star*, 17 August.

Alasia, S., 1988. 'Big man and party politics: the evolution of political parties in Solomon Islands', *Pacific Perspective*, 13(2):72–84.

——, 1989. 'Population movement', in H. Laracy (ed.), *Ples Blong Iumi: Solomon Islands, the past four thousand years*, Institute of Pacific Studies, University of the South Pacific, Suva:112–20.

——, 1997. *Party politics and government in Solomon Islands*, Discussion Paper 97/7, State, Society and Governance in Melanesia Program, Research School of Pacific and Asian Studies, The Australian National University, Canberra. Available from http://rspas.anu.edu.au/papers/melanesia/discussion_papers/ssgmalasia.pdf (accessed 11 April 2007).

Andrusiak, K. and Merritt, C., 2006. 'Fear for Einfeld as new résumé flaws revealed', *The Australian*, 31 August.

Australian Broadcasting Corporation (ABC), 2006. *Lateline*, ABC TV, 12 September.

Bennett, J.A., 2002. *Roots of conflict in Solomon Islands. Though much is taken, much abides: legacies of tradition and colonialism*, Discussion Paper 2002/5, State, Society and Governance in Melanesia Program, Research School of Pacific and Asian Studies, The Australian National University, Canberra. Available from http://rspas.anu.edu.au/papers/melanesia/discussion_papers/bennett02-5.pdf (accessed 13 May 2006).

Brown, T., 2005. Current issues in Solomon Islands politics: RAMSI and beyond, Paper presented to the State, Society and Governance in Melanesia Program Seminar Series, The Australian National University, Canberra, 7 July 2005. Available from http://rspas.anu.edu.au/papers/melanesia/seminars/05_0707_sp_brownNotes.pdf (accessed 11 April 2007).

Chen, A.C.S., 2006. ROC (Taiwan) is Solomon Islands' Most Reliable Partner, Press release, Embassy of the Republic of China (Taiwan), Honiara, 3 May.

Concerned Students, Woodford International School, 2006. 'We have the power', *Solomon Star*, 3 April.

Dinnen, S., 2002. 'Winners and losers: politics and disorder in the Solomon Islands, 2000–2002', *Journal of Pacific History*, 37(3):285–98.

Eremae, O., 2006. 'Is Moti the right choice?', *Solomon Star*, 25 August.

Fraenkel, J., 2004. *The Manipulation of Custom: from uprising to intervention in the Solomon Islands*, Victoria University Press, Wellington.

Fullilove, M., 2006. *The testament of Solomons: RAMSI and international state-building*, Analysis, Lowy Institute for International Policy, Sydney. Available from http://www.lowyinstitute.org/Publication.asp?pid=351 (accessed 11 April 2007).

Grand Coalition for Change Government, 2006. Policy framework document, Honiara.

Hereniko, V. and Wesley-Smith, T. (eds), 2003. 'Back to the future: decolonizing Pacific studies', *The Contemporary Pacific*, Special issue, 15(1).

Kabutaulaka, T.T., 1999. 'Political reviews: Solomon Islands', *The Contemporary Pacific*, 11(2):443–9.

—, 2005. 'Australian foreign policy and the RAMSI intervention in Solomon Islands', *Contemporary Pacific*, 17(2):283–308.

Keilor, P., 2006. 'Re "Streetman" to editor, "PM & Moss saga"', Letter to editor, *Solomon Star*, 3 April.

Kenilorea, P., 2006. 'Sir Peter Kenilorea to editor', *Solomon Star*, 31 August.

Lamani, J., 2006. 'PM sworn in secretly', *Solomon Star*, 21 April.

Larmour, P. (ed.), 1979. *Land in the Solomon Islands*, Institute of Pacific Studies, University of the South Pacific, Suva.

Larmour, P. with Tara, S. (eds), 1983. *Solomon Islands Politics*, Institute of Pacific Studies, University of the South Pacific, Suva.

Mamu, M., 2006a. 'More register to vote in election', *Solomon Star*, 28 March.

—, 2006b. 'Know who you're dealing with', *Solomon Star*, 31 March.

—, 2006c. 'Winds of change over Solomon Islands', *Solomon Star*, 31 March.

—, 2006d. 'Observers will be deployed to provinces', *Solomon Star*, 31 March.

—, 2006e. 'NZ to send 10 observers', *Solomon Star*, 31 March.

—, 2006f. 'C'wealth team pleased with election', *Solomon Star*, 7 April.

—, 2006g. 'Sir Allan back in', *Solomon Star*, 10 April.

—, 2006h. 'Election observers say it's free and fair', *Solomon Star*, 10 April.

—, 2006i. 'Women's council calls for quotas', *Solomon Star*, 11 April.

—, 2006j. 'AIMP hopes to lead next govt', *Solomon Star*, 11 April.

—, 2006k. 'Five members sign clean PM election pledge', *Solomon Star*, 13 April.

—, 2006l. 'New MPs caught in political tussle', *Solomon Star*, 13 April.

—, 2006m. 'Coalition formed', *Solomon Star*, 13 April.

—, 2006n. 'Breaking news—SI new PM', *Solomon Star*, 18 April.

—, 2006o. 'Retired judge to head commission of inquiry', *Solomon Star*, 1 July.

—, 2006p. 'Terms of reference of the commission of inquiry', *Solomon Star*, 14 July.

—, 2006q. 'Fono scorns PM's action', *Solomon Star*, 25 August.

—, 2006r. 'Hilly sacked over plan to expel over-stayers it was revealed', *Solomon Star*, 2 September.

Manimu, G., 2006. 'Letter to the editor', *Solomon Star*, 12 April.

Merritt, C. and Andrusiak, K., 2006. 'Two more groups deny that Einfeld holds posts', *The Australian*, 13 September.

Merritt, C., 2006. 'Einfeld grants in spotlight', *The Australian*, 29 August.

Moore, C., 2004. *Happy Isles in Crisis: the historical causes for a failing state in Solomon Islands, 1998–2004*, Asia Pacific Press, The Australian National University, Canberra.

—, 2005. 'The RAMSI intervention in the Solomon Islands crisis', *Journal of Pacific Studies*, 28:56–77.

Moti, J., 2006. 'Julian Moti to editor', *Solomon Star*, 1 September.

Nason, D., 2006. 'Uni can't find any record of Einfeld', *The Australian*, 28 August.

O'Callaghan, M.L., 2006. 'Solomon ministers sacked before Downer lands', *The Australian*, 19 May.

Rusa, D., 2006. 'PM's resignation greeted with joy', *Solomon Star*, 27 April.

Sanga, K., 2006. 'The MP as leader', *Solomon Star*, 31 March.

Sheridan, G., 2006. 'Bizarre insult that changes exactly nothing', *The Australian*, 14 September.

Skehan, C., 2006. 'Expulsion just part of the many rows bubbling along', *The Age*, 14 September.

Sogavare, M., 2006. 'Address to the nation', *Solomon Star*, 22 August.

Solomon Islands Government, 2006a. *New electoral system tested in the real world*, 6 April, Government Communications Unit, Solomon Islands Government, Honiara.

——, 2006b. Final Election Results, Press release, Government Communications Unit, Solomon Islands Government, 10 April.

Solomon Star, 2006a. *Solomon Star*, 16 March.

——, 2006b. *Solomon Star*, 17 March.

——, 2006c. *Solomon Star*, 4 April.

Sydney Morning Herald, 2006. 'Playing patience in the Solomons: Australia must keep its cool', Editorial, *Sydney Morning Herald*, 14 September.

The Australian, 2006. 'Something rotten in Solomons paradise: Honiara's corruption is hurting its island citizens', Editorial, *The Australian*, 19 September.

Tuza, E., 1977. 'Silas Eto of New Georgia', in G. Trompf (ed.), *Prophets of Melanesia: six essays*, Institute of Papua New Guinea Studies, University of Papua New Guinea, Port Moresby:65–87.

Wainwright, E., 2005. *How is RAMSI faring? Progress, challenges, and lessons learned*, Strategic Insight 14, Australian Strategic Policy Institute, Canberra. Available from http://www.aspi.org.au/publications/publication_details.aspx?ContentID=68&pubtype=6 (accessed 11 April 2007).

Walters, P., 2006. 'Maverick runs low on tricks', *The Australian*, 1 September.

Wasuka, E., 2006a. 'PM denies influence of Asian businesses', *Solomon Star*, 19 April.

——, 2006b. 'First test for Rini's govt', *Solomon Star*, 26 April.

——, 2006c. 'Rini bows out', *Solomon Star*, 27 April.

——, 2006d. 'Jailed MPs seek permission to vote', *Solomon Star*, 3 May.

——, 2006e. 'PM slams Downer for interfering', *Solomon Star*, 9 May.

——, 2006f. 'Acting ministers step in the right direction: Downer', *Solomon Star*, 22 May.

Wate, A., 2006a. 'Central Bank governor backs clean election', *Solomon Star*, 30 March.

—, 2006b. 'More people return to vote in home provinces', *Solomon Star*, 3 April.

—, 2006c. 'Forum observers on their way to SI', *Solomon Star*, 3 April.

—, 2006d. '44 international observers here', *Solomon Star*, 4 April.

—, 2006e. 'Interview with Sir Baddley Devesi', *Solomon Star*, 4 April.

—, 2006f. 'Clean election campaign receives public applause', *Solomon Star*, 4 April.

—, 2006g. 'Coalition govt predicted', *Solomon Star*, 4 April.

—, 2006h. 'Curfew lifted', *Solomon Star*, 28 April.

—, 2006i. 'Fino and Sogavare to vie for PM's post', *Solomon Star*, 1 May.

—, 2006j. 'Four coalition partnerships formed to contest PM election', *Solomon Star*, 1 May.

—, 2006k. 'A step further PM' , *Solomon Star*, 19 May.

—, 2006l. 'Fono urged to clarify allegations', *Solomon Star*, 25 May.

—, 2006m. 'Hilly denies report on mainland China', *Solomon Star*, 13 July.

—, 2006n. 'Terms of reference may interfere with trials: Suri', *Solomon Star*, 18 July.

—, 2006o. 'PM defends riot inquiry', *Solomon Star*, 19 July.

—, 2006p. 'Amendment to land law drafted', *Solomon Star*, 9 August.

—, 2006q. 'Mystery lawyer advises Sogavare', *Solomon Star*, 17 August.

—, 2006r. 'AG post', *Solomon Star*, 17 August.

—, 2006s. 'Prime Minister's address to the nation', *Solomon Star*, 22 August.

—, 2006t. 'Australia slams its door on MPs', *Solomon Star*, 14 September.

—, 2006u. 'Sir Allan says he will fight charges', *Solomon Star*, 26 October.

# Chapter 6
## The impact of RAMSI on the 2006 elections

Jon Fraenkel

The chains came off the doors of parliament and Governor-General Nathaniel Waena strode out at midday on 18 April 2006 to announce the results of the thirteenth prime ministerial elections since independence. To his right was former premier Sir Allan Kemakeza, whose government had proved the first since independence to survive a full term in office.[1] On his left was Snyder Rini, Kemakeza's former deputy, who was declared solemnly to be the newly elected prime minister. Surrounding them were the former cabinet ministers, fresh from their faction having prevailed over the opposition by 27 votes to 23 in a secret ballot held behind closed doors. The message of a triumph for the former government and of continuity in national politics was not lost on the crowds of spectators outside, who had been kept waiting in anticipation for hours in the baking sun. Before Rini had completed his acceptance speech, the protest had turned angry. Minutes later, rocks were raining down on the parliament building and the Australian police protecting it. A protracted siege began, which was eventually subdued with tear-gas. Rioting spread to Point Cruz, Chinatown and to Kukum, with many Asian shops and businesses and the Pacific Casino Hotel complex burnt to the ground. Eight days later, six MPs crossed the floor, triggering the collapse of the Rini-led government and a belated victory for the opposition—an event that transformed unrest into jubilation on the streets of Honiara.[2]

Black Tuesday—as the events of 18 April became known—generated familiar debates about the ultimate causes of the most serious urban disturbance since the arrival of the Regional Assistance Mission to the Solomon Islands (RAMSI) in July 2003. Why, after an election process unanimously declared free and fair by foreign observer groups, was there such a violent reaction to the outcome? Were the riots primarily a popular reaction against the perceived illegitimacy of the prime ministerial election result? Did disappointed opposition politicians instigate them? Were disturbances driven by anti-Chinese sentiment, or was the targeting of Asian businesses indicative of popular perceptions that the prime ministerial election had been bought with Asian cash? Was the key flash-point the premature use of tear-gas or, more generally, the poor tactical response to the initial protest by RAMSI police officers? Reports by the Australian Broadcasting Corporation (ABC) that, later that afternoon, RAMSI vehicles were ignited by youths carrying petrol-filled plastic squeeze bottles encouraged wild conspiracy theories in the Australian press: '[t]he protestors can be accused of many things but not spontaneity. Truckloads of rocks and water bottles were delivered outside parliament in the days before the violence began' (Maiden 2006).[3] Suggestions of 'prior planning and coordination' and of 'Taiwanese and Chinese influences behind the recent violence in the Solomons' were made by Australian Federal Police Commissioner, Mick Keelty (O'Callaghan 2006; PacNews 2006; ABC 2006b; Callick 2006; McKenna 2006). There was an extraordinary reluctance to look, in any depth, into the domestic political causes of the riots.

This chapter looks at the impact of RAMSI and the broader Australian presence on the outcomes of the April 2006 general election, and the subsequent prime ministerial election. It examines first the voter turn-out data and changes to the voting system before the 2006 poll. Second, it looks at the broader political divisions as they stood on the eve of the poll, and how RAMSI's arrival had shifted the balance between government and opposition. Third, the chapter analyses the variation in the number of candidates contesting compared with previous elections, the performance of women candidates, the turnover of sitting members and the political complexion of the various political parties. Finally, it examines shifting alliances in Honiara in the wake of the 2006 poll, how Rini emerged victorious in the prime ministerial elections on 18 April and the role electoral factors played in triggering the subsequent riots.

## The conduct of the polls

The 2006 Solomon Islands general election was the seventh since independence, and the first since RAMSI's arrival in mid 2003. It was potentially a key watershed on the road back to self-government. Parliament was dissolved on 20 December 2005, leaving Kemakeza's government to play a three and a half month long caretaker role.[4] The Solomon Islands Electoral Commission (SIEC) was in a weak state. Long-standing Chief Electoral Officer, John Babalu, had not had his contract renewed in 2005, and his successor, Martin Karani, had been fired for misappropriation of funds. The new supervisor, Musu Kevu, had been appointed only late in 2005. An AusAID-funded electoral assistance project brought seven advisers from the Australian Electoral Commission to assist the SIEC, which also ran an AusAID and NZAID-supported civic awareness program, which toured every ward and most of the major villages across the country. Unlike 2001, when donors funded the entire election, other costs of the 2006 election were met by the Solomon Islands government.[5]

The most serious problem was with the electoral roll. The final tally of 342,119 registered voters entailed an 85 per cent increase on the 2001 figure. With an estimated population of 470,681, this implied that 73 per cent of citizens were eligible to vote—an unlikely figure, given that about half the population was below the legal minimum voting age of 18. One reason for this was the absence of any 'cleaning' of the electoral register, that is, to remove those deceased or those who had changed constituency (SIEC 2006). Figure 6.1 shows the distribution of registered voters across the 50 constituencies, as well as the variation in turn-out across the country. The largest numbers of registered voters were in the three Honiara constituencies, but here the turn-out was only 28.6 per cent, well below the national average of 56.4 per cent. Many of those living in Honiara were registered twice—once in their place of residence, and again on their island of origin. Mobile town-dwellers regularly vote where they have land rights or strong kinship connections, rather than in the more ethnically inter-mixed urban centres. The Electoral Act contains no provisions for absentee voting. In the days before each general election, outward-bound vessels transport large numbers of islanders across the group—a process that enhances the political leverage of ship-owners, who often double as local logging magnates. The absence of any provision for absentee voting also disenfranchises the large numbers of mobile public servants, police officers and others engaged in the process of electoral administration, who are therefore unable to return to their homes to vote.

The most substantial change that occurred in electoral administration before the 2006 poll was the shift from a multiple to single ballot box system. In previous elections, polling stations had been organised with separate ballot boxes set aside for each candidate. The voter would collect an endorsed ballot paper from the presiding officer and then enter a private room to deposit this in their favoured candidate's box. The system eased the way for abuse.[6] The voter could pass through the booth without depositing the ballot paper and sell this outside the polling station to the highest bidder. Candidates or their agents might then cast their own vote towards the end of the polling day, but in the process deposit sizeable numbers of purchased votes into the ballot boxes. At previous elections, counting agents reported discovering large wads of stapled ballots with identical marks in the boxes. With the new single ballot box system, this method of vote buying became impossible, and the reform was applauded widely by returning and presiding officers, polling agents and many candidates, as well as by most ordinary voters. At about only 1.5 per cent, the rate of invalid (or informal) voting was lower than many had anticipated.

Unprecedented numbers of international observers arrived in the Solomon Islands before the 2006 election, including delegations from the Pacific Islands Forum, Australia, New Zealand, the United States and Japan, with the United Nations providing logistical coordination. The Commonwealth also had its own team and engaged in training domestic observers. Together, domestic observers and a Winds of Change Clean Election Campaign, inspired initially by Moral Rearmament Group activities in Kenya, ensured a stronger role for civil society activists than at previous elections, and served to focus attention on issues of personal probity, moral character and good governance.[7] Activists sought to have voters sign undertakings against corruption: 'I pledge that I will not accept bribes, accept any false promises, sell my vote or involve [sic] in any corrupt activity before, during or after the election' (Solomon Star 2006o). The AusAID-funded Clean Election Campaign, together with Winds of Change, generated anxiety among government ministers that this implied support for some cathartic sweeping away of sitting members. This was one of a host of new factors connected with RAMSI's arrival that influenced the habitually opaque and adaptable electoral processes of the Solomon Islands.

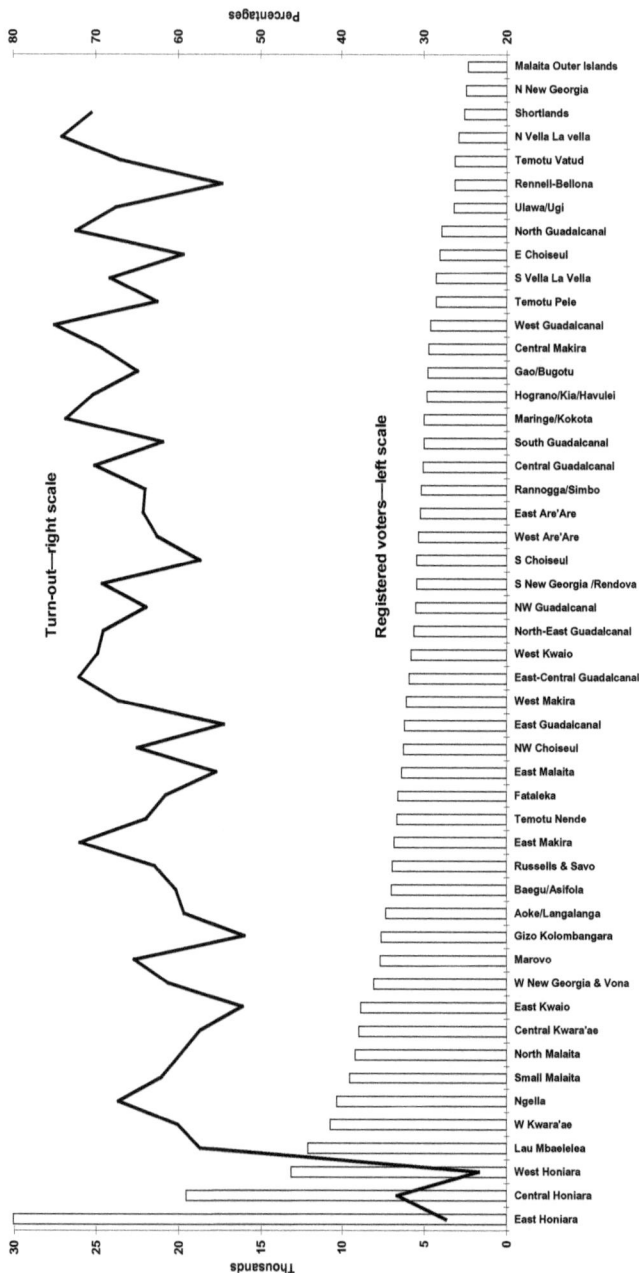

Figure 6.1    Solomon Islands election: registered voters and turn-out, 2006

# A shape of shapelessness

Sir Allan Kemakeza's chances of survival as prime minister depended on his repeating the coalition-building exercise that had given him the position back in 2001. His skills in this respect owed much to his political experience gained under the later governments of Solomon Mamaloni (1989–93, 1994–97). Kemakeza had entered parliament originally as the Member for Savo/Russells in 1989, and became Minister of Police in Mamaloni's People's Alliance Party (PAP) government. When Mamaloni abandoned the PAP in 1990 after an internal party revolt and stitched together a new coalition with opposition leaders, Kemakeza was one of the loyal ministers who accompanied him. At the 1993 polls, Kemakeza stood successfully as one of the candidates affiliated with Mamaloni's Government of National Unity and Reconciliation (GNUR) grouping. In 1994, he became Minister for Forestry, Environment and Conservation when Mamaloni returned to office, presiding over the most controversial phase of unsustainable round-log exports in the country's history (Bennett 2000:346–7).The Savo politician returned to cabinet for a third time after the June 2000 coup as deputy prime minister and Minister for National Unity, Reconciliation and Peace. Aboard HMAS Tobruk off the coast near Honiara, he was responsible for the handing out of SI$10 million to provincial politicians, most of which ended up in the hands of leaders of the Malaita Eagle Force (MEF) (Fraenkel 2004a:95). In the months after the October 2000 Townsville Peace Agreement (TPA), Kemakeza supervised the distribution of compensation money to militant leaders, including handling pay-outs from a SI$133.5 million (US$25 million) loan provided by the Taiwanese EXIM Bank. In the process, he awarded himself SI$851,000 (US$164,754), purportedly for damage to his property in Western Guadalcanal, and was sacked for embezzlement. Despite these episodes, in June 2001, Kemakeza received the Knight Bachelor award (KB) from the British Queen for 'services to policing and politics' (BBC 2001).

After the 2001 polls, Kemakeza exploited his newfound status to emerge triumphant in the race to be prime minister. Gathering together at the Honiara Hotel, Kemakeza's seamlessly rejuvenated PAP signed a memorandum of understanding with the Association of Independent Members of Parliament (AIMP). AIMP leader Snyder Rini consequently stepped aside as candidate for the prime ministerial post, ensuring victory for Kemakeza at the first count with 29 of the 50 votes—an event greeted with dismay by the crowds outside parliament. As prime minister, Kemakeza pursued a crisis-suited variant of the well-established Mamaloni strategy of building up networks of patronage and placating discontent by handing out personal favours.

Despite major failings of policy, including a confession of personal complicity in telling MEF leaders to hold onto their weapons in defiance of his own government's amnesty policy (Fraenkel 2004a: 141–2), Kemakeza's government survived. The continued release of successive portions of the Taiwanese EXIM loan during 2001–02 fuelled a debilitating process of harassment of finance ministry and treasury officials, with militants routinely hanging around outside the prime minister's office with guns, waiting for money to arrive. By December 2002, the economy had hit rock bottom, with gross domestic product (GDP) per capita about one-third lower than 1997 levels. Cabinet itself was under siege from distraught 'special constables'—ex-militants enlisted to serve alongside the regular police at the height of the tension. The prime minister's adviser, ethnic Malaysian businessman Robert Goh, was shot in the stomach during an assassination attempt. The increasing personal risk to the senior political classes encouraged renewed appeals for foreign intervention, and set the stage for what turned out to be an extraordinary political realignment.

The arrival of RAMSI in July 2003 strengthened the beleaguered Kemakeza government. After being flown to Canberra to agree to terms before the mission, Kemakeza steered the required enabling legislation first through cabinet and then through parliament, and reinvented his administration as the loyal ally of the new mission. Australian Prime Minister, John Howard, called Kemakeza a 'straightforward good man to deal with' (People First 2003a). With an armed protection force assigned to him after RAMSI's arrival, the Solomon Islands prime minister met accusations that he was one of the 'big fish' deserving of prosecution for corruption and complicity with the militants during the unrest of 1999–2003 with repeated rejoinders that he would allow the law to take its course (Solomon Star 2006c; New Zealand Herald 2003; SIBC 2003; People First 2003b; Sasako 2003a, 2003b). Three of Kemakeza's original ministers associated with the MEF were eventually convicted and, only after that, belatedly sacked. Several other ministers were prosecuted for corruption. Regular cabinet reshuffles, judicious distribution of Taiwanese aid and floor crossing by senior opposition leaders assisted the extraordinary survival of Kemakeza's government. Seeking a fifth term in office at the 2006 polls, Kemakeza embarked on a lacklustre campaign hoping to obtain credit for the arrival of RAMSI and the restoration of peace, stability and economic recovery.

On the other hand, the opposition entered the 2006 elections in a much-depleted state, leading some commentators to emphasise the absence of any meaningful distinction between the opposition and the 'old guard' in Solomon Islands politics (Hameiri 2006).[8] Yet that lack of coherence of the opposition in 2006 needs to be seen in a longer-term context. Solomon Islands politics has never revolved around clear-cut ideological distinctions, for example between left and right. Nor have ethnic, provincial or regional bases provided a workable basis for coalition formation or even for political parties. All governments have been alliances between MPs from different parts of the group, in particular balancing MPs from populous Malaita with those from Guadalcanal and Western Province. The polarisation of Solomon Islands politics in the 1980s around the struggle between the United Party (UP) and PAP ended with Mamaloni's 1990 abandonment of the PAP, and UP leader, Sir Peter Kenilorea's, decision to join the reconfigured Mamaloni GNUR cabinet. Party allegiances subsequently became still weaker, and 'leaders of the independents' turned from being kingmakers to potential victors in the all-important post-election tussle for the prime ministerial post.

The opposition-led governments that emerged at the 1993 and 1997 elections were fractious groupings, held together primarily by their efforts to prevent Mamaloni from returning to office. In 1993, leader of the independents, Francis Billy Hilly, became prime minister with a one-seat majority, and led a short-lived government that took steps to reduce the pace of logging activity, increase local processing and reform the forestry industry. Most of the ministers in the former Mamaloni government were connected closely with logging businesses and opposed the new reformist orientation (Bennett 2000:345). A no-confidence vote in November 1994 brought about the fall of the Hilly government—an event accompanied by what one Mamaloni ally admitted to have been a frenetic process of 'cheque or cash lobbying' (Alasia 1997:13). Deposed minister and former trade unionist Joses Tuhanuku alleged that Goh (later to become Kemakeza's adviser) had been the go-between in soliciting floor crossers for Mamaloni, and claimed to have been offered a SI$10,000 bribe to switch sides (Bennett 2000:345). Under the restored Mamaloni government (1994–97), duty was reduced on forestry products and licensing of local logging forms resumed. Despite the consequent acceleration of timber exports, government expenditure rose and debt increased (Bennett 2000:341–2; Fraenkel 2004a:40–1).

After the elections of 1997 Bartholomew Ulufa'alu became prime minister, again at the head of a loose coalition of small parties and independents. The Solomon Islands Action for Change (SIAC) government was committed to reform of government finances, greater regulation of the logging industry and down-sizing of the civil service with backing from the Asian Development Bank, the World Bank and the International Monetary Fund. For some observers, this implied a government committed to the pro-market ideals of the political right; however, arraying Solomon Islands politicians on a left–right spectrum has never been a particularly useful way of understanding the country's politics. The most characteristic appeal of the Ulufa'alu government was for reform away from the system of cronyism that was identified with Mamaloni's governments, which could hardly be identified as serving a leftist ideology. Those reforms met resistance from entrenched interests, particularly in the public sector (Hughes 2001:12); however, the Ulufa'alu government proved able to withstand several attempted no-confidence bids, in one case because tied votes left the government in office (Kabutaulaka 1999).

When the Isatabu uprising began in late 1998, ministers in the Ulufa'alu government rightly or wrongly interpreted those events as a conspiracy hatched by 'Mamaloni men' aimed at restoring the old guard to office; 'the tensions were being orchestrated to topple the SIAC Government in order to disrupt an ambitious reform programme' (Office of the Prime Minister 2000:7). The Isatabu Freedom Movement (IFM) evicted some 20,000 Malaitans from their homesteads in rural Guadalcanal. In November 1999, Ulufa'alu met Malaitan protestors demanding compensation for lost properties on the steps of parliament and publicly rejected their claims. Although some pilloried him for this response, the later opening of the compensation floodgates served only to encourage and even institutionalise the new-found role of the militants. In January 2000, the MEF raided the armoury in Auki (on Malaita) and, by April, the government had lost control of the security situation. The Ulufa'alu government was dislodged by the joint Police Field Force/MEF coup of 5 June 2000. In the wake of the coup, it was the grouping associated with Mamaloni that resumed office, although with Ulufa'alu's sacked finance minister, Manasseh Sogavare, as prime minister. Behind the scenes, the key power-broker was Malaitan politician Charles Dausabea, who was home affairs minister under Mamaloni in 1993 and chief whip in the 1994–97 Mamaloni government.

The 2001 elections found the opposition in a much-weakened state, owing largely to the fraught experience of coup and crisis. Gathering together at the Mendana Hotel, it comprised a loose association of former SIAC ministers, including the Liberal and Labour parties and those who had become known as 'independent of the independents' to distinguish them from those aligned with the only vaguely coherent AIMP (Sasako 2001). Deposed prime minister Ulufa'alu's leadership of the coalition was challenged, ostensibly on the grounds that his return to office might spark a further coup (SIBC 2001). Temotu politician Patteson Oti instead emerged as the favoured SIAC candidate for prime minister, leading Ulufa'alu to withdraw his small Liberal grouping and contest separately. The opposition split weakened its claim to office, and several drifting MPs instead joined the PAP/AIMP in backing Kemakeza. Claims that up to SI$50,000 had been offered to MPs circulated widely, although there were no prosecutions (Roughan 2001).

After RAMSI's arrival in July 2003, the coherence of the opposition group was weakened still further by defections. Even successive leaders of the opposition, first Oti and then John Garo, crossed the floor to join the Kemakeza government. Two no-confidence votes had failed in 2002, before RAMSI's arrival; the first was withdrawn before being put to a vote and the second was defeated. The likelihood of the Kemakeza government being dislodged after mid 2003 seemed ever more remote. Opposition leaders switching sides explained their action as driven by a desire for positions of responsibility, or pressure from constituents, but self-interest and hunger for power played their part. This consolidation of government was encouraged, particularly by the Australian High Commission but also by the European Union, although a desire to avoid accusations of foreign interference ensured that such advice was rarely formal. Routine informal diplomatic messages of approval or disapproval sufficed, whether or not these were driven by directives from Canberra or Brussels.

No-confidence votes were discouraged as destabilising, echoing the growing emphasis on establishing order along the Melanesian 'arc of instability'. Getting competent MPs into cabinet also appeared pragmatic, owing to the poor track record of the original grouping of PAP/AIMP ministers, demonstrated so vividly by the numerous sackings for corruption or complicity in militant activities during 1998–2003. One leading light on the opposition benches, Fred Fono, told supporters that he was encouraged to cross the floor by Australian and British High Commission requests to enable European Community STABEX funds to be transferred (Solomon Star 2005c, 2005g; Brown 2006). Yet another former minister in the SIAC government, Alfred Sasako, switched sides to assume sacked MEF minister Alex Bartlett's agriculture portfolio in September 2004 (Radio New Zealand International 2004). The short-term advantages of encouraging a 'national unity' cabinet under Kemakeza were readily apparent, but its longer-term political repercussions were to prove much more dangerous.

Anti-RAMSI ministers or politicians almost inevitably ended up, or remained, on the opposition benches, threatening a political realignment around the issue of support for or opposition to foreign intervention. Sogavare had, early on, established himself as a vocal critic of RAMSI, warning at the outset of the mission that ministers had become 'puppets of foreign governments' (ABC 2003; The Australian 2003). He remained on the opposition benches. In January 2005, Francis Zama was sacked as finance minister and Oti was sacked as communications minister for 'adverse reactions' after they criticised RAMSI during a debate on the mission's annual report (Solomon Star 2005a, 2005b).

Outside parliament, former leaders of the MEF sought to undermine the mission, and played on disquiet about aspects of the operation as a vehicle for their re-entry into parliament at the forthcoming elections. Charles Dausabea, who had lost his East Honiara seat in 2001, vigorously contested RAMSI's usurpation of Solomon Islands sovereignty, while former MEF supreme commander, Andrew Nori (also a candidate at the 2006 poll) sought to challenge the legality of RAMSI's immunity from prosecution under Solomon Islands law, unsuccessfully mimicking the constitutional challenge that had recently ended the first incarnation of Australia's Enhanced Cooperation Program in neighbouring Papua New Guinea. He came fourth in the race for West Are'Are, due partly to unpopularity arising from landowner resistance to his logging schemes in Waisisi. Demands by rebel militants hiding out in the interior of Malaita that Kemakeza resign (Solomon Star 2005e) were taken up by opposition spokesman for good governance and justice, Joses Sanga (Solomon Star 2005f). Even Ulufa'alu (once a vociferous enthusiast for Australian intervention) insisted on a time line for RAMSI's presence (Solomon Star 2005h). Labour Party leader, Joses Tuhanuku—whose strong support had been noted in the debates accompanying the start of the mission in Australia's parliament—accused Kemakeza of having become a 'puppet of Australia' (Solomon Star 2006f).[9] Elsina Wainwright, the Canberra-based author of the June 2003 Our Failing Neighbour pamphlet—which set out a justification for Australian intervention—now speculated that 'a realignment of political forces in Honiara could see political support for RAMSI evaporate' (Wainwright 2005:5).

The oddity was that the SIAC grouping had been the natural ally of the RAMSI operation; it was the victim of the June 2000 coup. Yet the absence of Australian intervention at that time left a legacy of bitterness. The apparent reluctance of RAMSI to pursue prosecutions against Kemakeza—and the practicalities of trying to dislodge a well-entrenched incumbent—potentially handed the opposition an otherwise lacking focal point for the 2006 campaign. The opposition was not, however, consistently or unanimously anti-RAMSI. Knowledge that political alignments were fluid, and that the ties that bound ministers to the Kemakeza government might evaporate in the wake of the poll, made a waiting game seem the more tactically astute option. The operation still had overwhelming public support, despite disquiet about Australian heavy-handedness, failure to respond to local anxieties and the absence of sufficient emphasis on the regional aspect of the intervention (Pacific Islands Forum Eminent Persons' Group 2005; Solomon Islands Government 2004, 2005a). Despite these good reasons, it stands to the credit of some leading opposition politicians that they did not seek to realign collectively around hostility to RAMSI. The better option was to use the hiatus occasioned by RAMSI to rebuild the potential for local leadership, and to seek to undermine the social weight of those still potentially powerful former militant leaders operating behind the scenes of Solomon Islands politics.

## Forces of fractionalisation

As the curtains rose on the 2006 poll, outcomes were highly uncertain, particularly given the widely expected high attrition rate for sitting members. Local-level contests turned out to be highly competitive—453 candidates stood for election, an average of 9.1 per constituency (up from 6.6 per cent in 2001). One result was that the average share of the vote secured by victors fell to 30.8 per cent—the lowest figure since independence. Half of all MPs obtained less than 30 per cent of the vote (Table 6.1). Only two MPs secured majorities of the constituency vote, although the unopposed Job Dudley Tausinga standing in North New Georgia clearly had unanimous backing from his constituents, who were renowned for solidly supporting the pre-selected Christian Fellowship Church candidate. He obtained 74 per cent of the vote in 2001, and in 2006 was embarking on his sixth consecutive term in office. More generally, the west of the country had lower than average numbers of candidates and higher than average victor vote shares, while Isabel, Guadalacanal, Malaita and Makira had larger numbers of candidates and lower victor vote shares—so too did Honiara, where the miniscule turn-out lent a particularly arbitrary character to electoral outcomes. The most contested constituency in the country was East Honiara, with 20 candidates, where Charles Dausabea emerged victorious with 23.4 per cent of the vote (or the support of 6.3 per cent of registered voters), retaking the seat he held in 1993 and 1997.[10]

One reason for the historically high level of candidates was the absence of distinctive political issues at the local level separating the candidates. Where elections pit acknowledged conservatives against reformist candidates or where other popularly accepted issues divide political parties, pressure is often exerted on weaker candidates to step aside to avoid splitting the vote for like-minded candidates (or parties). If there is no common consensus about what the electoral issues are, contests become a free-for-all, without much constraint on the number of contestants entering the race. Efforts to create a unified opposition to an incumbent MP did occur in some constituencies, such as West Kwara'ae, and in others sitting members bribed potential rivals not to contest. In most cases, however, there was little restraint on candidate proliferation.

Those national-level campaign issues that did emerge exerted a marginal influence on constituency outcomes. Rural development was championed

**Table 6.1    Selected features of Solomon Islands elections since independence, 1980–2006**

| Year of election | 1980 | 1984[1] | 1989 | 1993 | 1997 | 2001 | 2006 |
|---|---|---|---|---|---|---|---|
| Average no. candidates | 6.3 | 6.8 | 6.8 | 5.9 | 6.7 | 6.6 | 9.1 |
| Share new members (%)[2] | 68.4 | 56.8 | 52.6 | 42.6 | 52.0 | 64.0 | 50.0 |
| Incumbent turnover (%)[2] | 52.6 | 40.5 | 42.1 | 14.9 | 38.0 | 52.0 | 46.0 |

| Number of constituency victors by percentage of vote share | | | | | | | |
|---|---|---|---|---|---|---|---|
| >50% and unopposed | 6 | 9 | 8 | 17 | 12 | 10 | 3 |
| 40–9 | 5 | 6 | 6 | 5 | 7 | 7 | 5 |
| 30–9 | 14 | 12 | 13 | 14 | 15 | 15 | 17 |
| 20–9 | 11 | 7 | 10 | 5 | 10 | 16 | 25 |
| 10–20 | 2 | 3 | 1 | 6 | 6 | 2 | 0 |
| 0–9 | 0 | 0 | 0 | 0 | 0 | 0 | 0 |
| Total seats in parliament | 38 | 371 | 38 | 47 | 50 | 50 | 50 |

Notes: [1] No election held in East Kwaio in 1984. [2] Incumbent turnover and sitting member figures relate to general elections only, and are insensitive to by-election results.
Source: Compiled from data released by the Solomon Islands Electoral Commission.

particularly in Honiara and the west, but this was a program most aspiring politicians agreed on in principle—in the process, undermining its potential as a focal point for political crystallisation. Guale politician Francis Orodani launched a Solomon First Party, committed to pressing the government to make good on TPA commitments and enact the draft federal constitution (Solomon Star 2006p; The Pacific Magazine 2006). 'State government'—like rural development—was an issue of ostensible consensus, however much those who stood to lose from this sought to undermine the passage of the draft constitution through procedural complications, absenteeism and stonewalling.[11] Promises of devolution, greater provincial autonomy and reconciliation between Guadalcanal and Malaita were standard soap-box patter for politicians across the country. Solomon Islands recognition of Taiwan proved another potential focal point, owing to some opposition politicians engaging in negotiations with representatives from mainland

China and controversies about the influence of Taiwanese aid funding in the election. Rennell and Bellona MP Joses Tuhanuku (2006) claimed that, aside from picking up the tab for the Rural Constituency Development Funds (RCDF), the Taiwanese were funding clandestine 'special projects' through the prime minister's office, which were granted only to politically sympathetic allies.[12] Foreign entanglements were, however, scarcely a priority for hard-pressed villagers, despite an understandable readiness to accept assistance from any source.

Some local-level issues played a significant role in the campaign. The long-running strike by workers at Russell Islands Plantations Estates Ltd contributed to the fall of Kemakeza's vote share from 60 per cent in 2001 to 30 per cent in 2006 in his Savo/Russells constituency. Irate Russell Islanders refused to release the ballot boxes for passage to the Central Division counting centre at Tulagi off the nearby island of Gela, fearing official ballot rigging. East Malaita's Joses Sanga argued in favour of restricting naturalised citizens' rights to contest the election (Solomon Star 2006e). Similarly, one of the resolutions of the Guadalcanal Leaders' Summit at Balasuna on 14–18 February 2005 stated that 'non-indigenes and naturalised citizens should not be allowed to stand as candidates in any Guadalcanal constituency' (Guadalcanal Leaders' Summit 2005). This did not stop naturalised Chinese citizen Laurie Chan being returned as MP for West Guadalcanal. Most politicians promised constituency rewards if they were elected to office, and contests were decided by local verdicts about the personal integrity (or otherwise) of candidates. That type of focus was, to a greater degree than at previous elections, echoed at the national level, owing to the civic awareness program, the Winds of Change campaign, the impact of decisions by the Leadership Code Commission and the good governance agenda propagated by increasingly vociferous civil society organisations, with encouragement from RAMSI and the Honiara-based diplomatic fraternity.

Under first-past-the-post systems, as in Solomon Islands, candidate proliferation can prove self-reinforcing: the more candidates that enter the fray, the smaller is the share of the vote required for victory and the easier it appears to be for an aspiring candidate to win. Nevertheless, candidate proliferation does not mimic Papua New Guinea's long-term increase, election after election.[13] In Solomon Islands, the average number of candidates per constituency was always high—averaging 6.5 during 1980–2001—but it spiked in 2006 to reach 9.1 per constituency (Table 6.1). There were, therefore, specific reasons for the 2006 upswing in candidate numbers.

Most importantly, the arrival of RAMSI and the consequently transformed political situation generated enormous uncertainties about political leadership. Although there had been by-elections in the constituencies of the three convicted MEF ministers in the post-2001 cabinet and in the South Guadalcanal constituency of murdered MP Father Augustine Geve, most other MPs had held their seats since 2001. In the intervening period, many new influences affected the fortunes of local leaders. First, RAMSI's arrival, the arrest of militants and confiscation of weapons meant links with the militias or those carrying guns were no longer viable methods of controlling political power. Second, economic collapse during 2001–02—and the subsequent recovery of rural logging activity—had assisted some political aspirants, but damaged the fortunes of others. Third, regular cabinet reshuffles at Kemakeza's instigation left many casualties, for whom loss of prestigious portfolios potentially also entailed subsequent electoral defeat. Only half of those in the cabinet formed after the 2001 poll still held ministerial positions immediately before the 2006 election.

## The gender dimension

The Solomon Islands 2001–06 government had not a single woman member (Table 6.2). Since independence, only one woman has been elected to parliament in the country: Hilda Kari, 1993–2001. For the 2006 poll, 26 women contested, half of whom had the backing of the National Council of Women. This was the largest number of women candidates ever to contest a Solomon Islands election. Women had played an important role in the Solomon Islands peace process, and many hoped this would translate into representation in parliament; yet not a single female candidate gained a seat.

Some women contestants came close. Sarah Dyer—standing in West Honiara—came second ahead of well-known politicians such as the incumbent, Yukio Sato, and David Tuhanuku, but she lost to Isaac Inoke, who was able to draw on strong support from the sizeable Fataleka community in the critically important White River area. In central Honiara, three women candidates split the vote, and Nelson Ne'e emerged victorious through a crowded field. On Malaita, Afu Billy had in 2001 come within only two votes of victory. Back then, she had lost to Joses Sanga, who subsequently emerged as one of the more prominent new opposition MPs and who easily retook the East Malaita seat in 2006 with 46 per cent of the vote. Other new women candidates on Malaita—such as Rachel Fera in Aoke-Langalanga—notched up a significant share of the vote, but neither she nor civil society activist Mathew Wale could dislodge the well-known incumbent, former prime minister Bart Ulufa'alu. Where women candidates were not resident permanently in their constituencies, as with Alice Pollard in West Are'are and Doreen Kuper on Makira, they inevitably faced an uphill battle. In the aftermath of the election, the National Council of Women called for quotas for women in parliament—a proposal that, given the absence of strong political parties in Solomon Islands, would require the introduction of some seats reserved for women (Solomon Star 2006t).[14]

## Incumbent turnover

Historically, Solomon Islands has witnessed a high turnover of sitting members. In 1997, 52 per cent of those elected were new members, and, in 2001, an extraordinary 62 per cent of those elected had not previously been in parliament (Table 6.1). Since the 1990s, sweeping changes in parliament's

Table 6.2     Representation by gender group in Solomon Islands, 1980–2006

|  | Candidates | | MPs | |
|  | Women | Men | Women | Men |
|---|---|---|---|---|
| 1980 | 0 | 242 | 0 | 38 |
| 1984 | 1 | 245 | 0 | 37 |
| 1989 | 3 | 254 | 0 | 38 |
| 1993 | 11 | 269 | 1 | 46 |
| 1997 | 12 | 321 | 1 | 49 |
| 2001 | 13 | 315 | 0 | 50 |
| 2006 | 26 | 425 | 0 | 50 |

Note: No election was held in East Kwaio in 1984.
Source: Compiled from data released by the Solomon Islands Electoral Commission.

make-up have often, perhaps a little naively, been seen as indicative of popular backing for reform. Part of the reason for this view was because of the way government funds were deployed under the 1990–93 Mamaloni government to assist MPs to retain their seats, resulting, in 1993, in the lowest level of defeat of sitting members witnessed at any post-independence election (Table 6.1). Before the April 2006 elections, many had expected a high level of incumbent turnover similar to that in 2001. There were good reasons for this view. In July 2005, provincial elections in Choiseul and Western Province saw, respectively, 75 per cent and 85 per cent of members lose their seats (ABC 2005). In the 2006 general elections, however, the share of new members across the entire country was 50 per cent, closer to the historical average. Local economic conditions help to explain the variation in turnover rates in different parts of the group, owing to their impact on local leadership. On Choiseul and in Western Province, all MPs bar one were returned to office, and the one casualty lost by only two votes after a recount. On Isabel and in Honiara, all the incumbents lost their seats. On Malaita, Guadalcanal and Makira, the picture was much more varied.

Holding a ministerial portfolio exerted some influence over re-election prospects, but the potential downside was longer absence from the constituency on official business. At 55 per cent, the ministerial survival rate was only a little higher than the average rate of incumbent re-election (46 per cent). Of the nine ministers who lost, many faced popular hostility owing to incompetence or mismanagement, or because they supplemented their marriages with mistresses (popularly called 'O2s' and 'O3s' after the names of the Australian-donated patrol boats usually docked at the Point Cruz harbour in Honiara). High-profile casualties from the former cabinet included former mines minister Walton Naezon (Central Guadalcanal) and Michael Maena (Temotu Pele), who had been sacked as a minister by Kemakeza after being charged with embezzlement of US$150,000 (Radio New Zealand International 2005). Three government MPs who were found guilty of misconduct by the Leadership Code Commission—Alfred Sasako, Stephen Paeni and chairman of the government caucus, Jeffrey Teava—also lost their seats. The issue of good (or bad) governance had a discernible impact on outcomes. Minister of National Planning and Aid Coordination, Fred Fono, secured 55 per cent of the vote in West Kwara'ae (Malaita). His pre-election release of documents covering the expenditure of Rural

Constituency Development Funds was applauded widely in a campaign in which revelations of abuse of such funds regularly sealed the fate of sitting members (Solomon Star 2006i). Even Fono, however, was subsequently accused of offering cash for support before the 4 May 2006 contest for the prime ministership (Solomon Star 2006b). There were no public denials, confirming the view that this type of practice was extraordinarily widespread.

Political survival is perpetually precarious even for ministers, but judicious construction of patronage networks can stave off defeat. Long-term survivors such as Kemakeza carefully lavished expenditure on targeted voters (SIBC 2005). In March 2005, he handed over SI$20,000 cash to his main potential rival for the Savo/Russell constituency, former MP John Ngina (Solomon Star 2005d).

Former Minister of Finance Peter Boyers (New Zealand born but married locally and well versed in Melanesian ways) distributed water tanks across his West New Georgia constituency. Other well-endowed businessmen or recipients of plentiful logging revenues, such as Laurie Chan in West Guadalcanal and Snyder Rini in Morovo, were able to retain their seats in an election that, despite the new ballot box system, witnessed numerous allegations in the letters pages of the Solomon Star that MPs were buying votes.

On the opposition side of the house, veteran politicians who were household names—such as Ulufa'alu, Hilly and Leslie Boseto—kept their seats. There was one high-profile opposition casualty: Joses Tuhanuku came fourth in the race for the Rennell and Bellona constituency. Even before the election, he had claimed to be the victim of a concerted Taiwanese-funded effort to dislodge him (Solomon Star 2006k). More usually, defeated incumbents were the least well known at the national level, or were those long absent from their constituencies. As on the government side of the house, well-endowed opposition MPs with access to local logging revenue or other sources of income fared better than the more cash-strapped candidates. Even veteran MPs associated with reformist objectives found the procurement of political support difficult to avoid, and circulated small sums of cash to voters often on the night before the poll (the 'devil's night', see Alasia this volume), or flirted on the borders of legality by promising constituents monetary hand-outs at a fixed date after the election. Overall, the 2006 elections exhibited a familiar Melanesian pattern: extraordinarily high incumbent turnover at the rank-and-file level coupled with exceptionally low incumbent turnover for a small cluster of established political leaders.

## Parties and outcomes

Kemakeza's PAP launched its manifesto under the slogan 'Vote PAP to rebuild this nation', urging a platform of 'restoration of national unity and peace' and calling RAMSI a 'God-given gift to the people of this country'. The party promised to field 50 official candidates covering all of the nation's constituencies, as well as an additional collection of 'shadow candidates' (Solomon Star 2006a, 2006b). It charged SI$70 for a copy of the manifesto, suggesting some restriction of access to state coffers under the new tighter controls exercised by hard-nosed Australian officials. If, as some suggested, there was a substantial pot of Taiwanese cash funding Kemakeza sympathisers, there was little sign of this having any substantial impact on political allegiances. Most of those MPs and other officials affiliated with the PAP back in 2001 had drifted away in the intervening years, or saw the writing on the wall for Kemakeza. Robert Goh—the prime minister's prosperous so-called 'dollar-a-year' adviser since the 2001 polls—played little public role in the campaign, although his private residence was later burnt to the ground by angry rioters. The Solomon Star ran headlines such as 'PM urged to come clean' and 'Erase Sir Allan now', reinforcing the already strong popular perception of Kemakeza's government as corrupt (Solomon Star 2006m, 2006q). The prime minister made no major statements of policy or vision during the campaign. On many weekends, Kemakeza went to his home island of Savo or to Yandina in the Russell Islands, clearly focusing first and foremost on the anticipated tough battle to retain his own seat.

Other parties were just as diffuse. The Lafari Party—a new organisation appealing to public servants—secured two MPs and had, during the campaign, pledged to assist the PAP in stabilising the country. Its leaders, however (floor crossers John Garo and Alfred Sasako) both lost their seats, and the two successful Lafari MPs joined the PAP immediately after the election (Solomon Star 2006n). In February 2006, national president of the AIMP, Tommy Chan, launched a 'statement of policy 2006', pledging to assist with stabilisation, along with the usual platitudes about support for reconciliation and healing. The party never released a list of candidates, preferring to pursue the amorphous strategy of claiming to articulate the aspirations of those who failed to lodge any party affiliation. Party affiliations are always difficult to establish in Solomon Islands politics. Candidates often double list themselves, or shift allegiances, particularly in the days just before the prime ministerial vote. Table 6.3 provides affiliations given by the MPs themselves at the time of the prime ministerial election on 18 April.

On the opposition side, party affiliations were only slightly more meaningful. Ulufa'alu published conflicting listings of sponsored candidates for his Liberal Party in the Solomon Star (2006g, 2006h), several of whom responded by writing letters to the newspaper denying such allegiances. His party secured only two MPs, reducing Ulufa'alu's chances in the leadership contest. Francis Billy Hilly's Nasnol Pati (National Party) gained six members, including Hilly himself, Leslie Boseto, Patteson Oti and Joses Sanga. Sanga argued for legislation to strengthen the party system, including Papua New Guinea-style laws against floor crossing and provisions for public funding for political parties (Solomon Star 2006l). Ironically, Sanga, Oti and Boseto were all to resign from the Nasonol Pati shortly after the elections in the wake of Hilly's sacking (in a manner that might have been illegal had

---

**Table 6.3      Party affiliations of elected MPs as of 18 April 2006**

| | |
|---|---|
| Solomon Islands Social Credit Party | 2 |
| People's Alliance Party | 5 |
| Nasnol Pati | 6 |
| Solomon Islands Party for Rural Advancement | 6 |
| Solomon Islands Liberal Party | 3 |
| Democratic Party | 5 |
| Association of Independent Members | 12 |
| Independents | 11 |
| Total | 50 |

Source: Compiled by the author and David Kusilifu.

the legislation they proposed been enacted) (SIBC 2006b). Responding to national debates about the pivotal role villagers had played in leading the 2002–06 economic recovery, western politicians launched a Solomon Islands Party for Rural Advancement (SIPRA), led by former Permanent Secretary for Finance, Gordon Darcy Lilo. SIPRA was new, while the Liberal and Nasnol parties had been in hibernation since the 2001 poll. With 12 MPs altogether, these three parties formed the core of the opposition.

On the maverick fringe of Solomon Islands politics, Manasseh Sogavare launched a Solomon Islands Social Credit Party (Socred) in July 2005, backed by Filipino businessman Ramon Quitales. It campaigned on a platform of hostility to foreign banks as well as the Central Bank of the Solomon Islands, urging peculiar monetary reforms aimed at relieving national indebtedness (PacNews 2005a, 2005b). Only one Socred candidate other than Sogavare was successful: Temotu MP Clay Forau, a debutant MP who played the side-switching game with sufficient versatility to earn himself portfolios in Rini's and Sogavare's cabinets. By 18 April, five successful MPs had affiliated themselves with the Democratic Party, the brainchild of private lawyer Gabriel Suri. This barely figured as a cohesive entity, however, and party affiliations exerted little influence over candidates' subsequent alliances. Francis Orodani's Solomon First Party vanished without trace, as did several other 'virtual' parties that had made fleeting public appearances before the polls. Efforts to encourage a rebirth for the United Party of the 1970s and 1980s triggered denunciations after the chairman of the electoral commission and Speaker of the House, Sir Peter Kenilorea, assumed the presidency of the party. Kenilorea (2006a) responded that his actions had in no way violated the constitution, prompting Pacific Island Forum observers to respond that the issue was one of propriety rather than legality, and that the assumption of such a position 'damages the appearance of impartiality of the [electoral] Commission' (Pacific Islands Forum Secretariat 2006). In the event, none of the United Party candidates captured a seat. In total, only 26 of those elected as MPs had party affiliations or had acquired these by 18 April, implying that the remaining 24 were independents. Ten of these were associated with the quasi-formal AIMP grouping led by Rini and Chan, but 14 were genuinely unaffiliated or were watching closely which way the political winds blew.

The 44-strong international observer team found that 'the polling process was transparent and well conducted, and voters were able to exercise a free and secret vote' (International Electoral Observers 2006). Elsewhere in the world, election observation missions are, more usually, watch-dogs against gross fraud or ballot rigging, but are less well equipped to deal with the sort of subtle irregularities that occur behind the back of the formal election process in Solomon Islands. Despite substantial voter intimidation by armed militants, particularly on North Malaita and South Guadalcanal, the 2001 election was declared free and fair. In 2006, guns were not a factor influencing voting patterns, but efforts to purchase votes were nevertheless widespread—whether or not this breached the Electoral Act's un-enforced SI$50,000 limit on campaign expenditures. Despite the limited purview of the international election observers, their conclusions provided a confidence-building influence and a counterweight to some of the more outrageous 'tok stori' claims that circulated. Before the 5 April poll, former governor-general Sir Baddley Devesi had advised foreign observers to stay on to scrutinise the subsequent prime ministerial election. UN Observer Mission Coordinator, Steve Wagenseil, responded that the prime ministerial election process (conducted behind closed doors) lacked sufficient transparency to be susceptible to overseas observation (Solomon Star 2006j). Most international observers had left the country before the Easter weekend.

## The second election

As the election results flowed in to Honiara, so too did the newly elected and returned MPs. The alternative groupings settled in at the Honiara Hotel, owned by Chinese businessman Tommy Chan, and at the Iron Bottom Sound Hotel, owned by Alex Wong, another local Chinese businessman and naturalised citizen. Chan (national president of the AIMP) welcomed members with an advertisement in the Solomon Star (2006r) congratulating them and announcing that 'the people of Solomon Islands have again entrusted you with the responsibility of ensuring that this country they love to call home and its multiracial population is well governed and properly cared for. Your electors have given you the support you needed and now it is your turn to honour that support.' This was an attempt to generate consolidation in an otherwise fluid setting, a familiar Melanesian bandwagon strategy aimed at encouraging wavering MPs to gather behind a plausible victor. Of the 21 MPs listed in the advertisement, at least 11 had no previous association with the AIMP.[15] On the top of the list was Snyder Rini, and the next day the AIMP leader and Chan walked together into the Flamingo Nightclub (next to the Honiara Hotel) claiming 24 backers for an AIMP government, and announcing publicly the end of the coalition with Kemakeza. All 11 of the ministers who had secured re-election associated themselves with the Rini camp.

This was an unwelcome development for Australian diplomats. As an embarrassing leaked email from a subsequently hurriedly removed RAMSI official later acknowledged, Australian High Commissioner, Patrick Cole, had apparently been working hard behind the scenes to avoid Rini capturing the top job. 'Cole said he had talked to Tommy and [his son] Laurie Chan as to why Rini had been selected given that they had given him assurances that he wouldn't be,' wrote Mick Shannon (Solomon Star 2006y), '[l]ooks like Tommy Chan's main business interest is in getting a second casino licence and he can no doubt depend on Rini for that.' In itself, the revelation of Australian manoeuvring behind the scenes in Solomon Islands politics was hardly surprising. Perhaps more disturbing was the view expressed that, as a result of the anticipated loss of Peter Boyers as finance minister, 'we will end up with no effective voice in cabinet to guide economic and fiscal policy'. Cole refused to comment about 'what an individual may or may not have said about what may or may not have been going on' and faced down the calls for his resignation (Solomon Star 2006x). Cole viewed Kemakeza as 'the best of a bad bunch' and as an accomplished master at the parliamentary numbers game. He had long pursued a bilateral agenda that occasionally departed from the studied neutrality sought by RAMSI. Cole supported the adoption of Papua New Guinea-style integrity legislation in the Solomon Islands, including grace periods during which no-confidence votes could not dislodge governments and rules against MPs crossing the floor.[16]

The initial bid to assemble a rival coalition came from East Honiara MP, Charles Dausabea, who claimed the support of eight members and demanded an alternative to Kemakeza. This was still less welcome for Australian diplomats than having Rini as prime minister. The Prime Minister had 'crossed the line in terms of sovereignty', declared Dausabea, criticising Australian interference in cabinet decision making and associated breaches of national security (SIBC 2006a). Dausabea rejected having as prime minister someone from either Malaita or Guadalcanal—suggesting that this was 'too early after the ethnic tension' (Solomon Star 2006s) for such an outcome. That comment, as well as Dausabea's tarnished reputation during the 1998–99 unrest and as a behind-the-scenes power-broker after the 2000 coup, generated a flurry of hostile criticism (see, for example, Aqorau 2006). It played, however, to a familiar gallery in Solomon Islands politics. Even before the 1998–2003 tensions, candidates for prime minister who were not from Malaita or Guadalcanal—such as Makira's Mamaloni—had faced an easier ride than Kenilorea or Ulufa'alu (from Malaita) or Alebua (from Guadalcanal). In the wake of the Isatabu uprising, Sogavare (from Choiseul) and Kemakeza (from Savo) had traded off their origins. Disturbingly, the anti-Malaita directive ruled out as potential prime ministers the two politicians associated popularly with the younger generation and often perceived—rightly or wrongly—as promising a more competent, honest and reform-oriented style of leadership: Joses Sanga and Fred Fono.

On Thursday 12 April, a new coalition was announced, bringing together three former prime ministers: Ulufa'alu, Hilly and Sogavare. It claimed 30 members, including those from the SIPRA, the Nasnol Pati and the Liberals. Dausabea had also joined the group. In Solomon Islands realpolitik, having such a brutal presence as Dausabea belonging to the loosely knit, tactically ill-astute and soft-hearted opposition potentially made the difference in the fluid but hard-fought struggle for the prime ministerial post. Two opposition MPs arriving from the east were whisked away unexpectedly to the Honiara Hotel by Chan's henchmen. Oti fetched them away to the opposition headquarters at the Iron Bottom Sound Hotel. Police were stopped from collecting their personal possessions by hotel owner, Chan. It was Dausabea who then successfully physically obtained the luggage, and brought it to the opposition headquarters (Solomon Star 2006t).

The inauspicious 2001 splintering of the opposition due to conflicts about the leadership reappeared, although this time the group remained at least partially intact. Before the voting began, Sogavare broke away, leaving a number of disoriented supporters behind at the Iron Bottom Sound Hotel. The opposition continued its internal selection process and, after several rounds of elimination, settled on Job Dudley Tausinga as its candidate for prime minister. Other aspirants such as Ulufa'alu, Hilly and Oti held together behind the newly favoured leader, desperate as they were to avoid another term in the wilderness of opposition. The Sogavare breakaway, however, proved potentially devastating for opposition ambitions. This new group's headquarters was at the Pacific Casino Hotel, an enterprise owned by yet another Chinese businessman and naturalised citizen, Patrick Leong. It provided a convenient transit station for wavering opportunists, eager to take advantage of prevailing uncertainties to enhance their position in the struggle for prestigious portfolios and/or other rewards.

As realignments in the now tripartite contest began, the atmosphere became extraordinarily tense at the Iron Bottom Sound Hotel. The new MP for South Guadalcanal, David Day Pacha, was whisked away in a vehicle belonging to local businessman of Guale and Asian descent, Bobo Dettke, to join Sogavare's group. Dausabea's security guards manning the gates at the Iron Bottom Sound Hotel became greatly agitated and harried visitors, suspecting them of intending to snatch further opposition MPs. Three more of the Guale MPs had also shifted across to the Pacific Casino Hotel, as did several other debutant or previously non-aligned MPs. The rebel Guale bloc emphasised the presence of Dausabea—due to his notorious links with the MEF—as the reason for their flight from the opposition camp. It was widely rumoured that the bills for their rooms and expenses at the Pacific Casino Hotel were being paid by Dettke (reportedly at a cost of SI$2 million), and more secretive financiers could plausibly have been operating behind the scenes. A Winds of Change advertisement appeared in the Solomon Star (2006t) headlined 'Who will decide our PM?', and explained that 'there is a select group of business, logging and foreign interests that are currently attempting to corrupt our political process and manipulate the election of the new PM so that they can continue to control our nation'.

In the midst of this fraught coalition-building process, two Taiwanese naval vessels docked in port and sent sailors from the Wu-Yi's training squadron to perform kung-fu exercises for onlookers at the National Stadium. The event was accompanied by new announcements by Ambassador Antonio Chen of Taiwanese aid awaiting the incoming government (ABC 2006a). New and returned MPs were invited to come aboard the Wu-Yi that evening for a cocktail party. Only a few AIMP members attended, including Peter Boyers and Laurie Chan, as well as the outgoing prime minister. Kemakeza told the gathering that his government would be re-elected (Solomon Star 2006u), yet the celebrated 'numbers man' of 2001–06 no longer had sufficient party backing for a bid to remain prime minister. His PAP had been reduced to a rump of seven members. One of these, Fred Fono, immediately deserted and joined the AIMP.

According to the timetable set by Governor-General Sir Nathaniel Waena, nominations for the prime ministership were to close at 4pm on 11 April 2006, and the elections were scheduled for 9.30am on Tuesday 18 April. By the close of nominations, all three candidates were from the western part of the country: Rini, Tausinga and Sogavare. During the Easter long weekend, coalition fortunes waxed and waned. Numbers appeared increasingly to favour the opposition, and a greater sense of calm prevailed at the gates of the Iron Bottom Sound Hotel. On its own, the Honiara Hotel-based coalition did not have the numbers to win the prime ministerial election outright. When MPs finally gathered on Vavaya Ridge to select their new prime minister, Tausinga was easily ahead at the first count, but four votes short of a clear majority. It was the 11 MPs who sided with Sogavare at the first count who provided the crucial swing votes. In the second round of voting, 10 of these backed Rini—handing him victory by 27 votes to 23. It was to prove a short-lived triumph. Eight days later, responding to the political shock waves engendered by the riots, six MPs crossed the floor to join an opposition that regrouped around Sogavare as its new candidate for prime minister. Facing an impending no-confidence vote, Rini chose to resign. The Honiara Hotel camp chose Fred Fono as its candidate for the second prime ministerial elections held on 4 May, but he lost by 22 votes to Sogavare's 28. Sogavare consequently became prime minister, with Tausinga as deputy and Ulufa'alu as finance minister.

Table 6.4    The 18 April and 4 May 2006 prime ministerial elections

| 18 April | First round | Second round | 4 May | First round |
|---|---|---|---|---|
| Synder Rini | 17 | 27 | Fred Fono | 22 |
| Job Dudley Tausinga | 22 | 23 | Manasseh Sogavare | 28 |
| Mannaseh Sogavare | 11 | | | |

Source: Compiled by author.

## Conclusion: riots revisited

The riots that broke out on 18 April outside parliament were triggered by a deeply flawed prime ministerial selection process, which not for the first time generated an outcome that bore no relationship to any discernible popular mandate.[17] The previous government had earned itself a poor reputation among Solomon Islanders. As we have seen, many ministers had been sacked for embezzlement of funds or complicity in militant activities. Kemakeza's PAP performed poorly at the polls. Its coalition ally—the Rini-led AIMP—had also suffered high-profile casualties. In total, nine of the 20 ministers had lost their seats, as well as the bulk of pro-government backbenchers. Nevertheless, here was the former deputy prime minister leading the core of the old cabinet back into office. Whatever the role of disgruntled politicians in inciting the crowds, the causes of the Honiara riots ran much deeper. The intense level of popular antipathy to the outcome of the prime ministerial election—at least among the hundreds gathered outside parliament on 18 April—was captured in three hours of pilot footage for an intended new Solomon Islands TV station.[18] There exists no reason to believe that some reservoir of popular support for the former government existed anywhere else in the country.

This was not the first time a gathering outside parliament had reacted in a hostile way to the outcome of a prime ministerial election, even if the response this time was far more violent. Back in 2001, at the previous prime ministerial election, Kemakeza's victory had been greeted with such a stunned and disapproving silence that Sir Allan felt obliged in the midst of his post-election news conference to publicly dismiss his critics as articulating a narrowly urban response.[19] Previous government changes, for example in 1990 and 1994, were also outcomes of behind-the-scenes manoeuvring by top politicians, and bore no necessary relationship to popular enthusiasm or disdain with the performance of the government of the day. Cautious preparation for disturbances accompanying prime ministerial elections, including deployment of officers to Chinatown, had previously been standard Royal Solomon Islands Police procedure (Short 2006).[20]

Did disappointed politicians plan and spark the disturbances? Two opposition MPs—Dausabea and Nelson Ne'e—were subsequently arrested for inciting the crowds to violence. Some speculated about Dausabea's role in stirring youths to action the night before the riots (Wickham 2006).

Exiting parliament after Rini's election, Dausabea allegedly said '*mi fala
lose nao, iu fala doim what nao iufala likem* [we've lost, you go ahead and do
what you want]', which sounds more provocative in Pijin than in English
(Solomon Star 2006v). The less-seasoned Central Honiara MP, Ne'e, was
blunter: '*dynamitem parliment* [blow up parliament],' he is said to have told
the crowds (Solomon Star 2006w). Was this mere trouble making amid an
already occurring popular outrage-driven riot, or had frustrated political
leaders transformed an otherwise peaceful protest into a violent one? This is
a familiar issue, and one that also accompanied Solomon Islands urban unrest
in 1989 and 1996, the Isatabu uprising of 1998–99 and various Malaitan
demonstrations in Honiara during 1999–2000 (Fraenkel 2004a:64–5,
117–19). It is also—in all these cases—impossible to answer definitively,
for the Melanesian leader blends into the crowd and the instigator is rarely
separated easily from the instigated. At the time of writing, the courts are
entrusted with the responsibility of judging whether politicians incited the
riots and a commission of inquiry is supposed to establish the causes. Since
courts are responsible for establishing guilt or innocence, however, and not
ultimate causes, and since the commission cannot comment on matters
before the courts, it seems likely that neither will resolve the broader issue
of what was behind the Honiara riots.

The claims that trucks had delivered rocks, water bottles and fire-
bombs to parliament before the riots were all false (Maiden 2006; Morgan
and McLeod 2006:421–2).[21] Stones hurled at Parliament House were
available readily on the access road. The torching of the first RAMSI
vehicle, supposedly with the petrol-filled water bottles described in *The
Australian*, happened at least an hour and a half after the initial outbreak
of the disturbances outside parliament. Once the crowds veered towards
the town, numerous opportunist elements joined the melée. In the 1990s,
before their crisis-related exodus from Honiara in 2000–01, underemployed
youths hanging around aimlessly in Honiara (the notorious 'masta liu')
regularly joined urban disturbances. The renewed expansion of squatter
settlements on Honiara's fringes and the buildup of numbers of young and
aimless street-kids during 2002–06 were always likely to swell the ferocity
of even minor urban disturbances.

The claims that RAMSI police tactics sparked the disturbances were
overplayed and often inconsistent. Despite a heavy presence, Australian

police quickly lost control, and resorted to using tear-gas only about three hours after the disturbances outside parliament began. Providing a megaphone for respected senior statesman Sir Peter Kenilorea might have helped to calm the crowds, but it requires a big counterfactual stretch to suggest that this would have quelled the unrest. The Deputy Commissioner of Police, Johnson Siapu, claimed that 'the violence and attacks on property at Chinatown and other areas throughout Point Cruz had commenced prior to the deployment of tear gas' (Solomon Star 2006z). According to Police Commissioner Shane Castles, the timing was close: '[b]y 3.15pm...a crowd in excess of 200 began ransacking both the Sunrise and Wings Supermarkets', and 'at 3.22pm non-lethal [CS] tear gas was deployed at parliament house' (Solomon Star 2006aa). If so, the tear-gas was deployed seven minutes after the ransacking began. It takes about five minutes to run, without stumbling, down the steep hill from parliament to Point Cruz. Hence, if this timing was correct, those fleeing from the tear-gas outside parliament could have joined the rioting in the town centre only about 3.27pm, 12 minutes after it began.

Most extraordinary were the claims that Taiwanese funding somehow fuelled the riots. Taiwan had, at times, exercised an ill-advised influence on Solomon Islands politics: with regard to the misconceived EXIM loan in 2001, RCDF spending before the 2006 poll and selective payments routed through Kemakeza's office during the run up the 2006 poll. The diplomatic fiasco surrounding the ill-timed arrival of the Wu-Yi—and the cocktail party in the middle of government formation—encouraged increasingly shrill antipodean allegations of Taiwanese political interference in the electoral process. Many also claimed that Taiwanese money influenced the wheeling and dealing in the run up to the 18 April prime ministerial election. Money does change hands in such elections. Since such transactions are inevitably secretive in one sense—but well known in another—amounts often tend to become exaggerated. Solomon Islanders' evidence of receipts of bribes arises owing to ostentatious displays by recipients. In close-knit communities, politicians who are seen to suddenly mysteriously acquire a new four-wheel-drive vehicle, for example, or a fancy house are known to be in receipt of unusual sources of income. Such payments usually come from local businesses, would-be casino operators or logging companies seeking to influence the composition and policy direction of the incoming government.

The more important influence on the shaping and reshaping of Solomon Islands politics during 2003–06 was the Australian presence. Even that was limited, however, as the election first of Rini and then of Sogavare—neither of whom were candidates favoured in Canberra—clearly showed. Australian influence had served to strengthen the Kemakeza government, but it did not extend to determining the outcome of the post-election leadership contest. Nevertheless, the shaping and reshaping of government and opposition alliances during 2003–06 had showed itself to be extraordinarily susceptible to influence, whether deliberate or inadvertent. Neutrality was impossible, even if it appeared politically indispensable. No serious top-level consideration was given in Canberra to the political ramifications of the RAMSI operation, despite the parliamentary reconfiguration that ensued.[22] For the Australian High Commission, this was a positive consolidation around Kemakeza, even requiring additional legislation to further strengthen the position of the government. For RAMSI's special coordinator, it was perhaps more problematic, but unfortunately unavoidable owing to the role of the prime minister in legitimising the entire operation. Had the legislation recommended so strongly by some Canberra think-tanks—giving incoming governments a grace period during which they would be immune from no-confidence votes—been enacted and had it been accompanied by laws against floor crossing, the Rini government might have survived any parliamentary challenge, leaving RAMSI in the impossible situation of having to prop up a deeply unpopular government. Fortunately, such legislation had not been enacted. Nevertheless, the eventual triumph of a now heavily compromised opposition on 4 May 2006 bore all the scars of the reconfiguration of the political order during 2003–06. The way ahead will not be easy.

## Acknowledgments

Thanks to Johnson Honimae, Terry Brown, Peter Forau, David Chetwynd, Sarah Dyer, Josephine Taekeni, Ofani Eremae, Mary-Louise O'Callaghan and Tony Hughes for their comments.

# Notes

1   Solomon Mamaloni survived a full term as prime minister from 1989 to 1993, but his government did not. In 1990, Mamaloni abandoned his own People's Alliance Party and forged a new coalition with former opposition members. The 1984 United Party government also survived a full term, but its initial prime minister, Sir Peter Kenilorea, was forced to resign in 1986.

2   Rini in fact resigned, but only minutes before the vote on a no-confidence motion.

3   'The fact that elements of the pro-opposition crowd were already armed with petrol spray and fire bombs, and quickly set to incinerating RAMSI vehicles after the initial skirmishes, supports the contention that key members of the opposition group instrumentalised violence for political gain' (Morgan and McLeod 2006:421–2).

4   'There shall be a general election at such time within four months of every dissolution of Parliament' (Solomon Islands Government 1978:S.74).

5   I am indebted to Alistair Legge, of the Australian Electoral Commission, who managed the Civic Education Project, for details about these arrangements.

6   See the comments of SIEC adviser David Clarke in Solomon Star 2006d.

7   The Moral Rearmament Group grew out of the 1930s Oxford group and is known as Initiatives of Change in Australia. See http://www.au.iofc.org

8   Similarly, Morgan and McLeod (2006:420–1) reject the view that the prime ministerial election contest was 'a contest between the new guard who support political reform and the old guard characterised by money politics' on the grounds that many of the opposition politicians were also 'old' and because 'charges of money politics and maladministration may evenly be directed against members of Tausinga's camp' (my emphasis). For an alternative view, see Kabutaulaka 2006.

9   For the debates in Australia, see Australian Government 2003.

10  In the week before the election, Dausabea converted his house into a kind of hospitality centre for confirmed supporters and, on election day, he took them in groups of 20 to the polling station, bringing them back for refreshment thereafter (Bishop Terry Brown, personal communication, 31 August 2006).

11  The Constitutional (Amendment) Bill 2005 was defeated in November 2005—not due to direct opposition, but owing to the absence of so many sitting members that it proved impossible to reach the required majority (three-quarters of the house or 38 MPs) (Solomon Islands Government 2005b).

12  See also the rather inconsistent responses from Taiwanese Ambassador, Antonio Chen (2006), and Kemakeza (2006), and the subsequent contributions from Joses Sanga (2006), Alfred Sasako (2006) and Speaker of the House, Sir Peter Kenilorea (2006b).

13  In the wake of its 2002 elections, Papua New Guinea switched from first-past-the-post to a limited preferential voting system. For data on the number of candidates per constituency in Papua New Guinea, see Fraenkel 2004b. What is said here is also true of Vanuatu, although that country uses a single non-transferable vote system (see van Trease 2005).

14  For an analysis of the likely impact of quotas aimed at influencing party candidate selection, see Fraenkel 2006.

15  In some cases, only the constituencies were announced, presumably because when the advertisment was written the victors were still unknown.

16  Personal communications (Anonymous).

17  The issue of what reforms might prove effective in such circumstances, including the scope for strengthening political parties and reform of the process of electing prime ministers, is discussed in a separate forthcoming paper.

18  Raw DVD recording of Solomon Islands TV footage taken before, during and after the prime ministerial election result, including the subsequent disturbances outside parliament.

19  For some sense of the anticipation of the potential for hostility from the outcome of Solomon Islands' two-stage prime ministerial elections, and an account of the 2001 sequence of events, see Fraenkel 2004a:136–38.

20  Solomon Islands-born Mike Wheatley, the Assistant Police Commissioner, National Reconnaissance and Surveillance, during 1992–2000, explained: 'It is a standard procedure for the disciplinary forces of Solomon Islands to be on alert during any national election, stepping up as parliament is convened for the election of the Prime Minister. Forces were usually deployed at Parliament House, on the approaches to Chinatown and for other key locations on a direct route from Parliament House. Such a strategy allows one to block or deflect riotous assembly as opposed to the riskier strategy of following it into Chinatown' (Wheatley 2006).

21  See Note 4.

22  Personal communication (Anonymous).

# References

Alasia, S., 1997. *Party politics and government in Solomon Islands*, Discussion Paper 97/7, State, Society and Governance in Melanesia Program, Research School of Pacific and Asian Studies, The Australian National University, Canberra.

Aqorau, T., 2006. 'Letter', *Solomon Star*, 13 April.

Australian Broadcasting Corporation (ABC), 2003. 'Solomons parliament indicates support for intervention', ABC, 9 July.

——, 2005. 'Incumbent MPs routed in provincial elections', *Pacific Beat*, Radio Australia, 5 July.

——, 2006a. ABC Asia Pacific, 15 April.

——, 2006b. 'Australia's top cop says cash changed hands in recent poll', *Pacific Beat*, Radio Australia, 11 May.

Australian Government, 2003. *Hansard*, 12 August. Available from http://www.aph.gov.au/hansard/reps/dailys/dr120803.pdf

Bennett, J.A., 2000. *Pacific Forest: a history of resource control and contest in Solomon Islands, c.1800–1997*, The White Horse Press, Cambridge.

British Broadcasting Corporation (BBC), 2001. *Birthday Honours 2001*. Available from http://news.bbc.co.uk/2/hi/in_depth/uk/2001/birthday_honours_2001/1390944.stm (accessed 14 August 2006).

Brown, T., 2006. Email circular to Anthropology in Oceania network, 22 April.

Callick, R., 2006. 'Corruption the catalyst behind Pacific pattern', *The Australian*, 25 April.

Chen, A., 2006. *Solomon Star*, 21 March.

Fraenkel, J., 2004a. *The Manipulation of Custom: from uprising to intervention in the Solomon Islands*, Victoria University Press, Wellington.

——, 2004b. 'Electoral engineering in Papua New Guinea: lessons from Fiji and elsewhere', *Pacific Economic Bulletin*, 19(1):122–33.

——, 2006. The impact of electoral systems on women's representation in Pacific parliaments, Research to Advance Women's Political Representation in Forum Island Countries, Pacific Islands Forum Secretariat, April.

Guadalcanal Leaders' Summit, 2005. *Communiqué*, Guadalcanal Leaders' Summit, 18 February.

Hameiri, S., 2006. 'What really went wrong in Solomons', *The Age*, 24 April.

Hughes, T., 2001. Lessons from a false dawn: outcomes of the Solomon Islands police and structural reform programme, 1997–2000, Unpublished paper, 6 October.

International Electoral Observers, 2006. *Interim Statement*, 7 April 2006, International Electoral Observers (Pacific Islands Forum, Australia, Japan, New Zealand, United States).

Kabutaulaka, T.T., 1999. 'Political reviews: Melanesia—Solomon Islands', *The Contemporary Pacific*, 11(2):443–9.

——, 2006. 'Seeking answers in the ashes of Honiara', *Pacific Islands Report*, 20 April.

Kemakeza, A., 2006. *Solomon Star*, 3 March.

Kenilorea, P., 2006a. 'Letter', *Solomon Star*, 21 February.

——, 2006b. *Solomon Star*, 28 March.

Maiden, S., 2006. 'Leading questions', *The Australian*, 8–9 July.

McKenna, M., 2006. 'Corruption claims against new PM sparked violence', *The Australian*, 20 April.

Morgan, M. and McLeod, A., 2006. 'Have we failed our neighbour?', *Australian Journal of International Affairs*, 60(3):412–28.

New Zealand Herald, 2003. 'Militia tale symptom of sleaze', *New Zealand Herald*, 29 July.

O'Callaghan, M.L., 2006. 'Cash inflow into Solomons riots', *The Australian*, 11 May.

Office of the Prime Minister, 2000. *Beneath Guadalcanal: the underlying cause of the ethnic tension*, 24 February.

Pacific Islands Forum Eminent Persons' Group, 2005. *A Review of the Regional Assistance Mission to Solomon Islands*, Pacific Islands Forum Eminent Persons' Group, May.

Pacific Islands Forum Secretariat, 2006. *Report of the Pacific Islands Forum Observer Team*, 11 April, Pacific Islands Forum Secretariat, Honiara.

PacNews, 2005a. *PacNews*, 25 July 2005.

——, 2005b. 'Party blames government for poor economy', *PacNews*, 27 September.

——, 2006. 'Unusual cash deposited in Solomon bank', *PacNews*, 11 May.

People First, 2003a. *PFNet*, 26 August.

——, 2003b. 'Sir Allan risks both personal and political survival', *PFNet*, 15 September.

Radio New Zealand International, 2004. 'Solomons opposition MP replaces sacked agriculture minister', Radio New Zealand International, 10 September.

——, 2005. 'Sacked Solomon Islands minister refuses to go', Radio New Zealand International, 2 March.

Roughan, J., 2001. 'Joy to grief overnight', *Solomon Star*, 18 December.

Sanga, J., 2006. *Solomon Star*, 24 March.

Sasako, A., 2001. 'The election of Sir Allan', *Solomon Star*, 20 December.

——, 2003a. 'A bit more on my conversation with Pious and more', *A Private View*, 6 October, Lifhaus web site. Available from http://www.lifhaus.com/sasako2.htm (accessed 13 October 2003).

——, 2003b. 'Why immunity from prosecution for top ex-militants is so critical', *A Private View*, Lifhaus web site. Available from http://www.lifhaus.com/sasako.htm (accessed 14 October 2003).

——, 2006. *Solomon Star*, 29 March.

Short, F., 2006. 'Honiara riot warrants formal inquiry', *Pacific Islands Report*, 22 May. Available from http://archives.pireport.org/archive/2006/May/05-24-com.htm.

Solomon Islands Broadcasting Corporation (SIBC), 2001. SIBC, 15 December.

——, 2003. 'Kemakeza blasts accusations—then accuses', SIBC, 27 August.

——, 2005. 'Kemakeza gives $2,700 to home island in Solomons', SIBC, 9 March.

——, 2006a. SIBC, 16 April.

——, 2006b. 'Parliamentarians resign from National Party', SIBC, 18 August.

Solomon Islands Electoral Commission (SIEC), 2006. 'Commentary by Solomon Islands Electoral Commission', *Solomon Star*, 20 March.

Solomon Islands Government, 1978. 'The Solomon Islands Independence Order 1978', *Solomon Constitution 1978*, Solomon Islands Government, Honiara.

——, 2004. 'Report on the receipt, administration and management of the Regional Assistance Mission to Solomon Islands', *National Parliamentary Paper*, No.17 of 2004, December, Solomon Islands Government, Parliamentary Foreign Relations Committee, Honiara.

——, 2005a. 'Report of the Foreign Relations Committee on "The Report of the Forum Eminent Persons Group"', *National Parliamentary Paper*, No.3 of 2005, May, Solomon Islands Government, Honiara.

——, 2005b. *Daily Hansard*, 8 November.

Solomon Star, 2005a. 'Axed Solomon Islands minister blames Australia', *Solomon Star*, 4 February.

——, 2005b. 'Kemakeza fires two Solomon Islands ministers', *Solomon Star*, 4 February.

——, 2005c. 'Fono vows to tap Stabex fund', *Solomon Star*, 7 February.

——, 2005d. 'Leadership begins at home: PM', *Solomon Star*, 10 March.

——, 2005e. *Solomon Star*, 10 May.

——, 2005f. 'Solomon lawmaker calls for Kemakeza probe', *Solomon Star*, 13 May.

——, 2005g. 'EU to release $96m for 3 projects in SI', *Solomon Star*, 14 July.

——, 2005h. 'Ulu wants RAMSI to leave by 2010', *Solomon Star*, 16 December.

——, 2006a. *Solomon Star*, 27 January.

——, 2006b. *Solomon Star*, 6 February.

——, 2006c. 'Bishop challenged to prove allegations', *Solomon Star*, 8 February.

——, 2006d. 'Election managers train to conduct national election', *Solomon Star*, 10 February.

——, 2006e. 'Exclude non-natives: MP', *Solomon Star*, 14 February.

——, 2006f. *Solomon Star*, 17 February.

——, 2006g. 'Former MPs refute Liberal's claim', *Solomon Star*, 28 February.

——, 2006h. 'Liberals vie for 38 seats', *Solomon Star*, 28 February.

——, 2006i. 'Fono releases report on RCDF funding', *Solomon Star*, 9 March.

——, 2006j. 'Post-election observers unlikely: Wagenseil', *Solomon Star*, 9 March.

——, 2006k. 'Taiwan denies bribery claims', *Solomon Star*, 10 March.

——, 2006l. 'Nasnol Pati to legislate SI political party system', *Solomon Star*, 16 March.

——, 2006m. 'PM urged to come clean', *Solomon Star*, 17 March.

——, 2006n. 'Lafari pledges stability', *Solomon Star*, 21 March.

——, 2006o. *Solomon Star*, 21 March.

——, 2006p. *Solomon Star*, 23 March.

——, 2006q. 'Erase Sir Allan now', *Solomon Star*, 29 March.

——, 2006r. *Solomon Star*, 10 April.

——, 2006s. *Solomon Star*, 11 April.

——, 2006t. *Solomon Star*, 13 April.

——, 2006u. *Solomon Star*, 18 April.

——, 2006v. *Solomon Star*, 26 April.

——, 2006w. 'MPs' bail opposed', *Solomon Star*, 27 April.

——, 2006x. *Solomon Star*, 3 May.

——, 2006y. *Solomon Star*, 9 May.

——, 2006z. 'Police reject claims', *Solomon Star*, 10 May.

——, 2006aa. 'Police chief replies to criticisms', *Solomon Star*, 19 May.

——, 2006bb. *Solomon Star*, 25 May.

The Australian, 2003. 'We'll be puppets: Pacific leader', *The Australian*, 10 July.

The Pacific Magazine, 2006. 'One Nation Party wants agreement implemented', *The Pacific Magazine*, 16 March.

Tuhanuku, 2006. 'Aid or corruption', *Solomon Star*, 21 March.

van Trease, H., 2005. 'The operation of the single non-transferable vote system', *Commonwealth and Comparative Politics*, 43(3):296–332.

Wainwright, E., 2005. *How is RAMSI faring? Progress, challenges and lessons learned*, Strategic Insights, April, Australian Strategic Policy Institute, Canberra.

Wheatley, M., 2006. '"RAMSI Tuesday" wasn't due to intelligence failure', *Scoop Independent News*, 26 May. Available from http://www.scoop.co.nz/stories/HL0605/S00401.htm

Wickham, A., 2006. 'Pacific in custody & in cabinet', *New Matilda.com*, 10 May.

# Chapter 7
## RAMSI—the way ahead

Mary-Louise O'Callaghan

It is no small coincidence that the first to congratulate Solomon Islands' new prime minister on his election was a member of the Australian-led Regional Assistance Mission to Solomon Islands (RAMSI). Just four hours after Manasseh Sogavare had secured one of the most arduous jobs in the region, RAMSI Special Coordinator, James Batley—who, arguably, was holding down an equally challenging post—dispatched his congratulations to the man with whom he knew he must now attempt to forge an open and trusting partnership if RAMSI in its current form was to survive.

In reality, Batley and the government that put him there had little choice. Australia's grand vision was of a regional mission led and funded by Australia that could assist Solomon Islanders to rebuild and reshape their nation into a viable, modern state, which could be ruled and run effectively by its own people. If that vision was to be achieved, Australia needed not only the cooperation of the government of Solomon Islands, whoever that might be, it needed a meaningful working partnership with it. This is the case even if that government is headed, as it is today, by a politician who catapulted himself into office initially on the back of a coup in 2000 and who has been more recently on the rebound from the violent social unrest that razed Honiara's Chinatown in April 2006.

Solomon Islanders have no option. Most already know from the four agonising years of rule by the gun (from 1999 to 2003) just how bad things can get. While the majority of Solomon Islanders did not join in the ethnic tensions, as they are called, between the two largest islands of Guadalcanal and Malaita, they were forced to watch as any semblance of governance crumbled steadily under the weight of the guns and the criminals wielding them. Most also remain to this day uncomprehending of how their most powerful neighbour, Australia, could sit on its hands for those four long years.

In the first flush of the post-11 September new world order, Australia's John Howard-led government discovered an urgent imperative for neighbourly concern that eventually led to the formation of RAMSI. Arriving in the smoky dawn of 24 July 2003, RAMSI quickly wrought the miracle—the return of law and order and financial stability—that Solomon Islanders had been praying for. In the four years that have passed since, there have been great gains. Despite a lot of hard work, however, Solomon Islands is still far from free of the legacy of those dark days of neglect, nor, therefore, is RAMSI. In many ways, the challenges that RAMSI faces are the same as those that so daunt the future prospects of Solomon Islands, although RAMSI also has a separate set of challenges all its own, which will be discussed in this chapter.

In the 12 months since the Honiara riots, the Solomon Islands defied conventional wisdom and continued to grow. Real gross domestic product (GDP) grew by 6.1 per cent in 2006 and was forecast to grow by 6 per cent in 2007; employment was growing strongly and inflation had fallen to 6.9 per cent through 2006. This is largely due to a combination of smart economic reforms introduced by the government with the assistance of RAMSI's economic governance program and the almost doubling in the past year of revenue collected from logging. Even in the face of such facts, however, the harsh reality is that the Solomon Islands economy suffered so badly in the previous decade that it is estimated that an annual growth rate of 5 per cent will be needed for the next 20 years just to raise the standard of living for the fastest-growing population in the region back to where it was hovering in 1994.

Add to this the growing social problems that accompany a nation's declining capacity to look after itself and the deep-seated and as yet largely unresolved issues that were behind the years of strife and there is still a very, very long way to go before it will be possible to say that Solomon Islanders have wrested back control of their nation's destiny.

A key to turning any of this around is the requirement for rapid change in how Solomon Islands is attempting to fund, run and develop itself. This is a big ask anywhere but more so in a country where a combination of corruption, ignorance and naivety has combined with a poorly designed electoral system to produce successive governments that are barely representative of, far less accountable to, the people. The institutions bequeathed 30 years ago in the lead up to independence are still not understood clearly by most Solomon Islanders. Nor are these institutions without the need for reform and refinement themselves. RAMSI has already put enormous resources into doing something about Solomon Islanders' fundamental lack of knowledge of how their nation is intended to work, in 2005 funding a multi-million dollar nation-wide civic education project.

RAMSI's innovative programs to enhance rural livelihoods and develop provincial economies and infrastructure face a similar race against time and population growth. With 85 per cent of the Solomon Islands population living in non-urban areas, AusAID has focused some of RAMSI's efforts on improving the rural economic base, and to moving some of the quite active informal economy into the formal sector in time to cushion the nation from the impact of shrinking forestry revenues as Solomon Islands' ancient trees—once a sustainable resource—are finally exhausted in the next four to six years.

At the heart of RAMSI's efforts to assist with the restoration of governance and the institutions of state is a program of ambitious economic, legislative, public sector and electoral reform that is in various stages of design or implementation. It is here we start to see the rub of RAMSI. In stark contrast with the overwhelming support for the mission's quite extensive intervention into Solomon Islands' law and order, there has been resentment, suspicion and active undermining of RAMSI's reforms and, in particular, the policy of putting key RAMSI personnel into ministries such as finance and in positions in other departments, such as that of the accountant-general. The same resistance is evident in response to the mission's efforts to reform government practices, policies and the endemic corruption that so undermines much of the State's core business in Solomon Islands, particularly the delivery of services. RAMSI encounters resentment, suspicion and active undermining from the country's political and bureaucratic élite. The daily, endless and time-consuming struggle to push on with these reforms, with little or no support from all but a few of Solomon Islands' senior bureaucrats, was described by one RAMSI insider in 2005 as 'trench warfare'.

An interesting conundrum has developed since the riots of 2006: the ascendancy of Sogavare and his at times manic and virulent attacks on Australia and RAMSI. While the RAMSI/Solomon Islands government partnership at the political level remains fraught with complicated deceits, and not-so-hidden agendas to undermine the mission's effectiveness in moving the nation's institutions to a more accountable state, just below this a remarkably effective working relationship has developed between senior Solomon Islands bureaucrats and those programs under RAMSI's three pillars of reform: economic governance, machinery of government and law and justice.

In the year leading up to Sogavare's election, RAMSI had moved to meet the concerns of the Solomon Islands government that it was setting an agenda for these reforms and other RAMSI-funded government programs with little or no consultation or mechanism of accountability other than the agreement of the incumbent Solomon Islands prime minister and regular reporting back to Canberra, Wellington and the Pacific Islands Forum Secretariat. Under the initiative of the then RAMSI Special Coordinator, James Batley, a lot of work was done with the Solomon Islands government to establish jointly agreed targets for all three RAMSI pillars.

A joint consultative forum has been established. Co-chaired by the special coordinator and the secretary to the prime minister, the forum comprises the permanent secretaries of the seven key government departments and the head of the RAMSI programs in these reform areas. An annual performance report is now produced using 51 separate indicators, all developed in discussion with the relevant Solomon Islands authorities or counterparts. These draw on four different sources of data: program-level reporting; analytical surveys; surveys of the population; and capacity-building surveys for each of the reform pillars. The latest of these population surveys, commissioned by RAMSI but conducted by independent researchers, reveals an extraordinarily high level of support for the mission—more than 94 per cent among ordinary Solomon Islanders.

While the Sogavare government's close alliance with elements of the former Malaita Eagle Force's (MEF) criminal and militant leadership has predetermined its antagonism towards RAMSI's core goals, it has also highlighted for Solomon Islanders the critical value of RAMSI's efforts to stabilise and rehabilitate their nation. For instance, the disquiet fuelled in 2005 among informed Solomon Islanders by Canberra's ill-judged decision to impose an Australian Federal Police (AFP) officer as Solomon Islands' police commissioner has been all but forgotten two years later, amid Solomon Islanders' distaste for the politically compliant incumbent recently rustled up for this post by the Sogavare regime from the dregs of Fiji's now discredited post-coup police force.

A top priority of RAMSI is building the capacity of Solomon Islands' institutions of governance, including the police. Solomon Islanders, however, in sharp contrast with their government's rhetoric, remain wary of too fast a shift back to full localisation, lest they end up with nothing more than a smarter version of what undid the knot of statehood so effectively not so long ago. It is an open secret—discussed frequently by Solomon Islanders—that most politicians would like to get their hands back on the State's coffers with varying degrees of ill intent.

In what has become a large fillip for the mission's morale, the political implications of the continued widespread popular support for RAMSI are probably resisted least by the Solomon Islands government's newly appointed special envoy to RAMSI, former politician Michael Maina. Despite having himself been forced to step down as police minister in 2005 when arrested on, but later cleared of, charges of fraud, the special envoy appears to be working constructively to ensure the mission is able to fulfil its widest mandate.

A more sophisticated and coordinated approach to the induction of all members of RAMSI on their arrival in Solomon Islands, be they civilians, police or military, is still evolving but the importance of this to the mission's goals is now acknowledged. The significance and complexity of effective engagement with local institutions and their personnel—the mission's Solomon Islands counterparts—has been recognised as the touchstone for its efforts in capacity building. This is easier said than done in a cross-cultural environment in which there is often a radically different approach to communicating and imparting 'informations', as it is called in Solomon Islands Pijin. A lot of gains have, nevertheless, been made in the wake of the post-riot scrutiny applied to the mission from Canberra and from RAMSI practitioners on the ground. A good first step has been the encouragement given to young bureaucrats and other RAMSI personnel, especially members of RAMSI's Participating Police Force (PPF), to equip themselves with the precise skills they need for what is the extremely delicate task of working with Solomon Islanders to rebuild not only their country but their individual capacity to contribute to this process. Australians don't know how to sit in silence. Solomon Islanders rarely speak without it, that is, without the indication, through the respectful space provided, of the other's willingness to listen. The mission and its members are learning to listen and to learn from Solomon Islanders about how best to communicate with them, to listen to what they think, what they need, what they believe they can contribute and what they think we might be able to bring to the RAMSI table.

Nowhere was this need for a change in approach and preparation more apparent than in the pivotal area of law and order. Having secured most of the guns and prosecuted many of the hard-core violent criminals by the end of 2004, the PPF—led and staffed largely by officers of the AFP's International Deployment Group (IDG)—have grappled with how to relate to, let alone rebuild, a force decimated by the purge of officers involved in the recent lawlessness. The April 2006 protests outside parliament, where the predominantly Australian and New Zealand PPF officers could be seen acting in a seeming vacuum from the mood of the crowd and the senior-ranking local police officers who were present, was a chilling illustration of the dangers of trying to rebuild someone else's country without being steeped in understanding of that culture and the dynamics of that society.

Since the riots, a lot of work has been done to improve the PPF's ability to equip its members with the skills required for effective communication and capacity building. The idea that the most effective way to do this is through a common language is now accepted. While many Solomon Islanders are quite articulate in English, the absence of all but a few Pijin speakers in the civil—but particularly the police—arm of RAMSI was a major weakness before the riots. Now the benefits that fluency in Pijin can bring are recognised, with compulsory Pijin classes required for all new members of the PPF who are not from pidgin-speaking countries. More thorough training of those individual officers being posted to RAMSI is now carried out by a revamped induction process at the IDG in Canberra, which involves regular input from Solomon Islands police officers. There have also been some very good developments within the Solomon Islands Police Force under RAMSI. The resurgence of the Solomon Islands Police Academy and the positive impacts of its training programs throughout the force are examples of this.

At the heart of this are the efforts being made by the IDG to cope with the rapid changes that have been required of the AFP by the new demands of Australia's more proactive role in the region and the changes in the world in which the AFP must now operate. The formation of the IDG is in itself a function of these changes and it is currently deployed in nine missions throughout the world, none of which, bar Cyprus, existed a decade ago. While great achievements were made by RAMSI in the first 12 months after its initial deployment in July 2003—the surrender or seizure of most guns in the community and the arrest of most of the militant and criminal leadership—the organisation of the PPF's rapid deployment to the Solomons led to a lack of long-term planning, personnel management, skills matching and continuity of postings. All of these shortcomings had unintended consequences in other areas of RAMSI's operations. Already there has been an acknowledgement of the need for a wider skill set, particularly in areas such as community policing. Vacancies in the IDG are now advertised throughout Australian states and territories, Pijin classes are offered on a weekly and voluntary basis, the length of deployment has been stretched for many officers into cycles from 40 up to 60, 80 and 100 weeks, and family accommodation is being built in order to attract more stable, long-term officers to the force.

There is much at stake. If, as recent events suggest, the growing number of progressively more impoverished Solomon Islanders are no longer willing to tolerate bad governance as placidly as they have in years past, RAMSI forces could find themselves confronting the very people who should be their natural allies in these reforms.

The April 2006 riots required a rapid hike in the number of troops and police deployed under RAMSI, bringing the mission's military contingent to 430 personnel from the paltry 63 deemed necessary in the period leading up to the riots. Drawn mostly from Australia and New Zealand, they remain on the ground with the additional 120 police shipped in to boost the PPF's numbers above the 450 mark.

The absence of adequate military back-up for the PPF during the April riots raises another set of questions. The deployment of RAMSI's military contingency is intended to provide support to the PPF, not to lead the mission. Risk assessment is therefore one of the prime tasks of the mission's joint intelligence group. The peculiar role of the military in RAMSI limits the quality and depth of the contribution that can be made by the Australian

Defence Force (ADF)—a fact very much to the mission's detriment and evident at the time of the riots, when effectively no troops of the more than 60 in country were available (in any meaningful numbers) to support the increasingly overwhelmed police. Clearly, the deployment of about 60 troops was deemed commensurate with the assessed threat. The fact that the bulk of these troops were deployed to provide additional security at Honiara's main jail since a riot there in 2004 did not dissuade the mission from allowing those remaining, excluding headquarters staff, to make a non-urgent patrol to the country's Western Province.

Head of the PPF at the time, Will Jamieson, stated publicly that there was no intelligence to suggest the kind of orchestrated violence that the police ultimately faced. If not a failure of intelligence, this points, at the very least, to an alarming lack of institutional memory within the mission at the time. Although the precise timing of the assault could not have been anticipated by many Honiara residents, the possibility of the criminal forces aligned against RAMSI biding their time and making such an attempt to undermine public confidence in RAMSI, and to de-motivate and distract the mission, was expected by many Solomon Islanders from RAMSI's very inception.

Such confrontations between white foreign cops and angry black locals— as were witnessed in April 2006—not only left 25 RAMSI personnel injured, they dealt a severe blow to Solomon Islanders' confidence in the ability of the mission to guarantee public safety. Ironically, the vitriolic attacks and clear agenda of the prime minister that came to power through the riots have focused the community's attention on the strengths of the mission and why they don't want RAMSI to go home.

Last, but by no means least, RAMSI has become better, smarter and faster at getting its message out to all stakeholders. Particularly effective has been a new community outreach program, which puts teams of RAMSI personnel from all parts of the mission in regular contact with Honiara's disaffected settlement communities and the provincial population. The mission still has enormous support from the broad mass of Solomon Islanders who genuinely and whole-heartedly appreciate the turn around in their lives that RAMSI's deployment has wrought. There is, however, never an exhaustible supply of good will towards an intervention force. The people of Solomon Islands are now demanding good governance, and that also means they need to know what RAMSI, as their partner, might be prosecuting on their behalf. They also need reassurance about the nature of that partnership. Like any marriage in which desperate circumstances rather than real attraction dictated a continuing partnership, there were always going to be issues about managing mounting tensions generated by the presence and actions of an intervention force, even a regional one that was invited in so enthusiastically. The degree of honest self-examination, imagination and skill with which such issues continue to be addressed by RAMSI and its hosts—be it the Sogavare government or those that succeed it—will not only be pivotal to a successful RAMSI, they will determine the as yet uncertain future of Solomon Islands and its people.

## Acknowledgments

This is an updated version of a paper that was first presented at the 'Solomon Islands: where to now?' workshop, 5 May 2006, organised by the State, Society and Governance in Melanesia Program and The Pacific Centre, College of Asia and the Pacific, The Australian National University, and supported financially by AusAID. The author is a commentator and long-term resident of the Solomon Islands, who has also worked closely with RAMSI. She is currently the mission's public affairs manager.

# Chapter 8

## Kastom and theocracy: a reflection on governance from the uttermost part of the world

Jaap Timmer

> Solomon Islands has the highest Constitution that was ever written in human history which is the Holy Bible and was inspired by God's Holy Spirit. It directs man to the way, the truth and the life. It is the inherent and immutable word of God the Almighty Creator. There is no man made constitution or declaration which can or will ever excel its literary works, saying, truths, promises and unchangeable prophetic message which are now being fulfilled in these last days (Solomon Star 2005).

As of 1998, it became apparent to the wider world that many Solomon Islanders were prepared to violently oppose the central government—reacting to a long legacy of poor management of the country's resources. Honiara, Australia and the international media were alerted to what had gone wrong in Solomon Islands when long-standing tensions between people from Guadalcanal and Malaita sparked a violent campaign of forcible displacement of Malaitan 'settlers' from rural Guadalcanal and a subsequent backlash from Malaitan militants based mainly in Honiara. Thousands were affected by the 'tensions' and by skirmishes between opposing ethnic militias. A coup by Malaitan militants and renegade police officers in June 2000 resulted in the forcible removal of the incumbent Prime Minister, Bartholomew Ulufa'alu. Progressive deterioration in the economic and security situation culminated eventually in the intervention of the Australian-led Regional Assistance Mission to the Solomon Islands (RAMSI) in mid 2003.

The crisis did not, however, end with the arrival of RAMSI. The mission restored a level of law and order by disarming people, sentencing and imprisoning criminals, bringing to justice a number of corrupt government officials, providing some level of security to the national airport, policing the streets of Honiara and so on. Efforts were also put into recruiting and training new police and prison officers, training public servants and reforming government departments, but surprisingly little was done to address long-standing local concerns about the structure of the State. RAMSI seemed reluctant to address Solomon Islanders' long-standing aspirations for greater local autonomy and to tackle the intricacies of the devolution of power from Honiara.

When centralised government was introduced, colonial authorities acknowledged 'tribal links' by establishing four administrative districts and, after the Local Government Act in 1964, by allowing for the creation of local councils. As Corrin Care (2005:163–4) points out, however, the local councils were never set up properly. Plans for the devolution of power from Honiara to local chiefs were not implemented and regulations for the election of chiefs and governance of the functioning of the councils were never drawn up. People simply continued organising their communities and resources in ways they deemed appropriate—adapting to the changing circumstances that came with migration to the coast, the construction of roads, the introduction of coconut-tree plantations and the developing market for copra. At the same time, people began to think differently about leadership and gender relations as a result of Christian and state education.

After independence in 1978, a number of sometimes-conflicting statutes covering provincial government were passed (see Corrin Care 2005:163–4 for an overview). While these considered the role of traditional chiefs, they did not address the involvement of non-elected chiefs and elders. As a result, popular aspirations to involve local leaders or chiefs in government dating back to the colonial period were never accommodated.

As became clear during the violent uprisings during 1998–2002, grievances about the division of resources between the government in Honiara and the provinces constituted a critical focus of Solomon Islands politics. Despite the arrival of RAMSI, this grievance against national government control remains marked. The April 2006 riots in Honiara likewise gave vent to grievances against central government politicians and reflected perceptions that the government had failed to respond adequately to its citizens. In this chapter, I discuss one such localised popular reaction to central government control from the northern part of Malaita. The case also indicates that a general tendency among foreign observers to separate custom and Christianity precludes a good understanding of Solomon Islanders' perception of the State and its crisis.

The relevance of this chapter to the broader themes in this volume is the qualification it provides to overly static or romanticised conceptions of *kastom* and Christianity in current discussions about the challenges of governance in Solomon Islands and appropriate solutions. Analysts, policymakers, government and aid officials operating in Solomon Islands need to avoid depictions of *kastom* and Christianity as stable and conservative forces or, alternatively, as important for nation building. *Kastom* and Christianity are inherently dynamic world-views and, moreover, have come under considerable stress in recent times.

## Alternative constitutions

Since independence, federalism—or the state government system, as it is popularly known—has been discussed regularly as an antidote to perceived over-centralisation. During the 1998–99 disturbances on Guadalcanal, indigenous militants demanded the establishment of a federal system, reacting against the dominance of Malaitans on their island and within the headquarters of the central government. Politicians from Western Province also strongly supported federalism (Kabutaulaka 2006).

A Constitutional Review Committee advocated the federalist option in 1987. As a federal republic, Solomon Islands would be a nation-state in which more power would be given to the proposed states than would coincide geographically with existing provinces. In this formula, particular importance was placed on establishing new financial arrangements, as the provinces felt that under the existing system control of resources remained concentrated among the small political élite in Honiara. The most contentious aspects of more recent proposals for federalism have been the allocation of revenue-raising capacity between the states and the federal government, the sharing of revenue between Honiara and the states and the fiscal equalisation between the states (Le Roy 2004:20).

What frustrates many people, in particular those living in rural areas, is that while there is constitutional recognition of customary land and resource ownership, practical arrangements do not deal adequately with conflicts over land and property. There is also a lack of guidance on how modern state laws should be applied in the local realm, where traditional rules are also under debate and revision. Many disputes arise from contested land rights. A source of enduring tension between landowners relates to plots of land with potential development value as sites for government or commercial ventures. This tension can result in conflict and is complicated further when some parties seek to apply state court rulings while others resort to traditional forms of resolution. The two approaches are, however, incommensurable as manifested in the recurring complaints heard in Solomon Islands (as in its neighbours) about the inappropriateness of modern law in a Melanesian context. These arguments are then extended to the incommensurability of the central state and Westminster model and indigenous systems of governance.

Some observers consider that poor governance and corruption in Honiara are a legacy of the British colonial government and failed attempts at giving more power to local chiefs. At the same time, there are immense practical challenges in determining who the chiefs are and how to organise communities with respect to modern issues relating to land tenure and the distribution of wealth from commercial enterprises. Nevertheless, there is a feeling that prosperity will come only if the government in Honiara changes its attitude, curtails corruption and gives the provinces a fair share of the wealth it controls. Consequently, any perceptions that officials in Honiara are engaged in dealings that are inconsistent with local norms about justice, and that are felt to disadvantage one's own region, are likely to generate considerable opposition in the region concerned.

This opposition is expressed in a variety of ways. First of all, there are the continuing demands for more autonomy in the provinces, in particular in Malaita. After the recent conflict, Malaita rejected the plan for a federal system of government discussed during the Townsville peace negotiations (Corrin Care 2005:167) and demanded its own executive governor and legislative assembly. Secondly, there have been violent attempts to change the current system of governance. The 1998–2002 conflict, as with the events in April 2006, represented, in part, instances of protest against powerful vested interests concentrated in the national capital and the marginalising effect these had on rural people.

Among those with vested interests in the islands' resources are a number of Asian investors and businesspeople. It is no surprise that popular protest against corruption and unequal sharing of wealth is directed also at them. Moreover, Asian companies were believed widely to have increased their exploitation of Solomon Islands' natural wealth during and after the recent crisis (see Moore, this volume). People recognise that the principal Solomon Islands beneficiaries of this form of plunder are their own politicians. The outrage expressed in April 2006 was part of the tension intrinsic in growing economic disparities and the manifest failure of governance on the part of the Solomon Islands State.

In explaining these tensions and the resulting protests and outbreaks of violence, there is a common tendency among many outside observers to separate matters of church and religion from issues concerning state, society and governance. In practice, the meaning ascribed to *kastom* (custom) by Solomon Islanders and outsiders is often very different. To illustrate the differences, I will describe a religious movement in North Malaita that appears to offer a radical alternative to prevailing discourses about state-centred notions of governance. Although this is only one regional perspective out of many, it seeks to explain the particular concerns of many North Malaitans and the emotional dimensions of their experience of the modern state, Christianity and *kastom*.

Most explanations of the 'ethnic' conflict that broke out in 1998–99 offered by North Malaitans include references to the negative influence of introduced Western ways of government (in particular, the juridical system that clashes with customary ways), growing levels of individualism, unbridled criminal behaviour among élites and the progressive descent into a Babylonian apostasy, often taken as one of the many signs presaging the end of time. It is out of this broader experience of crisis and uncertainty that people often search for alternative ways of governing themselves and, in doing so, reflect on the power and usefulness of *kastom*. Some can even begin to revitalise traditions of relative freedom allegedly enjoyed in the past or promised in Christian lore in terms of redemption (see, for example, Lattas 1998).

In contrast with these indigenous explanations, those of outsiders stand rather sharply. Many of the external analyses of the Solomon Islands crisis have been offered by political scientists and historians and generally draw on accessible secondary sources, such as newspapers and Internet chat rooms.

They seem to agree that improved governance in Solomon Islands requires fuller participation of rural groups or communities, communal leaders, civil society, women, churches and customary ways of doing things (Amnesty International 2004; Corrin Care 2005; Douglas 2003, 2005; Weir 2000).

In general, an idealisation of *kastom* in these outside views figures as a remedy for alienating state structures. Fraenkel (2004:187) notes that for many foreign observers *kastom* is identified as an authentic and thus desirable foundation. As such, *kastom* is also juxtaposed with the role of Christianity in processes of reconciliation and for rectifying the immoral behaviour of politicians. While Christian charity is seen as informing successful reconciliation after violent conflict, the restoration of *kastom* (devoid of Christian influences) is viewed as a socially appropriate way of restoring old balances. In contrast, many Solomon Islanders, in particular those of evangelical denomination, see Christianity and *kastom* as being inextricably linked (see, for example, Burt 1994; White 1991; Scott 2005).[1]

When looking at popular concerns and politics at the community level in Solomon Islands, *kastom* and Christianity are not merely layers of identity capable of uniting people, making them peaceful or otherwise serving as a foundation on which nationalism can be built. Rather, they are resources that are employed dynamically and creatively in people's everyday politics, whether to support peace or to exacerbate existing fault lines between ethnic and religious groups, and between national élites and rural communities.

## *Kastom* out of balance

In the wake of the ethnic tensions in Solomon Islands, two books appeared that attempted to explain the conflict and its dynamics (Fraenkel 2004; Moore 2004). One of these authors, Clive Moore (2005), returned recently to the main arguments in his book *Happy Isles in Crisis* (2004) and, as well as providing an update, presented a critique of the Australian-led RAMSI.

While balanced at the level of political analysis, Moore provides a less satisfactory account of *kastom*. For example, when addressing the violence of the tensions, he suggested that there was disturbance to Solomon Islanders' 'cosmological balance' (Moore 2005:62). This cosmological balance comprises the complex symbolic links that people recognise 'between human relationships, lands, gardens, music, dance, everyday thoughts, speech, their ancestors and now Christianity' (Moore 2005:62). The configuration of activities and expressions is labelled generally as *kastom*.

The disturbance of *kastom* is what Moore sees as the root cause of the outbreak of violence during the crisis. He goes on to observe that these old balances are hard to accomplish because '[m]alevolent spirits circulate in the winds, and constantly try to get in...RAMSI chased out the malevolent spirits, but this was hardly a cosmological solution. What is needed is a large-scale programme of restorative justice or transformative justice' (Moore 2005:62). This program is what Moore sees as customary, involving a complex knowledge of kinship and status and no final fixed adjudication. Only through this *kastom* program will the old balances be restored. The kind of *kastom* referred to implicitly here comprises kinship and social status and thus is not the *kastom* that is deemed important when people amalgamate or juxtapose *kastom* and Christianity. Consequently, Moore observes that '[t]oday's peace and reconciliation involved customary ways in combination with Christian faith and Western-educated leadership, but the old balances still need to be achieved' (Moore 2005:65).

Moore (2005) quotes Sinclair Dinnen's introduction in the latter's *A Kind of Mending* (2003), a volume on restorative justice practices in Melanesia, to substantiate his claim that *kastom* is an important foundation for a prosperous future for Solomon Islanders. Dinnen (2003:11–18), however, acknowledges that *kastom* is variable and dynamic, that when power changes so might *kastom* and that adaptation of local courts and restorative justice systems to *kastom* can itself become a source of injustice. This approach to *kastom* is in line with the view of most anthropologists and is also reflected nicely in the other book on the Solomon Islands crisis, Fraenkel's *Manipulation of Custom* (2004).

Fraenkel's account of the role of *kastom* in the ethnic conflict in Solomon Islands builds fruitfully on the extensive literature on the invention of tradition in the Pacific (see Otto and Pedersen 2005 for an overview). The author's methodology underlines explicitly the historical and cultural fact that 'introduced institutions have been thoroughly indigenised' (Fraenkel 2004:43, 185). Fraenkel (2004) notes that the juxtaposition between externally driven and indigenous influences continues to be prominent in the way Solomon Islanders understand the tension within their community, region and nation.

The meanings of *kastom* that come to the fore in current discussions include: *kastom* as 'authentic and rooted' (and thus good); 'destructive' *kastom*, in the case of the permeation of the 'customary' *wantok* system (networks based on common linguistic or kinship bonds) into the bureaucracy; and *kastom* as 'powerful', evidencing that a local group relates to the roots of power and knowledge. In this last meaning, *kastom* relates to the particular *kastom* of one group and is seen as belonging authentically to that group. For that group, *kastom* underpins its rights, its access to resources and its identity in the local and wider world. This meaning of *kastom* is prominent in the religious movement discussed in this chapter.

Fraenkel focuses on *kastom* in relation to the compensation payments that played such a debilitating role in the Solomon Islands during the tensions of 1998–2003. He gives less prominence to the mobilising force of *kastom* as a basis for the assertion of indigenous rights and access to natural resources. Nevertheless, Fraenkel (2004:77) does acknowledge the growing sense of Malaitan difference and the urban anomie that is expressed increasingly in revived foundation myths, including the idea of the 'lost tribe of Israel'. These revived or, in some cases, invented foundation stories are themselves *kastom* and are part of long-standing local knowledge traditions, one of which I will detail below.

## Deep-sea canoe

In this section, I discuss a religious movement among To'abaita speakers of North Malaita for which Christian lore provides the narrative and moral terms of reference. The connection that people see between Christian lore and *kastom* feeds a belief that serves to oppose mainstream churches and the government. This particular movement originated in the South Sea Evangelical Church (SSEC), established in 1966 out of the South Sea Evangelical Mission. The mission was brought back by Solomon Islanders from their 'blackbirding' experience in Bundaberg in Queensland, where they had worked on sugar plantations since the beginning of the previous century (Griffiths 1977; Hilliard 1960).

In early 1984, a group of elders of the SSEC was meeting to consider starting a new congregation in one of the suburbs of Honiara. During prayer time, one of the elders, Michael Maeliau, began to receive a vision from

God. This typical end-time prophetic vision told the story of a massive wave that began in the Solomon Islands, travelled around the globe and ended up in Jerusalem (Hess 2003b:68–9; Maeliau 1998).

The vision begins with a valley that fills with crystal-clear (unpolluted) water, which develops into a flood and later becomes a cloud. The cloud travels to Australia and returns to Solomon Islands from where it goes to all the nations in the South Pacific. As the cloud reaches Papua New Guinea, it changes into a three-pronged powerful current that heads eastward towards the west coast of the United States. As it arrives in the United States, the central current continues towards the east coast then turns 180 degrees and develops into a mighty wave that eventually stretches from the North Pole to the South Pole.

The wave then rolls back and travels westward. The wave is so great that it submerges all the nations in its path and is so high that it floods even Mount Everest. It covers everything in its path as it moves over the Pacific and Asia until a circle encompassing the globe is complete. With the completion of the circle, the wave zooms in on Jerusalem and shoots up into the heavens like a mighty pillar. As it reaches high in the sky, it opens like a great mushroom that gradually spreads until it envelops the Earth. At this point, a voice comes from the cloud saying, 'And the Glory of the Lord shall cover the Earth as the waters cover the sea.'

A collection of stories about the spread of the gospel by South Pacific island missionary Alan Tippett (1994:9) explains that the term 'deep-sea canoe' relates to a Fijian and Tongan symbol for canoes that plied from island to island with trade goods, warriors and tribute. With the advent of Christianity in the region, the use of deep-sea canoes 'steadily shifted from the business of war and cannibalism to the transport of missionaries from one island to another' (Tippett 1994).

Peter Ambuofa, a local missionary, returned to North Malaita in 1894 to spread the gospel after two years' training in Bundaberg, Queensland (Hilliard 1960:45). The return of Ambuofa was seen by many as a great moment in Malaitan history, embodying simultaneous images of the past and the future. Official church history views his return as signifying an important turning point in the conversion of Malaitans from heathens to Christians. From that point onwards, the people of Malaita were expected to follow the line of becoming good Christians and modern Pacific islanders. Most followers of the Deep-Sea Canoe Movement, however, see the return of

Ambuofa as an act of God to remind the people of Malaita of their unique role as inhabitants of 'the uttermost parts of the world'.

In the Sermon on the Mount (described in Matthew 5:7 and Luke 6:17–49; and see Acts 1:8), Jesus referred to the uttermost parts of the world as the geographical ends to which God's word should be spread. For most Christians in North Malaita, this is the most significant aspect of the sermon apart from its listing of codes of conduct or moral rules for social living. In the evangelical group of North Malaita who wish to prepare the world for the return of Jesus, the sermon is considered to replace the rules outlined in the *thora* (law). Only strict adherence to these rules will enable the restoration of Jerusalem and the eventual return of the Saviour.

The social and economic marginalisation of Solomon Islands—its (almost) 'uttermost distance' from Jerusalem—and the fact that people observe that the world around them is falling into apostasy, confirms their theory that Jesus had Solomon Islands in mind when He used the phrase 'the uttermost parts' in His Sermon on the Mount. Ambuofa is thus the key figure in the transformation of Malaita in the official and mainstream church narrative and in the widespread North Malaitan story about historical links between Malaita and Israel. In both stories, the Malaitan missionary brings about change, but in the latter the change is not from heathen to good Christians but involves the restoration of a temporarily discontinued link with the genesis of the world. Below I will explain the related Malaitan ideas about the promised land, the scattering of the people of the covenant and their present position in the Solomon Islands and in the world at large.

This particular interpretation of the Old Testament and the light it purports to shed on the origins of certain groups on the island of Malaita does not suggest that they are members of a lost tribe. Instead, they claim to be those people referred to in Jesus's Sermon on the Mount, who were the last and most distant group to receive the word of God. At the same time, however, people trace their ancestry back to figures in the Old Testament.

As indicated above, Michael Maeliau is a major figure behind the dissemination of and support for these beliefs. While many see him as a prophet, he also derives his status from his role in international evangelical networks. Regionally, he leads the Evangelical Fellowship of the South Pacific. He is also a member of the board of reference of the International Prayer Council, which believes it is compelled by God to seek Christ's glory worldwide for the blessing, healing and transformation of all nations (IPC n.d.). He is also affiliated with Tom Hess's Prayer Assembly movement (Hess 2003a).

Apart from his role in religious circles, Maeliau has also been active in national politics. In the mid 1990s, he was Minister of Home Affairs and in that capacity was responsible for approving a licence for the Honiara Casino (Alasia 1997:12), an act that appears to be inconsistent with his belief in a God-fearing community living according to God's commandments (see below). In 2006, he stood as an independent candidate for the elections for the national parliament. His program of reform promised a God-fearing and non-corrupt government, but his electoral campaign was ultimately unsuccessful.

In the religious sphere, he appears to have met with more success. In the past two decades, Maeliau's vision and movement has attracted a growing number of adherents, in particular from the SSEC churches in North Malaita and Honiara. On the basis of interviews I have conducted with adherents and excommunicates of the Holiness Church, people's understanding of the deep-sea canoe theology appears to be noticeably consistent. This theology is based largely on the dramatic events and laws detailed in the Old Testament.

The reason why some Malaitans adhere to old Jewish rules is that they consider themselves to be a covenant people with an ancestry going back to the biblical kings. Proof of this link with God's chosen people and an earlier movement of people from the Mediterranean to the Pacific stems from the belief that the Ark of the Covenant lies buried in the mountains of Malaita. When telling this story, people talk in similitudes. Thus, original Malaitan *kastom* (tradition) is viewed as the same as old Jewish forms of worship and specific proscriptions regulating social life.

In this sense, the core narrative of the Deep-Sea Canoe Movement is similar to that of the Remnant Church as described by Burt (1983). Visionaries among the Kwara'ae-speaking people who live near Auki, south of the To'abaita, founded the Remnant Church in the 1950s. The church was small and never attracted many more than 100 men and their families. To the present day, there are still only a handful of members. Adherents of the Remnant Church trace their ancestry to certain Old Testament migrations of the tribes of Israel and they remain committed to observing old Jewish religious laws.

Observers have identified parallels between *kastom*—understood as old practices of sacrifice to ancestors, ideas about traditional ritual pollution and laws for upholding good community living—and Christian ways. For example, Burt (1983:338) explains that 'theological parallels between the two religions have enabled Christian Kwara'ae to sustain some of the underlying premises of the pagan religion, which are reflected in the ideology of the Remnant Church'.

The Deep-Sea Canoe Movement and the Remnant Church position their theologies in the zone of friction between local ideas about *kastom* and the mainstream Christian teaching of the SSEC, the Roman Catholic Church, the Anglican Church and government. The local theology, or *kastom*, cannot be labelled simply as 'pre-Christian beliefs and practices' or 'traditional cosmology', as the people's interpretation of *kastom* is framed contingently in relation to Christian teachings and reflections on recent developments in the region.

In his analysis of the Remnant Church, Burt (1983:336) defines *kastom* as 'a set of values which Kwara'ae, like other Malaitans, regard as central to their traditional way of life, a perception reflecting the changes wrought or threatened by colonial domination'. When the seeds for the Remnant Church were sown originally by Zebulon Sisimia after an experience of possession by the Holy Spirit in 1955 in a broader context of mounting anti-colonial sentiment, much of the meaning of *kastom* had been recast in terms of a loss of sovereignty due to government control.

As Sisimia explained in a letter to Burt in 1981, his studies of the Bible showed him 'that the world had been ruled successively by the kingdoms of the Assyrians, Babylonians, Medo-Persians, Greece, the Romans and ten others to the present day, under three types of government; Monarchy, Oligarchy and Democracy. Sisimia saw that an alternative to these "tyrant" regimes of man was "Theocracy", the government of God given to Israel in the Old Testament' (Burt 1983:339). The Deep-Sea Canoe Movement follows this line of thinking while also expressing a deep-seated longing for autonomy and self-determination.

## Theocracy or the inversion of the nation

Many people on Malaita are deeply concerned about the Holy Land and this is reflected in their changing interpretation and perception of the Scripture and their position in the region and larger world. The tradition of internalising biblical vocabulary—'uttermost part', 'promised land', 'chosen people' and 'Jerusalem'—and applying it to visions of Malaita, To'abaita and Kwara'ae, evoke a powerful sense of ambivalence towards the modern state and its formal system of governance. Popular religious culture, in other words, is crucial to the construction of an oppositional political discourse in this part of the Pacific.

Many Malaitans claim that the Ark of the Covenant and the Temple of the Lord or Lost Temple of Jerusalem are buried at various locations in the mountains of Malaita. According to the Old Testament, the ark was placed in the holy of holies—the innermost room of the tabernacle. Those Malaitans who map features of the Holy Land onto their own territory say that the shrines for ancestor worship on the mountain tops in the interior of Malaita contain three sections.[2] They call the most sacred and powerful section the holy of holies and they see the shrines as tabernacles. The innermost place was where ritual leaders offered pigs to the ancestors and where the remains of deceased leaders were buried.

Some claim that at these worship shrines, original Jewish worship to God was practised. Due to influences from outside, and, in particular, the introduction of cannibalism, these holy practices gradually disappeared. This happened between four and five generations after the first arrival of migrants from the Holy Land. As a result, people lost their memory of how to perform the appropriate rituals and, because of this, a generational conflict erupted. The generation that was supposed to follow in the footsteps of the ritual leaders was so diverted by the conduct of raids against others and severing the heads of enemies that they lost interest in the older practices that had originated in Israel. They shifted their belief in the powers of God to the powers of great ritual and war leaders. As a result, they began to make offerings to them and buried the bodies of their heroes in the innermost part of the shrine. Practices such as the offering of human flesh to ancestors aroused fierce reactions among elders and divided previously more or less united groups.

In light of this widespread deterioration in morals in present times, many people are reflecting deeply on what constitutes a God-fearing community. According to Deep-Sea Canoe theology, becoming holy is central to the restoration of the world to a previous divine order as narrated in the Old Testament. Mainstream churches and worldly governments are incapable of achieving this level of holiness. As a result, the Deep-Sea Canoe Movement seeks to overthrow the government and replace it with a theocracy that is executed by God-fearing leaders.

Moreover, the movement criticises mainstream churches, in particular the Roman Catholic and Anglican churches, for collaborating with the corrupt élites, mimicking Europeans and failing to acknowledge the spiritually founded sovereignty of Malaitans.[3] So instead of bringing people together and uniting them to build a better future, the Deep-Sea Canoe Movement actively foments religious fault lines in society. In particular, tension between Jehovah's Witnesses and the Deep-Sea Canoe Movement is mounting. The Watchtower people (Jehovah's Witnesses) denounce strongly pagan practices and the idea of a return to old rituals is abhorrent to them, whether Jewish or otherwise. Another matter of concern to them is that the followers of the Deep-Sea Canoe Movement disassociate themselves completely from social contact with 'non-believers' or people who are considered not holy.

Central to my argument in this chapter is the contention that the Deep-Sea Canoe Movement's narrative of nation emphasises the limits of the modern state. Its explanation of Malaitan people's origin and the roots of their *kastom* and identity can be seen, at one level, as an inversion of the official Solomon Islands narrative of nation. In seeking holiness and claiming that it will play a central role in the reconstruction of the nation of Israel, the Deep-Sea Canoe Movement employs a powerful metaphor. In a situation in which most Solomon Islands political leaders describe their national character in terms of a Christian nation, the critique offered by the movement of mainstream Christianity and referred to regularly in nationalist rhetoric also turns the official version of Solomon Islands nationhood upside down and presents theocracy as the preferable alternative (cf. Collins 2004).[4]

## Conclusion

In light of the themes of the current volume, one can conclude that the Deep-Sea Canoe Movement among To'abaita speakers on Malaita springs from people's deep-seated frustrations with decades of unfulfilled promises of development and the continuing deferral of the crystallisation of these promises (cf. Bennett 2002). Most Malaitans remain exceedingly sceptical about what a Westminster system of centralised government can offer them.

As the movement shows, some among them have begun to actively redefine their sovereignty and individual aspirations in terms that depart markedly from the official language of post-conflict recovery and national progress.

Most Solomon Islanders are familiar with the modern rhetoric of progress. This rhetoric derives, in turn, from two main sources: the colonial and post-colonial government, and the churches. The government teaches about hard work, community development, good leadership and efficient infrastructure. Church teachings denigrate aspects of people's *kastom* such as ancestor worship, witchcraft, sorcery, primitive attire and so on, which are deemed to be heathen, shameful and belonging to the past, that is, to tradition or *kastom*. These two dimensions of modern reflection on the past come together in a variety of ways in ponderings on good governance.

At the same time, most Malaitans remain oriented strongly towards modern government. Despite their sustained criticism of present-day and colonial governments, the majority of rural people on Malaita seek connection with developments in Auki, Honiara and other parts of the world. As elsewhere in Solomon Islands, Malaitans have expressed strong demands for good health care, proper education and infrastructure that will facilitate economic and labour investment. Their aspirations for tangible progress are real and, as such, deserve recognition.

They share the concerns of many Solomon Islanders about a broad range of perceived threats to their individual lives, their communities and their country's future. These include growing individualism, declining morality, theft, corruption and 'money politics'. External observers have identified most of these as evidence of a weak or failing state. There is considerable consistency in people's identification of these threats, although there remain significant differences in perceptions about how they should or can be overcome.

Generally speaking, people in Malaita see threats to their well-being issuing from the predominance of Western ways of doing things and the related decline of customary ways (as defined nostalgically in response to the perceived threat), while many also see that as God's plan for humankind. The latter interpretation is most prevalent among evangelical Christians and is fed continuously by those who see signs of the end-time, thereby linking the Revelation to St John to events around them.

The Deep-Sea Canoe Movement reflects a widespread concern among North Malaitans with topology and the related moral foundations of society.

It is through connections with markers in their immediate landscape—the territory that belongs to one's kin group—that rural people articulate their position in the world and the pride and fame of their particular group. As the significance of the landscape changes, with land becoming an increasingly commoditised economic asset, the mapping of kin-group histories and their rights to land and wealth contained in or on the ground becomes ever more critical and people also accept new customary rules to regulate land rights.

The meaning of *kastom* in North Malaita is shaped in relation to the ever-growing divide between the élites in Honiara and Auki (including 'the Asians'). The case discussed in this chapter underscores the point that understanding the people of North Malaita entails not only documenting and analysing their past (or *kastom*) and their Christian beliefs, it involves acknowledging that these people respond in very particular ways to colonialism, the post-colonial state and long-delayed promises of development.

## Acknowledgments

Fieldwork for this paper was undertaken between December 2005 and March 2006, with the permission of the Ministry of Education, the Ministry of Foreign Affairs and chiefs in North Malaita. I am grateful particularly to George Hoa'au, David Suata, Adam Ulufa'alu, Francis Iro, Steward, Lawrence Luiramo, Peter Kwanairara, Frank Daifa and Terry Brown. I thank Sinclair Dinnen for his valuable comments.

## Notes

1   For a general discussion on the use of Christianity in people's empowering of the past in Melanesia, see Strathern and Stewart 2004:Ch.8.

2   See Burt and Kwa'ioloa (2001:29) for a drawn plan of such a shrine at Siale, on Kwara'ae land.

3   Similarly, Sabbath-keeping Anglicans oppose the mainstream Anglican Church in the Kwara'ae region. According to the Anglican Bishop of Malaita, Terry Brown, the Sabbath-keeping Anglicans form a direct line with the Remnant Church. Recently, the group burned the altar in the historical Anglican church in Fiu (Brown 2004:8–15).

4   Most recently, the Chief Justice of Solomon Islands, Albert R. Palmer, reflected on failed leadership in his country and noted that 'God has given this nation another chance to do it right' (Palmer 2005:4).

# References

Alasia, S., 1997. *Party politics and government in Solomon Islands*, Discussion Paper 97/7, State, Society and Governance in Melanesia Program, Research School of Pacific and Asian Studies, The Australian National University, Canberra.

Amnesty International, 2004. *Solomon Islands: women confronting violence*, 8 November. Available from http://web.amnesty.org/library/pdf/ASA430012004ENGLISH/$File/ASA4300104.pdf (accessed 17 June 2006).

Bennett, J.A., 2002. *Roots of the conflict in Solomon Islands. Though much is taken, much abides: legacies of tradition and colonialism*, Discussion Paper 2002/5, State, Society and Governance in Melanesia Program, Research School of Pacific and Asian Studies, The Australian National University, Canberra.

Brown, T., 2004. Christian contextual theology: a Pacific example—Malaita's Sabbath-keeping Anglicans and the hermeneutic circle, Keynote address to conference on Contextual Theology in the Pacific, Bishop Patteson Theological College, Kohimarama, Solomon Islands, 22–25 August.

Burt, B. and Kwa'ioloa, M. 2001. *A Solomon Islands Chronicle, as told by Samuel Alasa'a*, British Museum Press, London.

Burt, B., 1983. 'The Remnant Church: a Christian sect of the Solomon Islands', *Oceania*, 53(4):334–46.

——, 1994. *Tradition and Christianity: the colonial transformation of a Solomon Islands society*, Harwood Academic Publishers, Chur.

Clark, J., 1997. 'Imagining the state, or tribalism and the arts of memory in the Highlands of Papua New Guinea', in T. Otto and N. Thomas (eds), *Narratives of Nation in the South Pacific*, Harwood Academic Publishers, Amsterdam:65–90.

Collins, J.F., 2004. '"X marks the future of Brazil": protestant ethics and bedeviling mixtures in a Brazilian cultural heritage center', in A. Shryock (ed.), *Off Stage/On Display: intimacy and ethnography in the age of public culture*, Stanford University Press, Stanford:191–222.

Corrin Care, J.C., 2005. 'The search for a more appropriate form of government in Solomon Islands', in B.A. Hocking (ed.), *Unfinished Constitutional Business? Rethinking Indigenous Self-determination*, Aboriginal Studies Press, Canberra:159–69.

Dinnen, S., 2003. 'Restorative justice in the Pacific Islands: an introduction', in S. Dinnen with A. Jowitt and T. Newton Cain (eds), *A Kind of Mending— Restorative Justice in the Pacific Islands*, Pandanus Books, The Australian National University, Canberra: 1–34.

Douglas, B. (ed.), 2003. 'Women's groups and everyday modernity in Melanesia', *Oceania*, 74(1–2), Special issue.

Douglas, B., 2005. Christian custom and the Church as structure in 'weak states' in Melanesia, Paper presented at the Civil Society, Religion and Global Governance: paradigms of power and persuasion international conference, Canberra, 1–2 September.

Fraenkel, J., 2004. *The Manipulation of Custom: from uprising to intervention in the Solomon Islands*, Victoria University Press, Wellington.

Griffiths, A., 1977. *Fire in the Islands! The acts of the Holy Spirit in the Solomons*, Harold Shaw, Wheaton, Illinois.

Hilliard, D., 1960. 'The South Sea Evangelical Mission in the Solomon Islands: the foundation years', *Journal of Pacific History*, 4:41–64.

Herzfeld, M., 2005. *Cultural Intimacy: social poetics in the nation-state*, Second Edition, Routledge, New York and London.

Hess, T., 2003a. *God's Abrahamic Covenants with Israel—Biblical Road Map of Reconciliation: restoring the altars, foundations, and pillars—the mountains of Israel*, Progressive Vision International, Jerusalem.

———, 2003b. *Sons of Abraham: worshipping God together as a blessing on the Earth*, Progressive Vision International, Jerusalem.

International Prayer Council (IPC), n.d. http://www.ipcprayer.org/mission.html

Kabutaulaka, T.T., 2006. 'Melanesia in review—issues and events 2005: Solomon Islands', *The Contemporary Pacific*, 18(2):423–30.

Keesing, R., 1992. *Custom and Confrontation: the Kwaio struggle for cultural autonomy*, University of Chicago Press, Chicago and London.

Lattas, A., 1998. *Cultures of Secrecy: reinventing race in bush Kaliai cargo cults*, University of Wisconsin Press, Madison.

Le Roy, K., 2004. *Comparative constitutionalism: establishing legitimacy and understanding the options of federalism*, Discussion Paper, based on a presentation made at the University of the South Pacific, Suva, 15 November.

Maeliau, M., 1987. 'Searching for a Melanesian way of worship', in G.W. Trompf (ed.), *Black Theologies from the South Pacific*, Orbis Books, Maryknoll, NewYork:119–27.

——, 1998. *The Deep-Sea Canoe Vision*, End Time Prophetic Vision. Available from http://www.etpv.org/1998/seacanoe.html (accessed 19 June 2006).

Moore, C., 2004. *Happy Isles in Crisis: the historical causes for a failing state in Solomon Islands, 1998–2004*, Asia Pacific Press, The Australian National University, Canberra.

——, 2005. 'The RAMSI intervention in the Solomon Islands crisis', *The Journal of Pacific Studies*, 28(1):56–77.

Otto, T. and Pedersen, P., 2005. 'Disentangling traditions: culture, agency and power', in T. Otto and P. Pedersen (eds), *Tradition and Agency: tracing cultural continuity and invention*, Aarhus University Press, Aarhus:11–49.

Palmer, A.R., 2005. 'Foreword', in K.F. Sanga and K.D. Walker, *Apem Moa: Solomon Islands leadership*, He Parekerekere, Institute for Research and Development in Maori and Pacific Education, Victoria University, Wellington:3–4.

Robbins, J., 2005. 'The humiliations of sin: Christianity and the modernization of the subject among the Urapmin', in J. Robbins and H. Wardlow (eds), *The Making of Global and Local Modernities in Melanesia: humiliation, transformation and the nature of cultural change*, Ashgate, Hampshire:43–56.

Scott, M., 2005. '"I Was Like Abraham": notes on the anthropology of Christianity from the Solomon Islands', *Ethnos*, 70(1):101–25.

Solomon Star, 2005. 'An observer', *Solomon Star*, 22 February.

Strathern, A. and Stewart, P.J., 2004. *Empowering the Past, Confronting the Future: the Duna people of Papua New Guinea*, Palgrave Macmillan, NewYork.

Tippett, Alan R., 1994. *The Deep-Sea Canoe: Stories of the Spread of the Gospel by South Pacific Island Missionaries*, Christian Books Melanesia, Wewak.

Weir, C., 2000. 'The churches in Solomon Islands and Fiji: responses to the crises of 2000', *Development Bulletin*, 53:49–52.

White, G.M., 1991. *Identity through history: living stories in a Solomon Islands society*, Cambridge Studies in Social and Cultural Anthropology, 83, Cambridge University Press, Cambridge.

# Chapter 9

## The coup nobody noticed: the Solomon Islands Western State Movement in 2000

Ian Scales

The most significant political consequence of the conflict in Solomon Islands between 1998 and 2000 was the widespread shift in thinking towards a federal system of government. This chapter argues that long-held political aspirations for greater independence in the resource-rich Western Province were reactivated in a milieu of ethnic tension in the west, and that Western Province politicians used the visionless Malaitan coup in Honiara as a springboard for a calculated push towards their own enhanced fiscal autonomy through advocacy of a federal system. Although the west was the only region likely to increase its wealth from the kind of federalism reforms it proposed, most other provinces (after the collapse of the central government) adopted the west's well-articulated agenda. The outstanding success of the west in trumping all other parties, effectively gaining control of the negotiation on the redistribution of state power, and the lack of attention this drew, can only be admired. It was the coup nobody noticed.

Solomon Islands' political geography is inhabited by three heavyweight players: Malaita, Guadalcanal and Western Province. Popular commentary on the 1998–2000 armed conflict in Solomon Islands has understandably focused on the conflict over Guadalcanal land between groups associated with Malaita and Guadalcanal. This chapter takes a different focus, seeking to understand the outcome of a second, less bloody, conflict which erupted in the west and escaped international attention. This focus derives from first hand observation of events as they unfolded in the west during 1999–2000, when I was based on the Western Province island of Kolombangara.

Conflict in the west, beginning in 1998, resonated initially with that on Guadalcanal by centring on local resentment of Malaitan settlement in the province, but it transformed in a way that did not occur in Guadalcanal. Direct conflict between Malaitan and western youths subsided as western political leaders set their sights on an overarching and long-desired goal: wresting control of resources from the national government. Politicians in the west sought to revitalise the old regional autonomy movement, which had been mostly dormant since Solomon Islands gained independence in 1978. Their focus on wealth was consistent with the prevailing policy discourse in Solomon Islands, which had always been about development. As early as 1893, a main justification for establishing the colonial protectorate—the first form of state in Solomon Islands—was the self-serving proposal that development would pay for the protectorate's administration (Heath 1974; Bennett 1987). After independence, successive national and provincial governments launched development plan after development plan, while political candidates for national constituency and provincial ward seats invariably campaigned on development as the main issue. For voters in the west, development has meant largely service delivery, especially health, education and transport, and questions concerning its funding from the abundant land and sea resources of the province.

The customary landowning groups to which almost every westerner belongs hold most of these resources. These groups themselves are organised, for the purposes of major resource development of their forests and reefs, under leadership of 'landowners', who are often entrepreneurially inclined. Western people have also been successful in past decades in developing a large, well-educated professional force of development-oriented government officials and business entrepreneurs, some of whom are landowners in their own right, while others are allied with landowners in a common spirit of development. Often, however, all the talk of development has seemed to go nowhere. Development plans gathered dust, parties argued and donor partner schemes came and went. This, and certain grievances against the national government, built up frustration with development.[1]

Calls for greater regional autonomy have come from the western Solomon Islands since the lead up to independence. Westerners have seen the centralised state as taking too much of their resources without delivering sufficient services in return. They have long wanted to develop the resources themselves and use the profits to provide services more directly. After a thwarted pre-independence proposal by the Western Council in 1975 that a federal structure be adopted for the coming nation—and a flurry of activity around a Western secession movement on the eve of national independence (Premdas et al. 1983; Dureau 1998)—the issue largely disappeared from the formal political agenda for many years, although it was aired during successive reviews of the provincial government system.[2] From 1998, the Malaita–Guadalcanal conflict reignited the issues behind the autonomy movement. Concurrently, the national government concluded a long-running review of the provincial government system with a proposal to remove the provincial tier of government. In 2000, this combination of events propelled western political leaders to make a call (coinciding with the June *coup d'état*) for a federal system of government granting the west much greater autonomy.

Ethnicity played a greatly overt role in the 1998–2000 national conflict, including the way it played out in the west. Ultimately, however—as far as western interests were concerned—the conflict was based on the underlying economic relationship between the nation-state and the western people, particularly powerful landowners. The 1998–2000 conflict in the west began with ethnic violence, but was quickly channelled away from a specific conflict with Malaitans and propelled into a direct contestation with the national government over its failure to serve landowners' interests.

## Inequality between the provinces of Solomon Islands

Solomon Islands has nine rural provinces plus Honiara, which is statutorily a town council separate from Guadalcanal. Production from primary resources is almost the nation's sole means for earning money from exports. During the mid 1990s, logging made up about half of exports and fishing about one-quarter in dollar terms.[3] The resources contributing to this export revenue were distributed unevenly among the provinces in the pre-crisis period. Western Province provided 51 per cent of all log exports during 1995–96, Guadalcanal, Choiseul and Isabel contributed 10–12 per cent each, Malaita contributed just 6 per cent, and the others even less. As for fish exports, offshore joint-venture vessels took most of the catch, but among local players, Solomon Taiyo Limited in Western Province was the largest, taking 29 per cent of the 1998 catch.[4] During the 1990s, Solomon Taiyo's Noro-based cannery and fishing fleet was also the largest employer in the country other than government (Bank of Hawai'i 1994; Aqorau 2001). By the late 1990s, prospectors had located viable gold and copper deposits in Western Province, particularly in Vangunu. To the extent that tax revenue was collected and used for public goods, the Solomon Islands government used western resources to subsidise poorer provinces although, as a later analysis showed, of all available recurrent public revenue, only about 30 per cent went to the provinces anyway, the other 70 per cent being consumed in Honiara by central government and the town council (Schindowski 2004).

While resources are concentrated in some provinces, population is concentrated in others. Western Province's rich resource endowment is coupled with moderate population, while elsewhere—particularly in Malaita—high population is mismatched with poor export resources. Malaita had 30 per cent of the nation's population in 1999, while Guadalcanal and Western provinces had 15 per cent each. All provinces in Solomons are feeling pressure on land-tenure systems due to high population growth. From 1970 to 1999, the country's population grew 254 per cent (Solomon Islands Government 2002a, 2002b:8–11). Since the 1980s, land pressure has fuelled conflict throughout Solomon Islands—notably that created by the diaspora of Malaitans, with some ending up in 'New Mala' settlements located on old plantations and unoccupied customary land dotted around the country.

Apart from these land pressures, there have been underlying resentments, differing in each province, that the national government does not allocate treasury resources properly according to, variously, province of revenue origin or population size or cost of service delivery. Therefore, people in the west think they are being bled because their forest and fishery resources provide the majority of national revenue, but in their view they receive an inadequate return. The people of Malaita believe that they do not receive funds commensurate with their population size and people in Temotu (the most remote province) think they have been forgotten when it comes to services.

In the lead up to independence in 1978, Solomon Islanders representing rural interests challenged the presumption in Honiara that the central government should control the resources of the proposed new provinces. The old British Solomon Islands Protectorate's Western District—which was to become Western Province—instead proposed declaring its own national independence. In August 1977, a motion was moved in the legislative assembly that the central government 'amicably agree' to the west becoming a separate nation (News Drum 1977). The political situation in the west precipitated a crisis for the government, with a 'breakaway movement' developing, which led to Western Province boycotting Solomon Islands' independence celebrations, although it eventually did stop short of declaring its own independence. Western grievances about the distribution of resources and the failure to accommodate western autonomy were then buried, but not forgotten.

## Sub-national identity in the west

The 'west' in common parlance means the islands of the New Georgia Group and Shortlands, with Choiseul either included or named separately. Occasionally, the western end of Isabel (the Kia language area) is also alluded to as part of the western Solomons, but it falls into Isabel Province. The New Georgia Islands and Shortlands are the current members of Western Province, while Choiseul (formerly a part of Western Province) split off into its own province in March 1991.

It is useful to reflect on how, from indigenous viewpoints, the western region had become defined in political terms by 1978. Before colonial rule, the western Solomons—like any other part of island Melanesia—was a chain of small local polities not under any wider form of authority. The British clumped these together under districts, including the Gizo District in 1904 which later formed much of the Western Solomons District, and gradually introduced a geography of governance in terms of sub-districts, districts and the protectorate as a whole.[5]

In 1975, the western submission to the Kausimae Committee on Provincial Government phrased the experience of defining a sub-national identity in terms of historical destiny as follows

[t]ake the formation of the Western Council. The move of the different local government councils in the Western District to form the Western Council was initiated by local leaders with government encouragement. These leaders, through the increased awareness of their people in knowing that the Western District is in fact for them all and not for the Choiseul

man or Marovo man only, came to realize that having one council would be better than having several. So the process of unity gradually grew. Many other factors contributed to the Western Council, but the process of unity and identity has spread from a tribe to a village, to a locality, to a whole island, to a district (Western Council 1975).

The main point here is that tribes and localities saw a common interest in amalgamating the five local councils in the west to form a more powerful identity-based political structure in 1972, the district council (Premdas et al. 1983:167). The effect of the British early on defining a 'Western District' was itself an important factor, because it was through this institution that the people of the west first experienced intimate colonial governance, back in the early 1920s. Coupled with this was the coterminous extent of the Methodist and Seventh-day Adventist missions, which in their early days operated exclusively in the west, adopting the western Solomons languages of Roviana and Marovo respectively as their *lingua franca*. Other parts of Solomon Islands were under different missions, adopting different local languages.

The third major factor in provincial identity is indigenous understanding of pre-protectorate history in terms of kin and custom. At that time, the islands of the western Solomons formed a maritime world of inter-island exchange, conflict and alliance, with little involvement with the east. Local populations in the New Georgia Islands by late frontier times comprised a mixture of people from all the islands of the west under the mantle of various local descent groups, each controlling their own area. This population mix included those intermarried from the New Georgia Islands themselves, as well as those abducted during raids or otherwise trafficked from Choiseul and western Isabel.[6] Therefore, in any modern village in the west, many people can trace their ancestry at great-grandparent level to all parts of the western Solomons, especially Choiseul, New Georgia Islands and western Isabel. At this level, cases of descent from eastern Solomon Islands are very rare. Since colonisation and formation of the nation-state, the borders of the broad cultural area in which western people live have expanded eastwards and there has been more intermarriage between west and east. Even so, the presence now of very large numbers of people in western villages who trace one of their parents to Malaita, Rennell-Bellonese, Guadalcanal or other eastern Solomons origin has little bearing on the sense of separate western identity.

In a more complex sense, the west is also a reference to that which is a general feature of ethnic identity anywhere: a third-person group that acts as a counterpoint in the construction of identity. The nationally powerful Malaitans have figured large as this 'other' to the western sense of identity during most of the post-independence period. The combination of shared kin and customs, the regionally specific colonial district and mission territories and the perceived difference in identity from the eastern Solomons bequeaths a rich set of referents to 'westernness' that can be worked and reworked according to the political needs of the day.

## Colonialism and sub-national geopolitics

Strategically, the crisis in the west hinged predominantly on relations with Bougainville and Malaita as other sub-national entities. Prior formation of attitudes to these entities is a critical factor, and these are now examined briefly in each case.

In early times, the Shortland Islands and southern Bougainville were together known as Sonto by people to their east, and by all accounts had much in common although this unity did not extend to Choiseul or the New Georgia Islands.[7] The Germans and English drew their revised border through the old unity in 1899 (Moore 2003). Bennett (2000) has covered the colonial history of the relations between Bougainville and the western Solomons. Despite bans on cross-border movement, relations of marriage, land inheritance and customary trade were maintained between the people of southern Bougainville and the Shortland Islands throughout the colonial period. In the lead up to independence for Papua New Guinea and Solomon Islands, secessionists in Bougainville and leaders in Shortland Islands canvassed the possibility of Bougainville joining the Solomons (BSI News Sheet 1974; Hannett 1975). This did not eventuate, but it underlined the general sense of affinity.

Expressions of connectedness between Bougainville and the western Solomons resurfaced dramatically during the Bougainville armed conflict of 1989–98, when refugees and casualties flooded into Western Province and received shelter and medical treatment.[8] The Bougainville militants were sustained partly by the supply links to Western Province markets, which in the early to mid 1990s brought invasion and attack on Solomon Islands civilians in Shortlands and Choiseul by the PNG Defence Force as part of its counter-insurgency operations.[9] These events cemented many links of friendship and sympathy between Bougainvilleans and western Solomons people during the 1990s. Even so, whereas other groups from Solomon Islands can migrate permanently to the west, Bougainvilleans cannot. Perhaps because affinity was held at arm's length by the international border, Bougainvilleans are not thought of as imposing, but rather are thought of in positive terms.

In contrast with Bougainville, relations with Malaita are seen as imposed and are portrayed negatively.[10] Of all Solomon Islands ethnic groups coming to the west, Malaitans have historically been the most contentious, with a long history of disharmony between Malaitans and locals. In colonial times, Malaitan plantation labourers came into the west as outsiders. The white plantation bosses thought Malaitans were more suitable labourers than the locals, and recruited them to live and work in labour enclaves separated from the indigenous westerners by space and cultural circumstances. Problems apparently arose early between the two groups in some regions: a district officer's report from 1913 details a fight between Roviana and Malaita youths on Rendova (Solomon Islands National Archives 1913; Bennett 1987:167–91). These enclave labourers remained working throughout the west until World War II, when the plantation days came to an end. Some remnants of Malaitan labour remained on the alienated land of plantations and, from the 1960s, more Malaitan labour came in for logging operations, but very little is known about the demography and history of such Malaitan immigration. By the 1990s, however, Malaitan settlements were dotted around the west, often on the so-called 'alienated land' areas. Title to these has been held by the Crown since colonial times, but often the land has been left dormant. Although all these areas are subject to indigenous claims stemming from various versions of pre-colonial ownership, development by people who regard themselves as the traditional landowners is frustrated by the Crown title. In the ensuing hiatus, Malaitan groups occupied some of these areas. It is resentment over these settlements that sparked conflict in the west in 1998.

Westerners often explain their resentment of Malaitans as being due to Malaitans' aggressive response if their customs are offended—and in some cases their ensuing demands for large sums of compensation money—which is not generally a western Solomons practice. Justly or not, many westerners also perceive thieving and sometimes sexual assault to be a trait of Malaitan settlers. While these are common themes when talking about Malaitans, it is also true that many Malaitans are married into western communities, thereby becoming in-law relatives. Malaitan–western children born to these marriages or through liaisons with western girls 'by the road' are integrated well into western communities and are usually not the target of such comments.

In the 1960s and 1970s, however, when marriages to Malaitans were novel, they led to much argument in villages. This was true on Kolombangara, where several local girls married Malaitan youths from Langalanga Lagoon in the 1960s.[11] Some hold that those marriages were never right, but since that time, the families concerned have matured and become integral to the village and the issue has largely ceased to matter. Integration proved ephemeral as, in Kolombangara and presumably elsewhere in the west, the anti-mixing attitude resurfaced during the 1998–2000 crisis. In some cases, young women were gathered together while their elders exhorted them not to marry Malaitans.[12] In terms of the geopolitics of the crisis, the stage was set by 1998 for the crisis to follow, with a benign, distant (and indebted) affinity to the west and an intertwined, resentful enmity to the east.

## The beginnings of ethnic tension in Western Province

In the east, ethnic conflict between Guadalcanal and Malaita groups—fuelled by Malaitan migration to Guadalcanal—emerged in November 1998 with a spate of violence and a number of demands by Guadalcanal leaders to the national government. In the west, the demands of the Guadalcanal people were heard generally with sympathy. The ethnic conflict on Guadalcanal intensified again in June 1999, when fighting encroached on the outskirts of Honiara and road-blocks isolated the capital from the rural hinterlands. At that time, large numbers of Malaitans were displaced from Guadalcanal rural areas, either camping in town or moving to Malaita or other islands. Guadalcanal people similarly left town for the rural areas. In the panic that swept Honiara, people from other provinces also returned to those provinces. Dinnen (2002), Moore (2004) and Fraenkel (2004) chronicle these events in detail. The flow of people into Western Province in June 1999 was compounded by the usual influx for the mid-year school and college holidays. A common perception (by hearsay if not by observation) was that large numbers of Malaitans were among the influx and were joining relatives in settler camps all across the west. In the same month, ethnic violence also began in Western Province, with reports of houses being burnt along the Noro–Munda Road in New Georgia, in the area known locally as Ziata. Youths around Munda—who had old grievances with Malaitan youths from squatter settlements in the bush in Ziata—apparently began the burnings with the aim of driving the Malaitans away, in much the same way as had occurred on Guadalcanal.

The Noro–Munda area continued to be the main hot spot of ethnic tension in the west. In early March 2000, police intelligence identified two Bougainville men living in Munda, who were alleged to have been collaborating with local men in either restoring World War II guns or producing home-made guns that worked with recovered 1940s ammunition. A number of these guns were distributed locally and, it seems, were connected to Guadalcanal militant activity (Western Province Assembly 2000b). Following a trend beginning to emerge in Solomon Islands, late the next month, the Munda Police Station was raided by 'unknown elements' and eight small-calibre rifles were taken.[13]

## Western political response to the ethnic tension

In June 1999, Clement Base, then Premier of Western Province, used a Solomon Islands Broadcasting Corporation (SIBC) radio interview to state the hard-line position of his province in relation to Malaitan people arriving there as a result of the recent inter-ethnic conflict in Honiara. In response, the western members of the national parliament met in Honiara with concerns that the interview could provoke an attack on Western Province people living in Honiara. Jackson Piasi, MP for Gizo/Kolombangara, made a media statement rebuffing Base's statement, and organised a national parliamentary representation to the premier (Solomon Islands Government 1999a).

The parliamentary committee consisted of Jackson Piasi, Nelson Boso (MP for Western New Georgia/Vonavona) and Job Dudley Tausinga (MP for North New Georgia). They met with the premier and executive of the Western Province government on 25 June 1999. The problem outlined by the premier at this meeting was increased agitation by western landowners over 'settlers' or 'squatters' from Malaita on or near their lands. The perception of many people in the west, he said, was that immigrants who were not rooted by marriage or work were responsible for much violence and theft, particularly around townships. Members of the meeting reported trouble in specific parts of the province, particularly the Munda–Noro region (including Ziata) and Gizo, with trouble also reported from Kolombangara, Ranongga and Rendova. They also identified towns, Temporary Occupation Licence (TOL) areas and old European plantations on alienated lands as being among the main places Malaitan settlers were to be found. The trouble reported had often to do with alleged theft by Malaitans of private or tribal-resource property (such as reef resources or timber), and Malaitan demands for high monetary compensation when wronged (Solomon Islands Government 1999a).

## Munda accord, July 1999

The meeting developed a set of resolutions known as the 'Munda Accord' (Solomon Islands Government 1999a), which more or less proposed further consultations and investigation into the problem by the province and the parliamentary committee. In addition, a set of conclusions to this document expressed guiding sentiments for future action. Among these were

- Western Province wants to restrict the movement of *lius* (unemployed youth) in their Province, especially people from outside their province

- Western Province wants to set down stringent measures against its own people who allow their land to be settled by outsiders

- direct allocation of land other than for the purposes of public interest must be stopped outright in Western Province (Solomon Islands Government 1999a).

In August 1999, the premiers of Malaita and Western provinces co-signed a communiqué on the ethnic tension (Malaita–Western Premiers' Excursion 1999). The premier of Western Province agreed to 'abide by the Munda Accord for a peaceful repatriation of undesirable settlers who have caused pain and suffering to his people'. The most salient of the five points agreed to by the premier of Malaita Province was a call to Malaitans 'not engaged in formal employment, nor in any productive activities and who are staying without proper legal arrangements to voluntarily return to Malaita Province and participate in the development of the Province'. Implementation of the Munda Accord resolutions was slow, but began when members for a new Western Province coordinating committee 'for spill-over effect' were chosen among the Western Province Assembly members at a provincial caucus meeting on 21–22 March 2000 (Western Province Assembly 2000a). As this was occurring, another potentially explosive situation was developing within the national government.

## The provincial government review and the western response

While never completely forgotten, the issues of regionalism were not dealt with decisively by any government in the Solomon Islands in the first 21 years of post-independence politics. The national constitution—drafted before independence—deferred the details of regional governance to a later time, when they could be debated in parliament on the recommendations of a review committee. This became the Kausimae Committee on Provincial Government which released its report in June 1979, 11 months after independence (Solomon Islands Government 1979). The report was equivocal on the issue of regional autonomy, and preferred not to mention the word 'state'. A Provincial Government Act was introduced in 1981, which, importantly, followed Section 106 of the constitution that 'no taxation shall be imposed or altered except by or under an Act of Parliament', limiting the power of the provinces to raise revenue. The act also gave the provinces no powers to make laws affecting trade and commerce with countries neighbouring Solomon Islands. Western aspirations were stymied.

A period of contradictory proposals for reform of the provincial system then followed. These vacillated between a nationalist preference for many local councils under strong central government (no provinces) and a sub-nationalist preference for strong provinces or states with a smaller central government. Sir Peter Kenilorea initiated the Provincial Government Review Committee in 1986, which culminated in its report and a white paper arguing for abolition of the provinces, produced after the new Alebua government had already taken office in December 1986 (Solomon Islands Government 1987, 1988b; Solomon Nius 1988b). Alebua ignored the continuing provincial review in favour of another process, in which he made former prime minister Solomon Mamaloni chairman of a new Constitutional

Review Committee (CRC) in 1987, to look at devolving legislative and revenue-raising power to the provinces (Solomon Islands Government 1988a).[14] Also equivocal in its recommendations, the committee introduced the idea of reforming provincial governments into states with expanded powers. Although the review raised expectations across Solomon Islands that a federal system of government would be introduced, the government changed again in March 1988, one month after the committee delivered its report. Even though Mamaloni had chaired the CRC, his new government chose to defer action on the review's recommendations in favour of minor reforms (Solomon Nius 1989a, 1989b). Then in 1996, Mamaloni—by then heading his third government—revisited the issue of provincial powers in a review of governance in Solomon Islands, passing a new Provincial Government Bill in which the provinces and local area councils were to be scrapped and replaced with provincial councils and area assemblies. Powers to the proposed councils were not increased; indeed, Western and Guadalcanal provinces argued that the reforms effectively diminished powers and the proposed changes were a bid by Mamaloni's government to increase its own power. After a legal challenge by Guadalcanal Province and further appeal by the government, the changes did not proceed because the Mamaloni government was voted out of office and the bill was repealed.[15] The failed bid to abolish the provinces served to sensitise provincial leaders of the late 1990s to apparent central government attempts at increasing its power to the provinces' detriment.

The new Ulufa'alu government elected in 1997 continued to work on provincial government reform as part of its commitment to overall structural reform of the national government and economy. It set up a Provincial Government Review Committee in May 1998, which began its work (after some delay) a year later. This proceeded as the ethnic conflict in Guadalcanal gained momentum, but was set haplessly in pre-conflict terms of reference. The national government completed a draft of the resulting Provincial Government Decentralisation Bill by late January 2000 (Solomon Star 2000b). The bill was due to go before parliament in April 2000 and was a topic of controversy as the government—amid rising ethnic tension—was keeping secret the contents of the bill, although rumours circulated that the legislation would indeed de-institutionalise the provinces.

Meanwhile, the Western provincial government elections were held in December 1999. In early January 2000, the new provincial assembly members elected their premier, Reuben Lilo (Solomon Star 2000a). Lilo was elected on a platform of reform echoing the concerns of the national Solomon Islands Alliance for Change (SIAC) government in Honiara. In his first assembly meeting in late March, Lilo told the members, 'The need is urgent to establish "good" governance and transparency, restoration of financial stability, improving the quality of Provincial staff…and more importantly the development of the private sector'.[16]

His speech clearly expressed tension over the old issue of resources distributed to the province by the national government: '[w]e have been handicapped by the limited areas devolved by the National Government in which to legislate and to collect much needed funds to finance our projects and programs.'[17]

Lilo was the west's man, representing the dominant entrepreneurial interests in the provincial town and among landowners and ordinary villagers. He spoke the language of development that the west liked to hear, and his success depended on how well he could carry it through.

Eventually, in mid March 2000, the draft Decentralisation Bill was sent to the provincial premiers for comment and, coincidentally, Lilo was invited to speak about the provincial government review at a conference in Honiara, where Milner Tozaka—at that time chairman of the review committee—was also making the first public presentation of the results of the review. The new system, Tozaka said, would be a 'two-tier constituency based system', removing the current provincial assembly and executive structures. Constituency Governing Councils (CGCs) would be formed instead, each covering a ward area (there are currently 26 wards in Western Province). A provincial congress made up of the presidents of the CGCs—headed by an elected governor—would coordinate the CGCs within a province while not forming a separate tier of government. The governor would take the place of the current premier and would mediate between the CGCs and the national government (Tozaka 2000).[18]

Various advantages were touted in Tozaka's paper for the new system, including greater grassroots participation in formal politics through the CGCs—whose members were to include chiefs, women and youth representatives—greater public benefit through articulation of provincial-level planning with nationally coordinated service delivery agencies and a more active role for MPs at the provincial level.

Criticism of the proposed system was heavy during the conference session, initially on the grounds that the government kept the bill secret rather than going through a 'green paper' public response stage. Then, led particularly by western Solomon Islanders in the audience, critics said that the proposal would lead to central government control with weak sub-national representation. The first critique from the audience came from Warren Paia—a successful Honiara businessman, influential civil servant and powerful Roviana landowner—followed by Tony Hughes, a former Central Bank governor now based in the west, who called the plan stupid. In his own response Lilo, while noting the national government's fault in not providing him with the document early enough for him to read it thoroughly, rebutted the proposed system as being the antithesis of regional autonomy, which he stressed was the wish of people in the west.

Lilo returned to the west concerned about the contents of the proposed bill. In response to the news the provincial assembly, which met a few days later, passed a motion calling for Western Province to attain statehood under a federal government system by 2005. The main rationale given for the motion by the member tabling it, Thornley Hite, was that the annual grant from the national government, on which the province based most of its budget, was insufficient to maintain provincial services. At the same time, the province had few powers to raise revenue itself. He raised the old theme that relative to other provinces, westerners 'produce more but receive less'. The discussion before passing this motion expressed sentiments that this was a long-awaited motion. The premier noted that, according to his reading of the Provincial Government Review Committee report, a number of submissions from other provinces had called for a federal system.[19] An interesting reflection by one member was that the issue of autonomy had been hard to raise since the separation of Choiseul from Western Province. As it was, the motion before the assembly included a clause for a new 'federal statehood' working committee to look into the re-amalgamation of Choiseul and Western provinces as one state.

## Western leaders' communiqué, April 2000

Coming out of the assembly meeting, Lilo set a joint meeting for the provincial and national political representatives to form a Western Province response to the issue (Western Province Assembly 2000a). The Western

Leaders' Consultative Meeting occurred in Gizo in early April, two weeks after the Honiara conference. It was attended by western politicians in national and provincial seats, provincial business professionals, town business leaders and a number of landowners from nearby islands (Western Leaders' Consultative Meeting 2000a).[20]

The Western Leaders' Consultative Meeting (2000b), which began the following week, developed a set of resolutions for delivery to the national government. The preamble noted that 'the way forward economically and politically lies in greater political and economic autonomy of the Province' and 'real and sustainable development can only occur in an environment of peace and security as well as in the ownership and control of all natural resources in the Province'. Following on from this, the crux of the resolutions were that

- a substantial portion of the revenue generated in the Western Province be retained in the Province and relevant legislation be amended accordingly.
- security issues should be addressed immediately in line with the Munda Accord.
- the National Government with immediate effect prepare the Province for the attainment of State Government by 2005, and that it should reconsider the implementation of the proposed Provincial Government Bill.
- the National Government immediately transfer all alienated land and other government assets to the government and people of Western Province (Western Leaders' Consultative Meeting 2000b).

The resolution also included a number of demands relating to economic development in the province, including building an international airport at Munda and implementing other provincial development projects previously agreed to, but never enacted, by the national government.

A second Western Leaders' Consultative Meeting occurred in late May. The call for a federal state government system was reiterated. In order to develop a constitution for the new state entity and to report the desired changes to the national constitution, this meeting established a task force for statehood that was to report by September 2000. Comments at the meeting made clear that security was deteriorating in Solomon Islands, with the police virtually incapable of operating independently. Another result of the meeting was initiation of a Western Province Security Council, membership of which included the police commander, Aloysius Ora; the premier; Jackson Piasi, MP for Gizo/Kolombangara; and Albert Laore, MP for Shortlands. They were to set up a plan that included recruiting a Western Province constabulary and put in place a 'security consultative arrangement' (Western Leaders' Consultative Meeting 2000c).

## Sub-national geopolitics and the 5 June 2000 take-over

On the same weekend as the leaders' meeting, a notice signed by 'Black Shark' appeared around Gizo telling Malaitans they had three weeks to get out of Western Province.[21] There was considerable speculation as to who posted it. One theory was that a Malaitan, John Fo'ogau—pictured a few days later on the front page of the *Solomon Star* in a Malaita Eagle Force (MEF) unit, holding an automatic weapon—posted the notice in order to destabilise the situation. Another theory had it posted by the Black Shark armed combatant group from southern Bougainville, who allegedly shot dead one of Fo'ogau's men soon after. This group was referred to also as 'Spear'.[22] Later allegations suggested Black Shark posted the notice in an effort to create a situation in which the province would contract the group to provide security.[23] The conflicting rumours flying around Gizo as to which outside force was to blame indicated how quickly things were becoming confused. The notice had a dramatic effect. Police were dispatched to various centres in the west, including Ringgi on Kolombangara, requesting people not to spread unsubstantiated rumours or exaggerated stories about anti-Malaitan activities. Their fear was that the MEF or other Malaitans in Honiara would hear those stories and retaliate against western people in the capital.[24]

Some days after the second leaders' meeting, the police armoury at Rove was overrun and Andrew Nori announced that the MEF and the joint operations force had 'declared war' against Guadalcanal's Isatabu Freedom Movement (IFM) (Nori 2000). This was the 5 June coup. By this time, various Bougainvillean combatant leaders had arrived in Western Province for negotiations. Ishmael Toroama, a Bougainville Revolutionary Army (BRA) commander from Central Bougainville, was in the area to provide security to one of the SIAC government MPs who had returned home from Honiara after receiving threats. Others, said to be from a southern Bougainville

BRA faction led by Cornelius Solomon, were in the Munda area.[25] The combatants from Bougainville were battle hardened, fully armed guerrilla soldiers who had been active fighters in the Bougainville insurgency against PNG Defence Force troops.

In the early morning of Sunday 11 June, a contingent of about 37 well-armed Bougainville men, accompanied by some western Solomon Islanders, arrived in Gizo by canoe. Most of these combatants were from southern Bougainville. They announced publicly their intention to protect Western Province in the case of any insurgency by Malaitans or attempt by the MEF to take over the provincial town. On the same day, Bougainville militants raided the police armoury in the Choiseul provincial town on Taro Island.[26] Their arrival in Gizo had at least the tacit support of the Western Province government and the police in Gizo. While not stated as such, this appeared to be part of the 'security consultative arrangement' mentioned in the western leaders' meeting of late May.[27]

A few days of mayhem followed. There was a general fear that the MEF would sweep in, take control of Gizo and thence the west. Some of the Bougainvillean combatants, who materialised suddenly, visited a house in Gizo looking for MEF sympathisers and their weapons, and shot a youth who was said to have produced a pistol (see, for example, SIBC 2000a). Simultaneously, some youths in Dunde, Roviana, ran amok, brandished 'home guns' (home-made light firearms), took outboard motors and demanded that people hand over their *kurukuru* (pigeon-shooting) guns. Bougainvillean combatants suppressed this group.[28] Meanwhile, the general secretary of the BRA, Robinson Asotau, issued a press statement that denied BRA involvement in the Gizo shooting, but said that a man from Buin (south Bougainville) was involved (SIBC 2000a). The president of the Bougainville People's Congress, Joseph Kabui, also denied BRA involvement in the Gizo events (Solomon Star 2000d). In any case, a large army of Bougainvillean counter-insurgents dressed in 'Rambo'-style, motley combat fatigues had occupied Gizo. More armed combatants in 21-foot Yamaha boats—a hallmark of the BRA—were patrolling the waters around the islands every night. '*Mae karangge nius*' (rumours) of an imminent MEF insurgency abounded in the townships and villages of the west.

Malaitans continued to leave the west in the face of threats to their safety. About 50 left the alienated land area of Kolombangara, while many left from the Koqulavata and Fishing Village areas in Gizo. Two months later, the Malaitan premier, David Oeta, claimed 500 Malaitans had fled the west (SIBC 2000i). It is difficult to determine the accuracy of that figure, but my impression is that most who fled did so during June. The outflow of Malaitans was matched by an inflow of westerners and their luggage from Honiara to Gizo and elsewhere in the province. Gizo began filling with taxis relocated from Honiara. Although people had been moving to the west for months as a result of the general unrest—a phenomenon seen first in June 1999—a new incentive for relocating was fear of reprisal attacks by Malaitans on western people in Honiara, for these had begun. A Malaitan church leader exacerbated tensions by declaring publicly later in June that Malaitans were being harassed to move. The premier desperately denied in the media 'that Malaitans leaving Western Province have been displaced due to threats from people of Western Province' (Solomon Star 2000f; SIBC 2000c). In Gizo town itself, an uneasy calm settled under the Bougainvillean 'assistance mission'. Talk turned to the question of 'what next'?

## Gaining the upper hand: the western state declaration under arms

The take-over of the central government apparatus in Honiara by Malaitan forces projected the ethnic dimension of the conflict holus-bolus into an issue of who should control the nation-state. The powerful underlying Malaitan 'labour' agendas stemming from their own long history of contest with the central government, notably including the Ma'asina Rule Movement of the 1940s (Laracy 1983; see also Moore 2007), confronted the western 'natural resources' agendas. On Monday 26 June, executives of Choiseul and Western provinces sat in a joint meeting and decided to declare on national Independence Day (7 July) their intention to form a joint, federal-style state government (Solomon Star 2000e; SIBC 2000b). This was the cementing of the Western and Choiseul province forces mooted back in the March provincial assembly meeting as necessary to invigorate fully the long-quiescent federal statehood agenda, which had been discussed in private ever since the MEF take-over of Honiara earlier that month.

It was well understood that to become a state within a continuing nation, there would still need to be a process of constitutional and legislative change by the national parliament. Nevertheless, for many, the nuance of an 'intention' to declare a state within a federation was too fine, and even the title of Lilo's public speech on national Independence Day was 'on the occasion of declaration of State Government in the region' (Lilo 2000a). The decision to advance the pace of the movement by the declaration reflected the growing currency of more radical views among the political community in and around Gizo. Despite his declaration, Lilo's opposition described him as too moderate. There was a mood of 'to hell with the national government' which, after the announcement in early July of Manasseh Sogavare (from Choiseul) as new prime minister and his new cabinet, many thought of as no more than a puppet regime of the MEF.[29] This was because the Ulufa'alu government had been deposed and the new government had come into office without election. With BRA militants in the background, Lilo expressed in his Independence Day speech the 'inalienable right' of Western and Choiseul provincial peoples to 'remove any threat' that 'interfered with' the ideals of peace and freedom, and to 'confirm...our very existence as a people, and our resources and other indigenous rights, as opposed to our constitutional rights and obligations'. Lilo stopped just short of an unambiguous unilateral declaration of statehood within a federation, saying instead

> That from this day on, we the people of Western Solomons do hereby renew our commitment to achieving State Government...
>
> We raise our flag today in recognition of our sincere and noble desire to have
>
> * Autonomy
> * Indigenised democracy
> * Rule of law
> * Legislative powers over our own resources and in the conduct of governance in the State of Western Solomons (Lilo 2000a).

Calls of 'God bless the state of Western Solomons' and 'God bless the sovereignty of Solomon Islands' followed and, despite the careful wording, a new State of Western Solomons flag was raised (Solomon Star 2000h). After this, 'State of Western Solomons' letterhead was used on official correspondence. The flag and the letterhead were further triumphs for those who wanted quick action on the issue.

Lawlessness in the west appeared to be rising during July. All banks in Gizo had closed due to an armed robbery, then a Solomon Taiyo fishing vessel was hijacked and a rest-house at Noro was held up (Solomon Star 2000i, 2000j; SIBC 2000f, 2000h). This in turn justified for many people the premier's position in his 7 July speech (and earlier) that the west should take care of its own security measures. Honiara, however, criticised this policy as illegal. Matters did not rest there. In response to the drying up of national funds to the provinces, Lilo then signed a memorandum on 2 August instructing the Gizo sub-treasurer of the Ministry of Finance to redirect all payments made by the public straight to the 'state treasurer'. These funds, he said, would be taken by the state government and used according to the provincial budget allocations already published in the national government's *Approved Recurrent Estimates* for 2000 and the other budget papers approved by the parliament (Lilo 2000b).

The national government showed consternation at this early declaration of western statehood. The Minister for Provincial Government, Nathaniel Waena, made a public statement later in the month that all provinces were still operating under the national constitution and the Provincial Government Act and that none had become a state (SIBC 2000g). Nonetheless, Waena and Sogavare took the statehood issue seriously, unlike Ulufa'alu before his house arrest. On Independence Day, Sogavare had mooted publicly the possibility of a shift to a state government system (SIBC 2000e). Waena organised the Solomon Islands government 'peace delegation' to Western Province to hold discussions in various places in the west, and visited Shortlands, Choiseul, Gizo, Noro, Munda and Marovo during mid August (SIBC 2000j).[30] Waena pronounced during the delegation's Gizo public meeting that 'the nation has got to a point of no return. The question is how to prepare the nation for a federal system of government or state government.' He and his official mentioned that a premiers' conference was planned for mid October to 'divide powers'.[31] By August, pressure had begun from most other provinces for a greater degree of decentralisation. Temotu began to negotiate separate trade and shipping arrangements with neighbouring Vanuatu, based on Temotu having not been part of the 1893 British protectorate; Makira-Ulawa wanted to become an independent nation; Isabel remembered that it had been German territory until the late 1890s; and Polynesian outliers Rennell-Bellona began preparing a constitution to become a state within a federal system. Even small Central Islands Province demanded more autonomous relations with the national government (Moore 2004:156–60).

During the whole period since the May leaders' meeting, four western state task forces—political and legislative, economics and commerce, human resources development and security—had been busy. Taking up a large, well-resourced office in Gizo, and engaging in many evening discussions in rooms of the Gizo Hotel, the most active members even created a multi-issue newsletter, *The Prunsvick*, between September and October, the title a reference to the Prunsvick Association of the 1978 Western Breakaway Movement (Premdas et al. 1983:54). A key reference document for the political and legislative task force was the 1987 *Constitutional Review Committee Report*, with its federalism recommendations. In mid October, the western state task forces presented their findings to the last of the Joint Leaders' Meetings, two days after the Townsville Peace Agreement (TPA) was signed by the MEF and IFM leaders, the prime minister and the provincial premiers, including Lilo. The great topic of the leaders' meeting, which was full to overflowing with members of the public, was the new western state's development plans. With the audience in high excitement, speakers bandied wild talk of millions in newly allocated foreign funds. The TPA had, however, included an agreement to halt unconstitutional action on state government pending a full constitutional review of a new prospective federal system. News of this filtered back, taking heat out of the movement just as expectations appeared to go beyond reasonable bounds. The threat of MEF incursion, which was looking unlikely by this stage, was also contained.

## The national government's response to the crisis

Under the TPA of mid October 2000, the Solomon Islands government was mandated to introduce a form of government that would give more autonomy to the provinces. As a first step, the government organised a week-long premiers' conference in Buala in mid November (Premiers' Millennium Conference Buala 2000a). Several reports were prepared for this conference, dealing with the legal and administrative requirements for the proposed changes, levels of provincial funding and a report on the provincial governments' own submissions (Saunana and Faluaburu 2000; Solomon Islands Government 2000; Teutao and Tuhaika 2000; Sore et al. 2000). It was noted that almost all provinces had commented on the need to devolve more legislative powers and functions, and provide extended powers of taxation and revenue raising and freedom to source their own funds. Among the most important of the background papers were the comprehensive western state government task force reports. At the conference's end, the premiers resolved that the national government adopt a 'Homegrown State System of Government for Solomon Islands whereby each respective province should become a State with its own State Constitution', and that the national constitution should be amended accordingly (Premiers' Millennium Conference Buala 2000b).

In response, Sogavare's national Peace, Reconciliation and Unity government set up a task force to revisit the constitutional review of 1987. In working through these issues, the task force developed a draft Constitution Amendment (Creation of the Federation) Bill in July 2001, along with budget estimates for the state government system (Solomon Islands Government 2001a, 2001b). The main proposals were presented a couple of months earlier in the *Report of the State Government Taskforce*. These proposals were largely an amalgam of recommendations from the 1987 *Constitutional Review Committee Report* and the 1999 *Report of the Provincial Government Review Committee*. Many of the Western Province demands were met. These, all of them important, gave many concessions to the powerful landowner–entrepreneur factions that had been at the forefront of western demands. Among the proposals were the following key reforms

- establishment of a federal republic of Solomon Islands
- state constitutions to be formed with strong legislative powers
- customary landowners to receive rights to all minerals in their land and to have unregulated rights over their land and resources
- alienated lands to be returned to traditional landowners unless excised for specific purposes (such as land for state headquarters)
- financial power to be devolved, including a provision that taxes can be raised and kept by the states
- states to share primary produce export levies with the federal government, and a finance council consisting of state premiers and national cabinet ministers to share other federal funds with the states.

The west gained all its key demands for control of its resources and revenue. In this way the bulk of recommendations suited the resource-rich provinces, notably Western and Choiseul. For the resource-poor but labour-strong Malaita, the recommendations did not support the inter-provincial labour migration on which many Malaitans depend.

Subsequently, consultations facilitated by the United Nations Development Programme (UNDP) were held throughout the nation and a draft federal constitution was prepared. The government of Sir Allan Kemakeza made slow progress and lost office before introducing the bill in 2006 as promised.[32] The draft was, however, discussed in parliament in December 2005, resulting in the instruction for the drafting process to continue. The incoming Grand Coalition for Change government under Sogavare proceeded cautiously by commissioning an audit of the draft constitution, but indicated in its policy framework of May (2006; see also Solomon Star 2006) that it regarded the reforms as a 'pressing issue' and it would 'pursue the adoption of a federal constitution forthwith' as part of its 'bottom-up approach'.

The draft federal constitution in its current form mirrors substantially the 2001 bill for the creation of a federation, in which the demands of western landowners and their entrepreneurial allies were largely met. At this point, it appears that the decades-old western struggle against Solomon Islands' central state has come into the field from behind and won hands down against the players fighting the bloody and ultimately pointless Guadalcanal conflict in the main arena of the 1998–2000 conflict. There are valid questions as to whether the entrepreneurial landowner interests that favour state government of the federal type proposed are the same interests as those of rural smallholders or those of resource-poor provinces. It has become a matter of faith, however, among Solomon Islanders that federalism of the type formulated by the western state task force during 2000 is the only alternative to the current form of national government. The few challenges and alternatives to this model have been left unheeded or disparaged by Solomon Islanders, who see in any of these only an attempt to subvert hard-won gains and reinforce the status quo of strong central government with weak sub-national government (Scales 2005). The belief in a state government system has, if anything, grown stronger in reaction to the views of foreign advisors, who appear to be concerned that the policy is flawed from administrative and economic points of view.[33]

## Conclusion

The west's brief flirtation with ethnic ideologies in 1998–99 was quickly overtaken by revitalisation of the western state movement, with its central goal of reclaiming control of western resources. By advocating sub-national autonomy against the backdrop of a mismanaged central state, the proposals of Western Province politicians in early 2000 struck an emotional chord across Solomon Islands to do with land, development aspirations and identity. These were, however, essentially the calculated, self-interested actions of a small élite group with a self-appointed task to reshape national governance. Perhaps the outcome would have been different if Malaitan politicians had presented their own detailed proposal for state reform, which articulated their best interests with respect to the all-important national geographic balance between natural resource distribution and population, or if any other province had similarly done so. In the event, we can ask if the real coup in Solomon Islands was that by the MEF on 6 June 2000 or if it was that of Western Province landowners, marked by the raising of the State of Western Solomons flag on 7 July 2000.

## Acknowledgments

The author would like to thank the Crawford School of Economics and Government at The Australian National University, Canberra, for support during the writing of this paper.

## Notes

1   For details of development issues in Western Province, see Foale 2001; Hviding 1996; Hviding and Bayliss-Smith 2000; McDougall 2005; as well as Scales 2004.

2   From time to time, breakaway ideas were also mentioned in the national Independence Day speeches in Gizo (see Tausinga 1987).

3   Central Bank of Solomon Islands (2001) and Foreign Exchange Department figures. For example, in 1996, the composition of exports in Solomon Islands dollars was: logs, 56 per cent; fish, 24 per cent; palm oil and kernels, 10 per cent; copra, 4 per cent; cocoa, 3 per cent; and all other exports, 3 per cent.

4   Data in Hand (1999:70–5) gives the share of the total fish catch in 1998 (in metric tonnes) as: Solomon Taiyo Ltd, based in Noro, 35,812; NFD, based in Tulagi, 19,546; various foreign-based joint ventures, 68,376; others, 1,775—making a total of

125,509. Gillett and Lightfoot (2002:Appendix 2, 193ff.), however, give an extended commentary as to difficulties with fisheries data for Solomon Islands in the 1990s.

5   The Western Solomons District was a post-war (April 1944) amalgamation of the Gizo, Shortland and Ysabel Administrative Districts. See District of Western Solomons 1951; also Bennett 1987:398.

6   On slaves sourced from western Isabel, see Jackson 1975.

7   For details, see Scales 2004; also Oliver 1955:17, 295. For mention of Sonto and its location, see Thurnwald (1909:527) and Hocart (1922:95)—the latter of whom says that 'Sonto appears to lie in Bougainville'.

8   The Solomon Islands Red Cross had care centres for Bougainville refugees in Gizo, Taro Island and Guadalcanal, while the Solomon Islands government provided asylum and free health care (see Red Cross 1999).

9   This included the killing of two Solomon Islands civilians in Kariki village about September 1992 (May 1993; Kabutaulaka 1998:40). Also see Office of the Prime Minister 1996; Spriggs 1992.

10  This imposition and negative sentiment is the crux of the argument in Dureau 1998.

11  Silas Bio, Ghatere Village, Kolombangara, personal communication, 1999.

12  I heard at the time that this had occurred in Hunda and Kena villages on Kolombangara in mid 2000.

13  The raid occurred on 26 April (Solomon Star 2000c).

14  For commentary, see Larmour's (1989) review of the report and his later summary— that the CRC was 'conservative, authoritarian and ethnically defensive'—in Larmour (1990). See also Ghai 1990. *Solomon Nius* (1988a) reported the presentation of the report to the prime minister.

15  The Provincial Government Bill 1996 (Pacific Manuscripts Bureau 1292) repealed the Provincial Government Act 1981—and itself was soon repealed by the Provincial Government Act 1997. For expanded treatment of the various reviews until about 1990, see Frazer 1995. For the early 1980s, see the treatment by Larmour (1985). For later developments, see Nanau 2002.

16  'Premier's address to the full assembly—March/April 2000' (Western Province Assembly 2000b).

17  Ibid.

18  I attended this conference. The full report (Solomon Islands Government 1999b) was soon after distributed to the provinces.

19  'Western Provincial Assembly: budget session [2000–01]' (Western Province Assembly 2000b).

20  I attended this and some subsequent leaders' meetings.

21  I did not see a copy of this notice and do not know what the exact wording was. Apparently, it was posted on the night of Sunday 28 May. Other reports say the notice was also posted in Munda and Noro (Fraenkel 2004:88).

22  A corruption of SBIA—the South Bougainville Interim Administration—an organisation that ceased to exist by late 1992 as a result of internal southern Bougainville power

struggles. These had occurred when hard-line pro-Bougainville Revolutionary Army (BRA) elements close to Francis Ona gained ascendancy and a number of SBIA moderates were killed—upon which other moderates joined the PNG Defence Force-aligned Bougainville Resistance Force (BRF). The term 'Spear' (SBIA) perhaps gained currency in western Solomons to describe continual border crossing into Solomon Islands by southern Bougainvilleans involved in fighting in the associated complex, difficult to understand, internal battles in Buin and Siwai during 1991–92. The term Spear continued to circulate in western Solomons well after SBIA disappeared—perhaps in distinction to the 'legitimate' BRA involved in negotiations in Honiara, which had formal links with the Solomon Islands government and whose members were mostly from Central Bougainville (Tony Regan, personal communication, 2007).

23  In a later commentary, Andrew Nori, a leader of the MEF coup in Honiara, claimed Black Shark had formed with the encouragement of the Western provincial government, 'together with some prominent businessmen in Gizo and in the Noro/Munda area', and was joined later by 'criminals and mercenaries from South Bougainville…to provide security for the people of Western Province from any imminent attacks by the MEF' (SIBC 2001). While Black Shark eventually became a code name for the armed groups in Gizo and Munda, it evidently began before the 5 June coup and might or might not have had early backing from the provincial government or other political leaders in the province.

24  Two police officers visited Ringgi on the weekend of 3–4 June with this message.

25  I heard this information at the time. Solomon was a member of BRA from Buin, who in 1997 was listed in BRA documentation (dated 26 December 1997) as the Company Commander, BRA Southern Marine (Tony Regan, personal communication, 2007).

26  This information is partly from rumours I heard while staying on Kolombangara at the time. Fraenkel (2004:88) and Moore (2004:13–14) provide further details based on news reports.

27  Two unrelated people I have spoken to say they have held a copy of the security arrangement document, which they both say was between the Western Province government and BRA militants from Bougainville.

28  Email from (name suppressed), 25 June 2000.

29  Sogavare was declared prime minister on 30 June (SIBC 2000d). Ministers in the new Sogavare government swore their oaths in early July 2000 (Solomon Star 2000g).

30  Waena was Minister for Provincial Government in Mamaloni's second government (March 1989–June 1993)—ironically, responsible for deferring action on the then widely expected federal system proposed in 1988.

31  Meeting notes, 10 August 2000, Gizo. This eventually became the Buala Premiers' Conference.

32  National community consultations were held between January and March 2003. See Solomon Islands Government 2003, 2004; Solomon Star 2005.

33  The most systematic critique is that of the audit commissioned by the Solomon Islands government in August 2006 (Institute of Policy Studies 2007).

# References

Aqorau, T., 2001. 'Sustainable management and development of Solomon Islands fisheries resources', *Pacific Economic Bulletin*, 16(2):120–6.

Bank of Hawai'i, 1994. *An Economic Assessment of Solomon Islands*, July.

Bennett, J.A., 1987. *Wealth of the Solomons: a history of a Pacific archipelago, 1800–1978*, University of Hawai'i Press, Honolulu.

——, 2000. 'Across the Bougainville Strait: commercial interests and colonial rivalry, c.1880–1930', *Journal of Pacific History*, 35:67–82.

BSI News Sheet, 1974. *BSI News Sheet*, (22), 6 December.

Central Bank of Solomon Islands, 2001. *Annual Report 2000*, Central Bank of Solomon Islands, Honiara.

Dinnen, S., 2002. 'Winners and losers: politics and disorder in the Solomon Islands, 2000–2002', *Journal of Pacific History*, 37(3):285–98.

District of Western Solomons, 1951. *District of Western Solomons Annual Report 1951*, BSIP 7/I/DCW 140A, Solomon Islands National Archives, Honiara.

Dureau, C., 1998. 'Decreed affinities: nationhood and the Western Solomons', *Journal of Pacific History*, 33:197–220.

Foale, S., 2001. 'Where's our development', *Asia Pacific Journal of Anthropology*, 2(2):44–67.

Fraenkel, J., 2004. *The Manipulation of Custom: from uprising to intervention in the Solomon Islands*, Victoria University Press, Wellington.

Frazer, I., 1995. 'Decentralisation and the postcolonial state in Solomon Islands', in B.V. Lal and H. Nelson (eds), *Lines Across the Sea: colonial inheritance in the post-colonial Pacific*, Pacific History Association, Brisbane:95–110.

Ghai, Y., 1990. 'Constitutional reviews in Papua New Guinea and Solomon Islands', *The Contemporary Pacific*, 2(2):313–33.

Gillett, R. and Lightfoot, C., 2002. *The Contribution of Fisheries to the Economies of Pacific Island Countries*, Asian Development Bank, Manila.

Grand Coalition for Change Government, 2006. *Policy Framework Document*, May, Honiara.

Hand, T., 1999. *A Review of Fisheries Taxation and Licensing in the Solomon Islands*, Asian Development Bank, Manila.

Hannett, L., 1975. 'The case for Bougainville secession', *Meanjin Quarterly*, 34(3):286–93.

Heath, I.C., 1974. Charles Morris Woodford of the Solomon Islands: a biographical note, 1852–1927, M.Qual. thesis, The Australian National University, Canberra.

Hocart, A.M., 1922. 'The cult of the dead in Eddystone of the Solomons', *Journal of the Royal Anthropological Institute of Great Britain and Ireland*, 52.

Hviding, E. and Bayliss-Smith, T., 2000. *Islands of Rainforest: agroforestry, logging and eco-tourism in Solomon Islands*, Aldershot, Ashgate.

Hviding, E., 1996. *Guardians of Marovo Lagoon: practice, place and politics in maritime Melanesia*, University of Hawai'i Press, Honolulu.

Institute of Policy Studies, 2007. *Report of the constitutional audit of the draft Federal Constitution of Solomon Islands*, Institute of Policy Studies, School of Government, Victoria University, Wellington.

Jackson, K.B., 1975. 'Head-hunting in the Christianization of Bugotu 1861–1900', *Journal of Pacific History*, 10:65–78.

Kabutaulaka, T.T., 1998. *Pacific islands stakeholder participation in development: Solomon Islands*, Pacific Islands Discussion Paper Series, World Bank, Washington, DC.

Laracy, H.M., 1983. *Pacific Protest: the Maasina Rule Movement, Solomon Islands, 1944–1952*, Institute of Pacific Studies, University of the South Pacific, Suva.

Larmour, P., 1985. 'Solomon Islands', in P. Larmour and R. Qalo (eds), *Decentralisation in the South Pacific*, Institute of Pacific Studies, University of the South Pacific, Suva.

——, 1989. 'Book review of *1987 Constitution Review Committee Report*', *The Contemporary Pacific*, 1(1–2):203–5.

——, 1990. 'Ethnicity and decentralisation in Melanesia: a review of the 1980s', *Pacific Viewpoint*, 31(2):10–27.

Lilo, R., 2000a. Speech delivered by the Premier of Western Province, Hon. Reuben Lilo, on the occasion of the declaration of State Government in the region on 7 July, TS.

——, 2000b. Memorandum to Sub-Treasurer Gizo, from Hon. R. Lilo, Premier Western State, 2 August.

Malaita–Western Premiers' Excursion, 1999. Communiqué: the Western Province ethnic tension: Malaita–Western premiers excursion, Three-page document, signed 18 August 1999 by Hon. David Oeta, Premier for Malaita Province, and Hon. Clement Base, Premier for Western Province (Pacific Manuscripts Bureau, 1292).

May, R.J., 1993. *The changing role of the military in Papua New Guinea*, Papers on Strategy and Defence, No. 101, Strategic and Defence Studies Centre, Research School of Pacific and Asian Studies, The Australian National University, Canberra.

McDougall, D., 2005. 'The unintended consequences of clarification: development, disputing, and the dynamics of community in Ranongga, Solomon Islands', *Ethnohistory*, 52(1):81–109.

Moore, C., 2003. *New Guinea: crossing boundaries and history*, University of Hawai'i Press, Honolulu.

——, 2004. *Happy Isles in Crisis: the historical causes for a failing state in Solomon Islands, 1998–2004*, Asia Pacific Press, The Australian National University, Canberra.

——, 2007. 'The misappropriation of Malaitan labour: historical origins of the recent Solomon Islands crisis', *Journal of Pacific History*, 42(2):211–32.

Nanau, G., 2002. 'Uniting the fragments: Solomon Islands constitutional reforms', *Development Bulletin*, 60:17–20.

News Drum, 1977. *News Drum*, 28 August.

Nori, A., 2000. Transcript of radio broadcast by Andrew Nori, SIBC News, 7 June.

Office of the Prime Minister, 1996. *Reports on Border Incursions 1996*, 6 December, Office of the Prime Minister, Honiara.

Oliver, D., 1955. *A Solomon Island Society: kinship and leadership among the Siuai of Bougainville*, Harvard University Press, Cambridge, MA.

Premdas, R., Steeves, J. and Larmour, P., 1983. 'The Western Breakaway Movement', in P. Larmour and S. Tarua (eds), *Solomon Islands Politics*, Institute of Pacific Studies, University of the South Pacific, Suva:164–95.

Premiers' Millennium Conference Buala, 2000a. *Premiers Millennium Conference Buala, Isabel Province: Day 1: Monday 13 November 2000 Proceedings, &c.*, Five volumes (Pacific Manuscripts Bureau, 1292).

——, 2000b. *Communiqué*, 17 November.

Red Cross, 1999. International Federation of Red Cross and Red Crescent Societies. Available from www.ifrc.org/docs/appeals/annual99/013499.pdf.

Saunana, J. and Faluaburu, S., 2000. A report on provincial governments' submissions on the proposed federal system for Solomon Islands, October, Bound reports from the Ministry of Provincial Government and Rural Development, Honiara (Pacific Manuscripts Bureau, 1292).

Scales, I., 2004. The social forest: landowners, development conflict and the state in Solomon Islands, PhD thesis, The Australian National University, Canberra.

——, 2005. 'State and local governance in Solomon Islands: building on existing strengths', *Pacific Economic Bulletin*, 20:140–7.

Schindowski, D., 2004. The implications of the constitutional reform from an economic point of view, TS dated July 2004 for United Nations Development Programme consultancy. Available from www.vanuatu.usp.ac.fj/library/Paclaw/SolomonIslands/SIConstitutionDraftIMP.pdf (accessed September 2005).

Solomon Islands Broadcasting Corporation (SIBC), 2000a. SIBC News, 12 June.

——, 2000b. SIBC News, 26 June.

——, 2000c. SIBC News, 28 June.

——, 2000d. SIBC News, 30 June.

——, 2000e. SIBC News, 6 July.

——, 2000f. SIBC News, 14 July.

——, 2000g. SIBC News, 25 July.

——, 2000h. SIBC News, 27 July.

——, 2000i. SIBC News, 9 August.

——, 2000j. SIBC News, 14 August.

——, 2001. '5th June 2000 in perspective', SIBC, December. Available from www.sibconline.com.sb/Analysis%20archive.asp

Solomon Islands Government, 1979. *Report of Special Committee on Provincial Government, December 1977–May 1979*, Solomon Islands National Parliamentary Paper 14/79 (Pacific Manuscripts Bureau, 1190).

——, 1987. *Report of the Provincial Government Review Committee 1986–1987*, Ministry of Home Affairs and Provincial Government, Honiara.

——, 1988a. *1987 Constitutional Review Committee Report*, Three volumes, Solomon Mamaloni (chair), Honiara.

——, 1988b. *Provincial Government Review White Paper*, Ministry of Home Affairs and Provincial Government, Honiara.

——, 1999a. Western Provincial Headquarters, Gizo: report of the spill-over effect and contingency plan, 15-page document, 5 July (Pacific Manuscripts Bureau, 1292).

——, 1999b. *Report: Provincial Government Review Committee on Provincial Government in Solomon Islands*, November, Department of Provincial Government and Rural Development, Honiara (Pacific Manuscripts Bureau, 1292).

———, 2000. A report outlining the views of the provincial governments on the proposed federal government system for Solomon Islands, Provincial Institutional Strengthening and Development Unit, Honiara.

———, 2001a. *Constitution Amendment (Creation of the Federation) Bill 2001*, July, Ministry of Provincial Government and Rural Development, Honiara.

———, 2001b. *Solomon Islands State Government System Budget*, July, Ministry of Provincial Government and Rural Development, Honiara.

———, 2002a. *Report on the 1999 Population and Housing Census: analysis*, Solomon Islands Government, Honiara.

———, 2002b. *Solomon Islands: human development report 2002, Volume 1: building a nation*, Main Report, Brisbane.

———, 2003. *Summary of the provincial community consultation team reports*, Government of Solomon Islands and UNDP Constitutional Reform Project, SOI/02/003, Honiara, March.

———, 2004. *Draft Federal Constitution of Solomon Islands, 2004*, Government of Solomon Islands, Honiara.

Solomon Islands National Archives (SINA), 1913. 'Report, District Officer, Gizo to Resident Commissioner', 10 January 1913, BSIP 21/1/7, Solomon Islands National Archives, Honiara.

Solomon Nius, 1988a. *Solomon Nius*, 12 February.

———, 1988b. 'Premiers further discuss provincial govt review white paper', *Solomon Nius*, 22 August.

———, 1989a. 'Provincial government to remain says Waena', *Solomon Nius*, 16 May.

———, 1989b. 'Gov't to devolve more powers to provinces—Waena', *Solomon Nius*, 11 August.

Solomon Star, 2000a. 'Premier Lilo appoints new executive govt', *Solomon Star*, 18 January.

———, 2000b. 'Draft law completed', *Solomon Star*, 24 January.

———, 2000c. 'Raid of Munda Police Station', *Solomon Star*, 4 May.

———, 2000d. *Solomon Star*, 14 June.

———, 2000e. *Solomon Star*, 28 June.

———, 2000f. *Solomon Star*, 29 June.

———, 2000g. *Solomon Star*, 3 July.

———, 2000h. *Solomon Star*, 11 July.

———, 2000i. *Solomon Star*, 14 July.

———, 2000j. *Solomon Star*, 27 July.

———, 2005. 'PM says federal system in 2006', *Solomon Star*, 4 March.

———, 2006. 'Grand coalition pursues adopting new constitution', *Solomon Star*, 30 May.

Sore, R., Givoro, B. and Ene, E., 2000. Consultancy on State Government Systems: research on the functions of central government systems (Pacific Manuscripts Bureau, 1292).

Spriggs, M., 1992. 'Bougainville update: May to October 1991', in M. Spriggs and D. Denoon (eds), *The Bougainville Crisis: 1991 update*, Department of Political and Social Change, Research School of Pacific Studies, The Australian National University, Canberra and Crawford House Press, Bathurst:192–5.

Tausinga, J.D., 1987. 'Independence anniversary speech', *Sunset News*, 7(8), August.

Teutao, R. and Tuhaika, J., 2000. The legal requirements for a change from provincial government system to state government system in Solomon Islands and manpower management in the new state/federal government system (Pacific Manuscripts Bureau, 1292).

Thurnwald, R.C., 1909. 'Reisebericht aus Buin und Kieta', *Zeitschrift für Ethnologie*, 41.

Tozaka, M., 2000. Provincial government review, Paper presented to the SICHE–ANU Governance and Economics Update conference, 16–17 March, Honiara (Pacific Manuscripts Bureau, 1292).

Western Council, 1975. *Submission of the Western Council*, Background Paper, No.28, August, Special Committee on Provincial Government, Mimeo. (Pacific Manuscripts Bureau, 1190 as 'SCPG, Background Paper 28').

Western Leaders' Consultative Meeting, 2000a. *Program*, Western Leaders' Consultative Meeting, 3–4 April (Pacific Manuscripts Bureau, 1292).

———, 2000b. *A Joint Communiqué by the Leaders of the Western Province*, 4 April 2000, Western Leaders' Consultative Meeting, Gizo (Pacific Manuscripts Bureau, 1292).

———, 2000c. *Diversity in Unity*, Resolution of the Western Leaders' Consultative Meeting, 31 May (Pacific Manuscripts Bureau, 1292).

Western Province Assembly, 2000a. Minutes of the third caucus meeting of Hon. R. Lilo's government, 21–22 March.

———, 2000b. *Western Provincial Assembly: Budget Session 1999/2000*, Proceedings of the Western Province Assembly meeting, 25 March–3 April (Pacific Manuscripts Bureau, 1292).

.

# Chapter 10
## Crisis in Solomon Islands: foraging for new directions

Transform Aqorau

Solomon Islanders are fed up with the constant politicking and petty bickering of their politicians and the manipulative behaviour of Asian loggers, which has resulted in the corruption of the entire fabric of Solomon Islands society save for the judiciary. Speaking to the former legal adviser to the Department of Forestry recently, I was told that he had grown tired of brown envelopes being handed to him. On one occasion, as he was getting out of his car, a group of Malaysian loggers turned up and—before he could wind the window closed—threw a bundle of neatly folded cash onto the passenger seat. They told him that it was for him to keep. On returning to his office, he told the commissioner, who instructed him to return the money. The legal adviser has since left to work in the Marshall Islands. Just recently, a former government minister (currently a member of the opposition) told me that when he was acting Minister for Mines and Energy, he was asked by a couple of his fellow ministers just before the elections to approve the application of a Chinese prospecting company and they would each be paid SI$50,000. The minister told me that the elections were closing in, and the two ministers said that the money could help their campaign. When I was legal adviser at the Ministry of Foreign Affairs, I received a call from the prime minister asking whether I could assist in developing drafting instructions for a proposed communications bill. I said that I would be willing to help out and he asked whether I wanted to be paid additional money for the service. I said no, since I was a civil servant and was already being paid by the government.

If Solomon Islands is to get anywhere, if it is to prosper, if it is to have a secure future, if it is to have a sustainable future with its people enjoying a standard of living that its natural wealth can generate, it must overcome—first and foremost—the terrible legacy of corruption that has permeated every inch of Solomon Islands society. The corruption that has been spawned largely by Asian logging companies has infiltrated the highest echelons of government and reaches down to the common man on the street. Solomon Islanders have gone berserk over logging, and it is being fuelled largely by the lavish way in which Asian logging companies bribe, cajole and unduly influence Solomon Islanders.

This chapter seeks solutions to the crisis that has beset Solomon Islands. Notwithstanding the presence of the Regional Assistance Mission to Solomon Islands (RAMSI), Solomon Islands still has a long way to go to bring back accountability, transparency and good governance to its institutions. Current conditions of peace and stability are only superficial and there remains deep-seated resentment between former adversaries from Malaita and Guadalcanal. The unfortunate situation in which Asian logging companies have become so powerful is only a small part of the problem. The biggest problems are poverty and social and economic inequities.

This chapter proposes a number of policy options for the Solomon Islands government. These are by no means exhaustive. With the problems that Solomon Islands has experienced, finding solutions has become akin to dragging oneself up from a bottomless pit. The dilemma that the Solomon Islands government faces is where to start: which sector should take priority, should it be education, health, law and order, land review, constitutional restructuring, rural development or provincial government strengthening? The list goes on. This chapter offers some ideas about some areas that can be addressed as a matter of priority. It concludes that Solomon Islands is still foraging for new directions. On the one hand, there is the political rhetoric of Prime Minister Manasseh Sogavare, who often says one thing and does another. On the other hand, there is a lack of resources to do the things that the government wants to do. Solomon Islands is torn between two competing forces: the desire to get on with life, and a lack of resources to establish the basis for this.

## The Asian logging connections

Logging in Solomon Islands has been well established since colonial days. In the beginning, most logging operations took place on government land, therefore there were none of the issues confronting the industry today. Customary land was preserved for Solomon Islanders. The trees and forests on customary land were well conserved and provided Solomon Islanders with a source of building materials, herbal medicine and other traditional needs, which were met from whatever the forests could provide. Tribal communities were largely undivided and the social ills associated with large-scale logging were unknown.

When logging on government land declined in the early 1980s because of reduced numbers of trees, logging companies started to look at gaining access to customary land areas. At the same time, the Government of Malaysia tightened its laws governing the large-scale exploitation of its forests. This compelled Malaysian logging companies to look offshore to supply their clients. Solomon Islands offered ready prey. Cyclone Namu, which hit a large part of Solomon Islands in May 1986, destroyed much of the country's rice and oil-palm plantations. Solomon Islands' economy was hit hard. The government was, therefore, compelled to pursue other forms of economic development activities and large-scale commercial logging provided an easy alternative.

According to Kabutaulaka (2006), between 1980 and 1983, there was a fourfold increase in the number of logging licences issued to foreign companies. One of the problems of the surge in logging is the perception that it delivers real development to ordinary villagers. I have firsthand experience of the devastating social and environmental impacts of logging and have witnessed the manipulation by Asian logging companies, and the ineptitude of Solomon Islands government officials to stand up to the undue influence that logging company officials can exert. Since 2000, I have made my home in Rakutu, Ziata, which is a good two hours' walk from Munda on the south coast of New Georgia. The island of New Georgia has been the site of some of the most extensive logging operations in Solomon Islands' forestry history. Rakutu is situated in the bush along the Munda–Noro road. Noro hosts two important companies providing much-needed revenue for the coffers of the Solomon Islands government: the Soltai Fishing Company and NFD Fishing Company Limited. Unbeknown to me, a timber rights agreement was signed in November 2004 between five trustees—three of whom are closely related to me—and Delta Timber Company to log areas within Kazukuru Left Hand land, including the area where I live. This did not come as a surprise to me because logging is on the minds of almost everyone who has a piece of land. It was, however, saddening because of the inevitable loss of biodiversity in the pristine tropical forest and the fact that people will be poorer, not richer, as a result of logging. Delta is a subsidiary of Earthmovers, one of the largest logging companies in Solomon Islands and owned by Malaysian business interests. Delta Timber Company was established by an employee of Earthmovers and its local consultant, who was also a serving member of parliament at the time of Delta's establishment. The individual concerned is now a minister in the Sogavare government. The association between provincial and national politicians and logging companies makes it very difficult for the government to address the corruption that this industry has caused.

The extraordinary way in which Asian logging companies have permeated almost all levels of Solomon Islands society is illustrated by two cases with which I am acquainted personally. The first is my own futile endeavour to get information from the Department of Forestry and the Western Province government about Delta's operations on Kazukuru Left Hand land. After learning about the agreement, I visited the Forestry Department in Honiara several times and asked to see the relevant file, which would have allowed me to see the terms of the agreement and also see a copy of the licence. The information would have helped inform me about the nature of the operation and determine the legal action I could take against the so-called trustees, the Forestry Department and Delta. I also wrote to the secretary of the Western provincial government to receive confirmation of the minutes of the timber rights hearing, which is required under the Forest Resources and Timber Utilisation Act (Solomon Islands Government 1999:Cap.40).

All my inquiries were, however, in vain and I kept getting all sorts of excuses about the relevant file. I was told that the file was with the commissioner. The next time it was with the minister, and then again it was with the AusAID-funded project personnel. Each time I went to inquire at the forestry department, the file was with someone else, but I was assured that they would find it and make it available. I eventually wrote to the permanent secretary but, like his counterpart in the Western provincial government, he deemed me not worth responding to. I did, however, find out from the assistant administrative officer at Munda (the officer responsible for all administrative matters pertaining to the provincial government at Munda) that no timber rights hearing had been convened at Munda in respect of the timber rights granted to Delta. Section 8 of the Forest Resource and Timber Utilisation Act requires the executive of the provincial government to fix a place within the area of its authority and a date—no earlier than two months and no later than three months from the date of receipt of the copy of the application—for a meeting to be held with the appropriate government, the customary landowners and the applicant. The purpose of the meeting is to determine: whether or not the landowners are willing to negotiate for the disposal of their timber rights to the applicant; whether those proposing to grant the timber rights in question are the people, and represent all the people, lawfully entitled to grant such rights and, if not, who such people are; and the nature and extent of the timber rights, if any, to be granted to the applicant. I was also able to subsequently confirm with the principal forestry officer in charge of the Forestry Research Station at Munda that to the best of his knowledge no timber rights hearing had been convened, as was required by law.

Recently, the premier of Malaita Province called for an investigation into all timber rights hearings for logging operations in Malaita. I can only imagine what such an investigation would reveal. What most logging companies have done is bypass the timber rights hearings and simply negotiate directly with so-called landowners. The Forest Resources and Timber Regulations specify that when a timber company negotiates with a community, it must do so 'with the chosen representatives of the landowners in public' and that the negotiations must take place in the presence not only of the landowner's legal adviser but also of representatives of the province and the Forestry Division. If the two sides agree, the agreement is to be signed in the approved form by 'the Company and not less than 5 representatives chosen by the landowners'. One copy of all such agreements must be deposited with the province and one copy with the Forestry Division within 14 days of being signed (Solomon Islands Government 1999).

While this is required under the regulations, it does not negate the requirement under the act to determine the right of those who can grant timber rights.

The second illustration concerns the influence that logging companies have even over such things as chartering planes for deceased relatives of the trustees. I know of one recent case where relatives who travelled to their home village after the father of a trustee passed away had their costs reimbursed. The company also contributed to the costs of food for those who had gathered in the village for the wake. This same company advanced money to the trustees. Whenever the trustees travel to Honiara, they are put up in hotels. To renovate their church, the trustees advanced money from the company to pay for the renovations. All of these advances are, of course, deducted from the agreed royalty so usually the landowners' proportion paid by the company is far less than what was originally agreed because of the deductions for advances. This story is, of course, repeated everywhere: the same thing happens in every logging concession.

In 1999, the government granted logging company Silvania Ltd permission to establish an oil-palm plantation on government land in Vangunu, New Georgia. Recently, the auditor-general's office issued a scathing report revealing that the oil-palm plantation was merely a disguise to enable the company to log the trees on the land. The company did not have any experience in growing oil palms and had no interest in developing a plantation. This happened under the government of Bartholomew Ulufa'alu.

Solomon Islanders at all levels, from the grass roots right up to the highest echelons of government, have become crazy about logging. It is easy money. The government's reluctance to take drastic measures to address the exploitation of Solomon Islands' forest resources is largely because of its misguided belief that logging contributes significantly to gross domestic product (GDP). It should not be interfered with because that would severely impact on the country's foreign exchange earnings.

> Apart from unsustainable log production, another issue that dominated discussions of the forestry industry was Solomon Islands' economic dependence on log exports. In 1990, logging contributed 34.5 per cent of the country's total exports. This increased to 54.9 per cent in 1993. In 1994, it contributed 56 per cent of the country's export earnings and 31 per cent of all government earnings...In the ten years between 1988 and 1998, timber made up a huge percentage of Solomon Islands' principal exports...From 1992 to 1996, receipts from log exports increased dramatically and dominated total exports. The average value of timber

exports in that period was SI$285.2 million per annum. In 1998, however, there was a dramatic decline in log export receipts: SI$196.3 million as compared to SI$290.7 million in 1997 and an average of SI$285.2 million in the period from 1993 to 1996...The 1997 and 1998 declines were due to the fall in export prices and volume as a result of the continued adverse developments associated with the Asian financial crisis. Despite this decline, the value of log exports was still well above that of other commodities (Kabutaulaka 2007:247).

The behaviour and practices of Asian logging companies have not helped make the situation any better. In a penetrating analysis of how the government and politicians have exacerbated the problem, Tony Hughes (2004) argues

[a]t the same time successive governments were making a famous mess of the arrangements for promoting and monitoring foreign direct investment in [Solomon Islands]. The process was heavily politicised from the start, with ministerial and prime ministerial involvement in interviewing and selection of investors and devising of investment conditions, with some of the more important and personal conditions apparently not being recorded. This long-winded and corruption-prone process has had a deterrent effect on a number of genuine would-be investors, some of whom have made their feelings known in Honiara, and has encouraged some obvious con-artists to try hijacking parts of the economy. Amazing statistics have periodically appeared about the number and value of incoming investments approved, but there has never been any serious attempt to follow [these] up to see what actually happened and publish the information.

The problem is not just how politicians manipulate the system. I also blame the self-interest of Asian logging companies. Just before the prime ministerial election in April 2006, Sean Dorney of Radio Australia interviewed Charles Dausabea, the Member for East Honiara. I heard the interview on Radio Australia. Dorney described Dausabea as a linchpin of Solomon Islands politics. I disagreed and wrote a letter to the *Solomon Star* newspaper (Aqorau 2006). It was aimed largely at the Asian logging companies and their role in making and breaking governments in Solomon Islands. The letter stated in part that

...the real linchpins in Solomon Islands politics are actually unelected. They are already busy manipulating the process, if not explicitly, at least implicitly. The full-page advertisement that appeared in Monday's *Solomon Star* is evident [*sic*] of the undercurrents already at play. There are also some fairly well known power broker(s) lurking in the background somewhere, seemingly oblivious to the situation, but certainly strenuously working in the background to influence next Tuesday's election results. There are possibly some very powerful entities who could potentially lose considerable leverage and advantage also working tirelessly at influencing the outcome so that they can continue to maintain their preferential status. The machinations of their operations are fairly well known. They are not elected and represent only their narrow interests which they will want to pursue through the outcome they are endeavouring to influence. These are the real linchpins and not, with respect, Hon. Charles Dausabea as alluded [to] by the media. With respect, [Dausabea] being himself as everyone who knows him, will lobby, will endeavour to form alliances, will make media statements, and will ostensibly appear as the power broker, but with further respect, his is a spent force, lacking the potency he once yielded, and certainly not as powerful as the unseen forces working in the background (Aqorau 2006).

Solomon Islanders confront many challenges. One of the biggest challenges facing the Sogavare government is restoring public confidence in the light of the total breakdown of government structures, institutions and processes. The Sogavare government has been making the right noises about transparency, good governance and accountability, but so far, Solomon Islanders have not seen any evidence of real progress on this front. Indeed, Sogavare himself has demonstrated dictatorial tendencies. Firstly, he took on the Director of Public Prosecutions (DPP) and accused the DPP and the judiciary of colluding to keep two politicians who were arrested after the April riots in custody longer than necessary. Secondly, he appointed the secretary to cabinet without advertising the position, and advertised for the positions of permanent secretaries but hand-picked them nevertheless. Third, he established a commission of inquiry into the April unrest to be headed by a retired Australian judge, who is himself under investigation. He also included in the terms of reference of the commission an investigation into whether the arrest and prosecution of the two politicians were politically motivated. At the time of writing, he was embroiled in a public disagreement with the attorney-general about the latter's application to the High Court to strike out the two controversial terms of reference relating to the circumstances of the politicians' arrests because the matter was the subject of court proceedings. Prime Minister Sogavare threatened to sack the attorney-general and replace him with a private lawyer from Australia, who is known to have political connections in Solomon Islands. (This is what subsequently occurred. See Chapter 1.) All this talk about good governance is at the moment just that—all talk and no action.

## Foraging for new directions: is there a way forward?

The scenes of rioting in Honiara in April 2006 were broadcast around the world. Now when I meet people and tell them about Solomon Islands, they know where it is because of the publicity the riots received. I listened to the reports on the radio and to analysis from various academics from Australia, New Zealand and Fiji. Funnily enough, there were not as many Solomon Islanders interviewed as there were Australians and New Zealanders.

I have often been bothered by the fact that Solomon Islands is a rich country, yet it is so undeveloped. It is true that being rich in natural resources does not necessarily translate into social and economic wealth; there must be political stability as well as an educated population. I think of the case of Oman, which, 30 years ago, had only three miles of paved road. Today, all its roads are paved. Although its sultan is very wealthy because of his country's oil, he has ensured that his people also improve their social and economic well-being. I have often pondered what could have happened in Solomon Islands.

As legal adviser to the Pacific Islands Forum Secretariat in 2003, I had the unique privilege of attending the forum's foreign affairs ministers' meeting in Sydney on 30 June. It was touching to hear the support and sympathy for Solomon Islands from regional leaders. They had gathered there under the auspices of the Biketawa Declaration, which allowed the forum to lend whatever support was necessary to assist a forum member. RAMSI was born out of this meeting. Having listened to the discussions in Sydney, I viewed RAMSI as the conduit through which Solomon Islanders could rebuild their shattered and war-torn country. The region was giving Solomon Islands a second chance. That opportunity, however, cannot be dependent on RAMSI. The responsibility to rebuild Solomon Islands, to re-establish its institutions and restore confidence in the country rests ultimately with Solomon Islanders. Only Solomon Islanders can rebuild their country.

As I watched and listened to events unfold from Suva, I began to see some worrying trends. These were reconfirmed when I returned to work in Solomon Islands. My major worry was that our political leaders would not use the opportunity afforded by RAMSI to put in place policies that would ensure Solomon Islands did not repeat the problems that resulted in the ethnic tensions. There was an almost total lack of direction as to where the country was heading. I have not changed my views about RAMSI in spite of criticisms about its response—or lack thereof—to the April 2006 riots. In an article on local perspectives of RAMSI, Matthew Allen argues that

> ...the RAMSI of 'state building' and 'nation building' is markedly different to the RAMSI which is seen and interpreted by Solomon Islanders. For the majority of people in Solomon Islands RAMSI means police and soldiers. Moreover, it is widely perceived as an Australian dominated enterprise, composed mostly of Australian security forces which are commanded by Australian officers (Allen 2006:199).

With respect, RAMSI cannot and never will be able to nation build and state build in Solomon Islands; only Solomon Islanders can legitimately and realistically do that. The onus is on Solomon Islanders and not on RAMSI to rebuild Solomon Islands. RAMSI, however, offers Solomon Islanders and its political leaders an easy target to blame for their own failures. I do not want to be construed as an apologist for RAMSI, but Solomon Islanders cannot just sit back, lament and complain about the inequities between their salaries and those received by RAMSI-supported personnel holding line positions without saying openly: this is what we want Solomon Islands to be in 50 years, and we will achieve it with RAMSI's support.

In the period leading up to the April 2006 general elections, I wrote an article that set out some of the critical issues that had to be handled by the incoming government. I wanted a broader readership in Solomon Islands to read my thoughts and I also wanted to participate in a debate about what issues should be addressed by the new government, so I sent the article to the *Solomon Star*. It was never published, so I sent it to *Islands Business* magazine. In the article, I argued that the Kemakeza government had been provided with an environment through the support of RAMSI in which to govern effectively. The two and half year time frame that the Kemakeza government had after the arrival of RAMSI was only long enough, in my view, for it to address governance structures and law and order issues. I argued that if it had attempted to address the underlying social and economic problems that had beset Solomon Islands in the past 27 years, it was not apparent.

The Sogavare government has announced that it will pursue rural development as one of its key policy priorities. Rural development without any infrastructure support to spur it will be hard to achieve. There remain, however, some very serious issues that the government needs to address. I have set these out without making any claim as to whether they are the only issues that need to be addressed. I like to think that Solomon Islands' problems are like falling into a bottomless pit: it is very hard to begin climbing out until you have hit the bottom. This is perhaps Solomon Islands' last opportunity to re-establish itself. The current members of parliament have only the next four years to lay a foundation on which to build Solomon Islands' prosperity.

The omens, however, are not good. Prime Minister Sogavare has already found himself in all sorts of self-inflicted disputes. He has made several contradictory statements, and seems bent on undermining the independence of the three arms of government. Already his government is unstable, with the recent sacking of his Minister for Commerce and former prime minister, Francis Billy Hilly. Six of his ministers have also resigned from the National Party. The signs are fairly ominous that Sogavare's government might not see out its full four-year term. Nonetheless, the challenges facing Solomon Islands remain, irrespective of who is in government. I set these challenges out below, as well as suggesting ways in which Solomon Islands can move forward. So what are some of these challenges? One of the biggest challenges facing Solomon Islands today is overcoming corruption and the influence of Asian logging companies, in particular, the negative influence this has had on the mind-set of ordinary villagers and government officials. The hand-out mentality that it has spawned and the idea that logging is the panacea for Solomon Islands' economic problems needs to be debunked. Solutions are not easy to come by. This is because government ministers, senior public servants, provincial politicians, village chiefs, community leaders, lawyers and ordinary villagers all have a stake in logging.

The other challenges pertain to addressing the underlying causes of the ethnic tension and Solomon Islands' rapid population growth.

## Underlying causes of ethnic tension not addressed

The social, political and economic factors that led to the ethnic tension and quasi-civil war have not been addressed. There should not be any pretence that all is well in Solomon Islands now that law and order has been restored, justice is being delivered and the Gold Ridge mine and oil-palm plantations are being revitalised. There are serious undercurrents simmering and feelings of mistrust that still exist among the former warring parties. If these undercurrents are not addressed, they could easily reignite the tension. It is common knowledge that not all the high-powered guns used in the conflict were collected by RAMSI. The notorious Edmond Sae is still at large and it is alleged that he and others hiding with him still have such weapons. After the rioting and immediately before the convening of parliament at which Sogavare was elected, Honiara was rife with rumours that Sae and his group from the 'bush' were hiding in the settlements on the outskirts of Honiara. Their mission (according to the rumours) was to ensure that Snyder Rini stepped down and to take on the military component of RAMSI. In light of the fact that guns are still in the community, such rumours have the potential to create instability. There are always rumours that once RAMSI leaves, the conflict will start again.

Much has been said about the economy and the confidence brought about by the restoration of law and order. The April riots severely shattered that momentum. Even before the riots, however, things were generally not what they were made out to be. The fire that burnt down the new oil-palm plantation headquarters early in 2006, the calls for greater resource-owner participation in the Gold Ridge mine and the demands for alienated land in Lunga and Tenaru to revert to the original landowners were evidence of the tensions that still existed. The only reason these issues have not resulted in violent confrontation is because of the presence of RAMSI. The proliferation of squatters in Honiara needs to be addressed. One cannot help but notice the exponential growth of unemployed people loitering in the town since the beginning of the year. There are now more squatters in the national capital than there were before the tension. What is more worrying is the encroachment of these squatter settlements on customary land just outside Honiara. Something must be done about rural development. The development of Malaita, in particular, is an important part of the long-term solution of some of the problems facing Solomon Islands. Naturally, because of its larger population and underdevelopment, Malaita supplies a greater proportion of people migrating to Honiara than other islands. This is in no way meant to be an indictment of Malaitans; it is simply stating a fact. What it means for the Sogavare government is that the Auluta oil-palm plantation, the Bina Harbour project and an international runway for Malaita must be pursued with vigour. It also means that land and resource owners from Malaita must be amenable to the idea that if they are to develop, they must allow their resources to be developed. This is true not only for Malaita; it is true for everyone else. It means that approaches to economic development must be different from what they have been in the past 27 years since Solomon Islands gained independence.

## Rapid population growth

Solomon Islands' population continues to grow at an alarming rate. It has one of the highest population growth rates in the world, which has serious implications for society. The effects of rapid population growth are quite visible in the areas of public health and education. Visitors will immediately notice the stench and filth of betel-nut stains and the piles of rubbish outside residential and commercial buildings in Honiara. Solomon Islands' capital provides a good illustration of the public health problems arising from the population explosion. There is generally poor sanitation and drainage, with the dusty and dirty general environment not conducive to healthy living. HIV/AIDS is also another threat that will have to be addressed with greater political vigour than has hitherto been the case. In education, the annual increase in the number of children attending school is obvious. There is overcrowding in schools, which generally are also under-resourced. Such an environment is not conducive to learning. There is also increasing poverty, especially in Honiara. Poverty fuels other social problems, such as petty stealing, ravaging in garbage dumps and prostitution.

It is not possible in a short discussion such as this to describe all the challenges facing Solomon Islands. I have often thought that there are so many challenges that one problem is knowing where to start. The key challenge, of course, is choosing a path that will avoid a repeat of the ethnic tension. Once again, I do not claim to have a monopoly on knowledge about what should be done. The following ideas are simply that—ideas about issues that should receive the government's attention

- establish a royal commission into the ethnic tension
- establish, as a matter of urgency, a commission of inquiry into land matters
- establish an appropriate population policy
- decentralisation of development projects
- raise education standards
- healthy environment
- free the public service of political interference
- address the fluidity of electioneering and politicking
- make it unlawful for members to switch political parties once elected
- introduce limited preferential voting
- make illegal the giving of gifts, money, airfares, assistance and demands for money within six months of an election
- find an alternative way of electing the prime minister
- enhance the role of the media.

**Establish a royal commission into the ethnic tension.** I have always felt that Solomon Islands' political leaders had something to hide, that they wanted memories of the ethnic tension to be swept under the carpet. The danger of such an approach is that we will never really know the full extent of the involvement of various individuals, including national and provincial politicians, and we will never understand fully the reasons for groups taking up arms. How can Solomon Islands be expected to move on without ensuring that the reasons for the ethnic tension have been addressed? The victims of the tension are still calling on the government for compensation. If nothing is done to understand and address the causes of the ethnic tension, it is possible that it will happen again. It is also dangerous to simply forget about it. The nation needs to know who planned and masterminded the ethnic tension. Those who tragically lost their lives should not be nameless victims of violence perpetrated by a few who held the entire nation to ransom. **Establish, as a matter of urgency, a commission of inquiry into land matters.** The outgoing Minister for Lands in the Kemakeza government announced the establishment of a commission of inquiry into land matters, but so far nothing has been done towards the creation of such a commission. Addressing problems of land tenure in Solomon Islands must be among the top priorities of the government. I believe that there is already a class of essentially landless Solomon Islanders. I say so, however, with some qualification, but there are people for whom returning to their ancestral land is no longer an option. This must be recognised. During the ethnic tension, many people were compelled to return to their ancestral land. Some of them had not been back since they were born. Initially, they were welcomed, but many of them were later forced to leave and return to Honiara because—having been away for a long time—their rights to land had diminished. The proliferation of squatters in and around Honiara attests to this. Sadly, many of these settlements are not serviced by proper public utilities—roads, water, electricity and telecommunications—creating a distinct class of citizens in Honiara deprived of the most basic services. The issue of squatters is sensitive and needs to be handled carefully. Having said that, I do not believe the government should shy away from it, hoping that it will just disappear. It won't—and left alone, it could be the trigger for further ethnic tension.

**The need for a population policy.** Solomon Islands' rapid population growth needs to be addressed through the development of a population policy that encourages smaller-sized families. The traditional idea that larger families mean more hands to provide labour is no longer valid. In fact, the converse is now true because the main struggle people face is finding the money to pay their children's school fees. In my village these days, it is almost not worthwhile celebrating a birthday because if you do have a party there are usually many more children than there is available food. While I do not advocate the birth-control methods used in China, I would suggest that the government could aim, as a matter of policy, to reduce the population growth rate by half over a defined period of time, say 20 years.

**Decentralisation of development projects.** One of the pillars of the Sogavare government is rural development. It was on this basis that Dr John Roughan was appointed secretary to cabinet so that he could spearhead the government's new development strategy. Roughan was director of the Solomon Islands Development Trust (SIDT), which worked for a long time to empower villagers. The test for the government is whether any new major development projects will be diverted to the provinces. What is sorely needed is infrastructure such as roads, bridges, telecommunications, wharfs and ports to spawn development. Two international-standard airport runways should be built in Western and Malaita provinces. The ethnic tension clearly showed the danger of centralising government functions in one location. With international-standard facilities in the provinces, Honiara could be divested of its primacy as the 'bright lights' of Solomon Islands and thereby reduce the inward migration of people to Honiara.

**Raising education standards.** I have also advocated the importance of education for providing better opportunities. The government should ensure education standards are raised to a level whereby Solomon Islanders can export their skills rather than cheap raw materials that damage the environment. In the past 10 years, the number of schools has increased but the number of qualified teachers has not matched this. The large number of untrained teachers in many schools throughout Solomon Islands has affected the quality of education. Education is a three-legged partnership between parents, students and teachers, whereby students should be taught to be creative, critical and thought provoking and not just to regurgitate what teachers/lecturers tell them. Too often students, including university students, lack creative, critical thinking abilities.

**Healthy environment.** The health of the environment is fundamental. The government and every Solomon Islander should ensure that Solomon Islands has a clean, healthy environment. In addition to the beautification of Honiara and villages throughout the country, a greening of Solomon Islands policy should be adopted by the government whereby every household, suburb, village and town is encouraged to plant trees, not just for beautification but to help the environment.

**Freeing the public service of political interference.** In the past 15 years, the politicisation of the public service has led to a lowering of standards within it. The government should ensure that the public service is free of political influence. The public service plays an important role in the fabric of Solomon Islands society. One of the first things the government should do is change the nomenclature 'permanent secretary' because there is nothing permanent about the position. A problem facing the public service is a lack of capacity in policy implementation, especially through legislating to implement government policy. This is evident by the extremely small amount of legislation that parliament has enacted in the past four years. This problem will, unfortunately, be compounded in the next few years because of the capacity gaps that now exist in the service. Having said that, I should point out that a number of very positive developments have taken place in the past three years. There are well-publicised manuals on the Solomon Islands People First Network's web site on various procedures, including the role of permanent secretaries, how to make legislation and the role of cabinet. These manuals are very useful tools that should enhance the capacity of the public service.

**Addressing the fluidity of electioneering and politicking.** Perhaps Solomon Islands' biggest problem is political instability. Electoral laws should be amended so that elections are contested only by political parties and not by independent candidates. This would eliminate the uncertainty of individuals standing with no particular political platform or policies. The counter-argument is that political parties have never worked, do not have a strong grass roots base, have no particular ideological leanings and, historically, once elected, parliamentarians have oscillated from one side of the house to the other. Greater political stability is needed so that Solomon Islands can have a secure future and this should be the overriding public policy concern. It would be better for Solomon Islands to have a grouping within parliament that already had its policies and strategies in place once elected, rather than a group that started to think about its policies and strategies only after forming government. We also need to move forward rather than being constrained by the uncertainties of the present system.

The idea of electing parties rather than individuals is certainly not new and can be found in a number of countries throughout the Commonwealth. It could be argued that Solomon Islanders are not yet ready for the election of parties because of the *wantok* system, low levels of understanding of government and the electoral processes. My response is that we need to start somewhere. The suggestion that Solomon Islanders are not sophisticated enough to appreciate a strong party system has two implications: firstly, Solomon Islanders are not intelligent and flexible enough to understand and accept change; secondly, it is best that Solomon Islanders be condemned to the same old uncertain, inherently weak system that we currently have. Most Solomon Islanders would be only too happy to see change that would realise greater political stability. The key to economic growth and greater social and economic well-being is political stability.

**Making it unlawful for members to switch parties once elected.**
Logically, it follows that if individuals are to be elected on the basis of their
party affiliation, they should remain loyal to the principles, policies and
strategies espoused by their party. Therefore, the electoral laws should
be amended to make it unlawful for any person who has been elected to
parliament as a member of one party to switch to another party. The counter-
argument is that it would be hard to discipline parliamentarians and such a
law would simply not work. My response is that there is an overriding public
policy interest in ensuring stability, reducing fluidity and tightening discipline
in the national parliament, which necessitates such change. Ensuring that the
sanctions and penalties were high would be incentive enough for members
not to change parties after they were elected. The system is applied in some
countries in the Commonwealth—for example, Papua New Guinea—and
could be tried in Solomon Islands as a means of addressing the problem of
members frequently crossing the floor and thereby creating instability.

**Introducing limited preferential voting.** The first-past-the-post system
of voting does not result in a democratically elected member who is truly
representative of the electorate. In the just-completed national elections,
only two members were elected with more than 50 per cent of the votes
cast. The election of the prime minister, on the other hand, requires that the
winner must obtain at least 51 per cent of the votes. Electoral laws should be
changed to ensure parity in the general principles underpinning the majority
required to elect a prime minister and MPs. Introducing limited preferential
voting whereby voters have a choice of up to three people can do this. If a
candidate receives more than 50 per cent of the votes cast on the first count,
he/she wins. If, however, no one wins an outright majority, the preferences
are distributed until such time as a candidate receives more than 50 per cent
of the votes. The counter-argument is that such a system is complicated, will
confuse voters and it will take too long to count votes. My response is that
there is a strong public policy interest in ensuring that a truly democratic
parliament is elected, which represents the majority of Solomon Islanders; it
is also something that is being implemented in Papua New Guinea.

While such a system would not eliminate bribery and vote buying, it
would certainly reduce these practices, because voters would at least have
more than one choice. The introduction of a limited preferential system
can be phased in through provincial assembly elections and eventually the

national elections. It is instructive to note that the introduction of the single ballot box system generated considerable debate in parliament. Indeed, there were suggestions that Solomon Islanders were not literate enough to understand this system. I think it is a fair observation that such comments were generated largely by fear among some leaders that any change to the system might lesson their chances of winning. I would argue that the main consideration should be the national interest—stability and ensuring elected representatives receive more than 50 per cent of the votes—rather than the narrow, self-centred interests of MPs. The idea is not new and is applied in countries throughout the Commonwealth, including the Pacific Island Forum countries. In fact, in 1995, I made submissions to the Electoral Review Committee to introduce a limited preferential voting system. I reiterated those same sentiments in the *Solomon Star* in 1998.

**Making illegal the giving of gifts, money, airfares, assistance and demands for money within six months of an election.** My observation of the general elections is that they are becoming more corrupt and routinely involve the exchange of goods and services. Voters have also exacerbated the problem by imposing all manner of demands on candidates. The tendency for voters to ask candidates for money, sea fares and airfares, food and school fees during the period leading up to elections has become progressively worse. The 2006 election was one of the most unclean in terms of the attitudes of the voters and candidates. The movement of supporters from one candidate to another depending on who gave them money was not obvious to the casual observer, but was an open secret in the constituencies. There is an overwhelming public policy interest in ensuring that election campaigns are conducted cleanly and fairly on a level playing field.

To ensure that money, goods and services are not transferred between candidates and voters, and to ensure that voters do not impose undue pressure on candidates by demanding money from them, the provisions on bribery and treatment under the National Parliament Electoral Provisions Act and the local government regulations should be made more specific by proscribing altogether any exchange of money, goods or services and voter demands up to six months before elections. As it is, the current laws require proof that such exchanges of goods and services are intended to induce a person to vote. The problem is that it is difficult to determine whether the distribution of water tanks and other forms of assistance a few weeks before an election constitute 'development assistance' or 'special treatment'. Perfectly legitimate arguments can be developed either way.

The counter-argument is that such a law is unduly prohibitive and would prevent MPs providing legitimate assistance to their constituents. My response is that the best form of assistance that MPs can offer is to deliver laws that will enhance the social and economic welfare of the people of the Solomon Islands. There is an overriding public policy interest for MPs to discharge their duties as parliamentarians rather than be bankers underwriting school fees, airfares, sea fares, plane charters and so on for their constituents, and in ensuring that elections are a time when issues affecting the social and economic well-being of Solomon Islanders are debated. It should not be a time when the greed, graft and cunning of voters and candidates are manifested so blatantly. Voters must not use the election campaign period as a pretext to milk candidates of whatever money they have set aside for their campaign. Even with tight laws in place, it is difficult to control the exchange of goods and services. The prohibitions should, therefore, be made broader so that they cover any form of exchange of goods and services six months before an election.

**Finding an alternative way of electing the prime minister.** It is said that the real politicking starts once elected members arrive in Honiara to choose the prime minister. Indeed, if one has been observing the election of prime ministers since independence, it might be fair to say that elected members have become more immature, irresponsible, childish, irrational and militant in their approach to the election of the prime minister. It is almost laughable the way that individual members are literally hijacked by the different groups. The MPs might not realise it, but to the members of the public, such behaviour is tantamount to lunacy.

Black Tuesday—as the April 2006 riots became known—underscored the need to find a more sensible, transparent, accountable and less divisive way of electing a prime minister. The reforms suggested above are a precondition for the proposals for choosing the prime minister. A couple of models are offered. Once again, these models are not new and exist within the Commonwealth, including Pacific Islands Forum countries. The first alternative would be for the head of state to invite the leader of the party or alliance of parties that commands the majority of MPs to form government. This would immediately address the hanky-panky that currently occurs. Fundamental to this, of course, is the strong representation of parties in parliament. The second alternative is for MPs to nominate two candidates—or such numbers as appropriate—and have them elected by the people of Solomon Islands. The public policy interest is to find a more stable and cohesive way of electing the prime minister. This would not necessarily eliminate the need for horse-trading, but it would certainly minimise the uncertainties in the present system and ensure a more transparent, accountable and cohesive way of choosing the prime minister.

**Enhancing the role of the media.** One of the major contributors to a free society is media freedom. Much has been said about the role of the media in Solomon Islands and it is not my intention, therefore, to go through what has been hammered home on several occasions. I was, however, disappointed with the media coverage during the April riots. In emails exchanged with Ofani Eremae, editor of the *Solomon Star*, after the April riots, I wrote that

> ...the media has a very important role to play in not only rebuilding the nation, [but in] galvanising public views on what could be incorporated into public policy. My views are only just one of the views that can be put across, but the most important thing in my mind are [sic] the views of ordinary Solomon Islands [sic] and how they will be affected. I don't want the exchange of views to become élitist only because some people can express themselves clearer than others. The important lesson that should be taken from this is that we should also learn to listen, and listen even more.

> In terms of the media, I know that there are limits to what the print media can do, but the real reach out [sic] is the SIBC [Solomon Islands Broadcasting Corporation] radio and I think they have failed. Yesterday I listened to your panel discussion through Radio Australia which was excellent, but I cannot understand why SIBC cannot be doing the same, and asking people questions, and searching for solutions. There is far too much music being played on the national broadcast service and not enough educational material from which we can learn. I really want to see a lot of pressure being put on politicians...[to] improve the connection between them and us, and the media must ensure that this happens over the next four years otherwise these 50 people will ruin [the lives of] the 450,000 who live here. Your coverage has been good and I understand perfectly

the limits that you have. I think that one piece of investigative journalism a month will go a long way to exposing corruption and keeping leaders on their toes (author correspondence with Ofani Eremae, 28 April 2006).

## Conclusion

One of the things I noticed immediately after the October 2000 cease-fire was that people were enthusiastic about rebuilding the country. They were desperate to find any form of work. During that time, I said that there was renewed energy to rebuild Solomon Islands from the ashes. I cannot speak for other provinces, but during that time I observed that people from my area in Western Province did not wait for government hand-outs in order to do something. Many people got into growing tree crops. It was also at this time that I built my own home in the bush—growing a small teak plantation, as well planting nail-nut trees, betel-nut and sago palm. I decided that there was no future in Honiara and that the ethnic tensions had taught Solomon Islanders some important lessons: it reaffirmed the importance of land and it demonstrated that you could not live on someone else's land. The Sogavare government's emphasis on rural development should be welcomed; however, it is easier said than done. Development cannot happen if Solomon Islanders expect others to do it. There has been a lot of criticism of RAMSI, but it is not for RAMSI to nation build in Solomon Islands. Just like the unrealistic expectations that Solomon Islanders have placed on RAMSI, there are unrealistic expectations that others will help Solomon Islands solve all its problems.

Corruption, graft, cunning, uncertainty and so on cannot be totally eradicated; they can, however, be minimised. The ideas offered above will certainly go a long way towards addressing some of the uncertainties in the current system. To those who would oppose change to the current system, I say: traditions, cultures and societal values change over time. While laws are intended to be forward looking, they become outdated, obsolete and inappropriate. That is why they should be changed to reflect how society has transformed. I would argue very strongly that the democratic processes espoused in the 1978 constitution and the National Elections Provisions Act are outdated and need to be changed. I would also question the moral authority of a democratic process that results in the looting, destruction and dislocation of Solomon Islands in a way that has never been seen before in the short history of this nation. If MPs are to raise their heads above the destruction, they must change the laws immediately. The test of whether parliament is interested in avoiding another Black Tuesday will be whether the legislative changes proposed above are deliberated on and enacted during the next four years. Failure to do so will be a clear demonstration that our political leaders do not have the national interests of Solomon Islands at heart.

Recently, a minister in the Sogavare government bought a car from a colleague of mine. When the cheque for the purchase of the car was delivered, the drawer was a Chinese shop owner. This was immediately after the April riots. Is there a way out of the crisis? I would argue that there is, but we are still foraging for it.

## Acknowledgment

The views expressed in this article are the personal views of the author.

## References

Allen, M.G., 2006. 'Dissenting voices: local perspectives on the Regional Assistance Mission to Solomon Islands', *Pacific Economic Bulletin*, 21(2):194–201.

Aqorau, T., 2006. 'The real linchpins of Solomon Islands politics', Letter to the Editor, *Solomon Star*, 14 April.

Hughes, A., 2004. The economy: past experiences, recent situation and pressing issues, paper presented at the Beyond Intervention: Navigating Solomon Islands' Future Conference, East–West Center–PIDP Workshop, Honiara, 14–16 June.

Kabutaulaka, T.T., 2007. 'Global capital and local ownership in Solomon Islands' forestry industry', in Stewart Firth (ed.), Globalisationa dn Governance in the Pacific Islands, ANU E Press, The Australian National University, Canberra:239–57. Available from http://epress.anu.edu.au/ssgm/global_gov/pdf/ch12.pdf (accessed 28 January 2007).

Solomon Islands Government, 1999. 'Forest Resources and Timber Utilisation Act', *The Revised Laws of Solomon Islands*, Solomon Islands Government, Honiara.

# Appendix 1

## The unrest in Honiara—an Australian government perspective

Anita Butler

Thank you for inviting me here today to talk about the situation in Solomon Islands, the Australian government's perspective on what has occurred and its implications for our engagement there. The situation is obviously still very fluid, and these are very preliminary thoughts, which is why I am speaking only for Australia at this stage, and not for the other contributing members of RAMSI.

Firstly, let me offer a brief update on the situation on the ground, as we understand it. Manasseh Sogavare has been elected prime minister. His election seems to have been received calmly thus far. He has yet to announce his cabinet, but details are expected to emerge over the weekend. In his acceptance speech, he noted that he would ensure responsible government for the country. This comment was welcomed. In addition, he has indicated to the media that he thinks RAMSI should remain in Solomon Islands, and that he will work with RAMSI. He has previously said he would like to review RAMSI's direction, and we of course know that he has been a critic of RAMSI in the past.

So let me take up this point, before going into more general discussion. We welcome Sogavare's comments, and we look forward to engaging with the new prime minister to learn his priorities and to take RAMSI forward. As far as we are concerned, RAMSI is under constant review, including now through a number of formal mechanisms, and we welcome the new government's interest in engaging in this process. This would have been our position, no matter who was elected. As we have said on a number of occasions recently, RAMSI is a partnership with the Solomon Islands government—whichever government is elected by the democratic and parliamentary processes of Solomon Islands. RAMSI came about at the invitation of the Solomon Islands government, and has its legal foundation in an act of the Solomon Islands parliament, which was passed unanimously in 2003. There is, therefore, no question that we would work with the elected government. We have no other choice if we wish to support the notion of democracy in Solomon Islands.

We recognise that the political processes are open to abuse and that corruption is a huge problem in Solomon Islands, including—and perhaps especially—within the political system. That is why, through RAMSI, we have focused on trying to rebuild and strengthen the accountability institutions: the Leadership Code Commission, the ombudsman's office and the auditor-general's office. In time, the hope is that these institutions will be strong enough to inspire faith in them, so that people will actually use them to report allegations of corruption and allow them to be investigated and dealt with in the courts. At present, while everyone is willing to talk about what this or that politician may have done, who they may have taken money from and who they may be giving money to, very few people are willing to put their name to that talk in an official report. Some people are willing to come forward, and as a result a number of politicians, including ministers, and senior public servants have been arrested and charged with corruption offences in the past two and half years. But, in relation to the recent election, police advise that they have not at this stage received any official report of corruption. Building trust and making a democracy work takes time.

Australia, New Zealand and the other countries of the region have committed to Solomon Islands for the long term. In Australia's case, not only do we have an unusual four-year budget pledge—beyond the life of our own government and with bipartisan support—our prime minister said publicly in 2003 that we would need to be fully committed to the task for at least 10 years. Recent events have not altered that long-term commitment. If anything, they have underlined the need for it, and reinforced the message that we have been putting forward since the beginning of RAMSI: that the changes needed in Solomon Islands, to ensure future prosperity, security and stability, will take many years, if not generations, to implement and embed. RAMSI, after all, has been in Solomon Islands for only two years and nine months. In that time, significant progress has been made on a number of fronts.

When RAMSI arrived in Solomon Islands in 2003, the problems faced by the country were immense. Although outright ethnic warfare had ceased, opportunistic criminal lawlessness was rife, the police force was so compromised by its links to former militants and criminal gangs that it was unable to keep the peace, corruption was widespread—remissions and illegal licences meant much government revenue was never collected, and that which did come in, mainly in the form of tax payments from the commercial banks, was immediately extorted at gunpoint by ex-militants and special constables and anyone else with a big enough gun. As a result, service delivery had faltered—nothing had flowed out to the provinces for some time, public officers, including teachers and nurses, were not being paid and, by 2003, even the compensation money that had kept at least the beer and mag-wheel sections of the Honiara economy afloat had dried up. Along with the collapse of the economy was a total collapse in public confidence in all the institutions of state.

So, when Australia, New Zealand and the other Pacific island countries agreed to respond to the Solomon Islands government's request for help with the law and order situation in 2003, we made it very clear that we were going to offer a package of assistance. It would not be enough to provide security—just as it had proven not to be enough to focus on basic service delivery or institutional strengthening in the context of such profound decline. If RAMSI was going to be successful, it would need to tackle a broad spectrum of problems, including the ones that could not be solved overnight, and including those that were politically difficult. This position has not changed, and it is one we will be reinforcing strongly with the new government.

Although RAMSI was always an integrated approach, there is no doubt that the first priority on arrival was the restoration of the rule of law. It is fair to say initial success in this regard—in relation to the arrest of militants and the removal of a large number of firearms from the community—was quicker and more significant than had been anticipated. There was also considerable early success in stabilising government finances. From the beginning, we made a concerted effort to reiterate that the real challenges were only just beginning and would take time and commitment. But, understandably, progress after that initial period has seemed slow in comparison. So before we look specifically at the implications of the recent riots—which have clearly had damaging effects in many areas—I want to highlight for a moment the progress made by the RAMSI partnership, which has not been undermined and which is still of value. I think it is important that we don't throw the baby out with the bath water.

Let's focus first on the area that may seem at a glance to have suffered the most significant set-back: police, law and order. Apart from the arrest of large numbers of law-breakers (the incredible number of 6,300 on more than 9,100 charges), successful support to the judicial system (which has enabled those arrested to be dealt with by an effective and impartial judiciary) and the removal of more than 3,600 firearms from the community (which no doubt contributed to the fact that no lives were lost in the recent unrest), the progress made since RAMSI's arrival in July 2003 on rebuilding the Royal Solomon Islands Police (RSIP) as a vital national institution cannot be discounted.

After a wholesale clean out of the police force—more than 160 former RSIP officers arrested and others removed through internal investigations—rebuilding has obviously been a mammoth task. Four rounds of new recruits—men and women from all provinces—have completed training at the RSIP academy at Rove and commenced policing duties. According to the police commissioner, these new recruits and junior RSIP officers performed very well in combating the recent riots. There is a long way to go, of course, but the progress in this area is what underlies the return to the rule of law that has occurred in Solomon Islands. What that means practically is that when security is undermined, and when people break the law, as occurred two weeks ago, order can be restored, and people can be arrested. It is true that widespread damage occurred before the situation was brought under control, and that reinforcements had to be called in from Australia, New Zealand and the region, but that tells us two things: firstly, that a riot is not an easy thing to control (even the Paris Riot Police, with all their experience, find it a challenge); and secondly, that the work on rebuilding the Solomon Islands police must be continued. The fact that two weeks after the riots Honiara is calm and more than 150 people have been arrested for their activities during the unrest tells us we have come a long way since 2003.

In RAMSI's two other main areas of work—economic governance and machinery of government—we can also point to significant progress that has not been undermined. The government's improved financial position and financial management means that, among other things, service delivery continues, public servant salaries are paid on time and essential economic reform is under way. The bureaucracy is functioning far more effectively than it was, with improved communication and coordination between different parts of government, better planning and management systems, improved understanding and implementation of processes and, importantly, recruitment and human resource development. With RAMSI support, the Institute for Public Administration and Management has been re-established, and public servants have received the first training they have undertaken in many years.

It is important for us not to lose sight of this progress, but I don't want to give the impression that we are complacent, or that we intend to ignore the implications of the riots. What has occurred clearly represents a significant set-back for Solomon Islands. It is a set-back in terms of the physical damage that has been caused (which has affected not only Chinese business people, but also the many ethnic Solomon Islanders who were employed by those businesses—estimated to have been 600 at the Pacific Casino Hotel alone) and also in terms of the damage to the international image of Solomon Islands (which has implications for tourism and foreign investment). More far-reaching, the riots have been a set-back to the process of peace and reconciliation in the country, and to people's sense of well-being and security. Australia, as the lead country in RAMSI, is very focused on examining what the unrest can tell us, which can inform our approach. This process has only just begun, and what I have to offer are some very preliminary thoughts.

The first obvious lesson we draw is that our job is a long way from being done, and we need to stay committed. We will therefore be working hard to engage with the incoming government and ensure its commitment to forward partnership. Our partners in the region have already reaffirmed their support for RAMSI, both publicly and privately.

Secondly, we are already reflecting—in our many internal consultative mechanisms—on the reasons for the unrest and what it tells us about the needs of Solomon Islands society.

In fact, it tells us a lot that we already know: first and foremost, that the situation in Solomon Islands remains fragile—as the literature says, 'a post-conflict society is a pre-conflict society'.

Much analysis remains to be done—and is being done by many people—on the factors that provoked this unrest. At this early stage, let me offer a nutshell take on what has occurred—in very simplistic terms—from which some initial thoughts can be drawn. One possible explanation is that a small criminal element, frustrated that increasing adherence to the rule of law has curtailed its interests, has preyed on and used to its own ends what are very genuinely felt, deep-seated resentments within the population—partly of corruption and mismanagement, partly a feeling that the politicians have been taking the people for a ride, partly of perceived Chinese interference in politics and, most significantly, resentment of Chinese commercial success and a feeling that it has been at the expense of Solomon Islanders' prosperity. All of these resentments fed into a ransacking mass element, stirred up by those with less worthy political motives than the elimination of corruption or wanting the bad guys out of government, and it all got out of hand.

This tells us a few things. Obviously, despite the fact that things clearly have improved since the bad old days, people do not feel they are getting their fair share of the benefits. They feel that others—politicians, Chinese business people, maybe foreign advisers—are taking more than their share, and they do not have faith in their political system, and specifically in their politicians' ability to elect a good prime minister. And what does this tell us? Perhaps that more work needs to be done in some key areas

- on building a sense of unity and nationhood, and on reconciliation
- on addressing the problems of corruption and lack of transparency in government
- on improving people's understanding of and ability to participate in the democratic process
- and on generating economic development and creating opportunities for young people in Solomon Islands.

Alexander Downer, during his recent visit to Honiara, urged both sides of politics to step up and take responsibility for tackling these issues. These problems cannot be solved by outsiders alone. But clearly, RAMSI has an interest in doing what we can to help address these issues, if we are to ensure that the progress RAMSI has made to date is sustainable.

None of this is new. We have all been discussing the need to address the underlying causes of conflict in Solomon Islands for some time. But quick fixes have not been easy to find. RAMSI is already working—through the civic education and parliamentary strengthening projects, through work on strengthening the accountability institutions and improving governance and through the various arms of the finance project—on addressing these deep-seated problems. But everything we are doing takes time: education takes time, building trust takes time, instilling good practices takes time. Clearly, if people do not sense that enough progress is being made in these areas, there is a risk that they will take matters into their own hands, with disastrous results. So we think we probably have to do more in these areas in an attempt to increase the pace of change and satisfy public expectations. Although we have been focused over the past two weeks on the task of again restoring order, we have already begun the process within the Australian government and in discussion with New Zealand of creative thinking with a view to presenting some concrete proposals to the new government as soon as possible. This process will be taken forward in discussion with our regional partners.

# Appendix 2

## Terms of Reference
## Commissions of Inquiry Act (Cap.5)
## Commission of Inquiry into the April 2006 Civil Unrest in Honiara

### Commission

**By the Honourable Manasseh D. Sogavare MP, Prime Minister of Solomon Islands**

TO: MR BRIAN DANESBURY BRUNTON of Alotau, Papua New Guinea;
MR WAETA BEN TABUSASI SIM CSI of Honiara, Solomon Islands;
MR NOEL LEVI CBE of Kavieng, Papua New Guinea; and
MR CHARLES LEVO of Honiara, Solomon Islands.

WHEREAS by virtue of Section 3 of the Commissions of Inquiry Act (Cap.5), the Prime Minister, whenever he deems it advisable, shall issue a commission appointing one or more commissioners and authorising them to inquire into any matter in which an inquiry would, in the opinion of the Prime Minister, be for the public welfare.

NOW THEREFORE by this commission, I, the Honourable Manasseh D. Sogavare MP, Prime Minister:

1   APPOINT Mr Brian Danesbury Brunton; Mr Waeta Ben Tabusasi SIM CSI; Mr Noel Levi CBE; and Mr Charles Levo as commissioners ('the Commissioners') to inquire into the civil

unrest which occurred in Honiara during the period between April 18, 2006 and April 20, 2006, following the election of the Honourable Snyder Rini MP as Prime Minister of Solomon Islands ('the April 2006 Civil Unrest');

2  AUTHORISE the Commissioners to:

a  investigate, probe, examine and analyse the background to the April 2006 Civil Unrest including all the incidents, events, activities and circumstances connected therewith and leading thereto;

b  investigate and determine the role played by the bodies, groups and individuals who planned, organised and participated in all activities relating to the April 2006 Civil Unrest;

c  identify the persons as well as political parties and groups who spearheaded and participated in the April 2006 Civil Unrest;

d  investigate, examine and determine the role of any Member of Parliament in the planning, organisation and execution of the April 2006 Civil Unrest;

e  investigate all the circumstances attendant upon and surrounding the damage and destruction of property as well as the arson and looting of commercial and business establishments in and around Honiara and identify the bodies, groups and persons who conspired, planned and executed such criminal activities;

f  investigate, examine, analyse, appraise and determine the role and responsibility of the Solomon Islands Police Force ('the SIPF') and the Participating Police Force ('the PPF') respectively, in the preservation and maintenance of law and order in Honiara during the April 2006 Civil Unrest;

g  consider and evaluate the response of the SIPF, the PPF and the emergency services to the April 2006 Civil Unrest and advise on the appropriateness, adequacy and coordination of that response;

h  review and consider the question of the liability or obligation of the Solomon Islands Government to rehabilitate and/or compensate any victims of the April 2006 Civil Unrest for damage, loss or destruction of their property occasioned thereby due to the failure (whether by omission or commission) of the SIPF, the

PPF or any other constitutional or statutory body entrusted with responsibility for the prevention, control and suppression of the April 2006 Civil Unrest;

i   review, examine, appraise and evaluate the nature, appropriateness, effectiveness and adequacy of existing arrangements for the prevention, control, immediate suppression and repetition of incidents, events and activities occurring during the April 2006 Civil Unrest;

j   investigate, appraise, evaluate and report on any other issue bearing or impinging on any of the foregoing; and

k   make recommendations as to the actions that ought to be taken to prevent a recurrence of the incidents, events and activities occurring during the April 2006 Civil Unrest.

3   DIRECT as follows:

a   that Mr Brian Danesbury Brunton shall be chairman of the Commissioners;

b   that the inquiry shall be held:

i.   in public;

ii.   as soon as practicable; and

iii.   at such place(s) as the Commissioners shall designate;

c   that the presence of the chairman and one of the Commissioners shall constitute a quorum for the proceedings of the inquiry while permitting the Commissioners to sit in panels of one or two to take particular evidence if a quorum considers it convenient or appropriate so to do;

d   that decisions of the Commissioners shall be by simple majority and in the case of equality of votes the chairman shall have a casting as well as a deliberative vote;

e   that the Commissioners shall:

i.   submit their written report on the result of their inquiry into each and all of the matters referred to in Paragraph 2 above as well as the reasons for their conclusions; and

ii.   furnish the full record of the proceedings of the inquiry to the Prime Minister within five (5) months of the commencement of the inquiry, or on or before such other date as the Prime Minister may determine;

f   that the Commissioners may, if they consider it prudent or appropriate so to do:

i.   prepare and submit to the Prime Minister interim or provisional reports on any aspect of the inquiry at any stage thereof;

ii.  keep any part of the transcript and their reports confidential to the Prime Minister and the Attorney-General;

g   that the Commissioners shall, in the performance of their functions, be assisted by:

i.   Mr Sam Tagana MBE who is hereby appointed as secretary to the Commissioners under Section 7 of the Commissions of Inquiry Act (Cap. 5);

ii.  one or more legal practitioners duly appointed by the Attorney-General to act as counsel to the Commissioners;

iii. transcribers, interpreters, investigators, technical advisers, researchers and any other persons whom the Commissioners may, with the approval of the Minister of Finance, engage to render services based on their recognised expertise, specialisation, qualifications, knowledge and relevant experience;

iv.  police officers who the Commissioner of Police is hereby directed under Section 17 of the Commissions of Inquiry Act (Cap. 5) to detail for the protection of the Commissioners and the orderly and efficient conduct of their inquiry;

v.   such other public officer as may be assigned from time to time by the Minister responsible for the public service;

h   that the Commissioners and the secretary shall be remunerated at a rate to be determined by the Prime Minister;

i.   that all ministries, servants, boards, agencies and instrumentalities of the Solomon Islands Government shall assist the Commissioners to the fullest extent in order that they may discharge their functions without any hindrance whatsoever.

ISSUED at Honiara this 24th day of April, 2007
The Honourable Manasseh Sogavare, MP
Prime Minister

# Appendix 3
## Forum Review of the Regional Assistance Mission to the Solomon Islands. Terms of reference

### Mandate

At the 37$^{th}$ Pacific Islands Forum, Leaders agreed, following a six-point submission from the Solomon Islands Government (SIG), to establish a Task Force to expeditiously review RAMSI and to report back to Foreign Ministers who would make recommendations to leaders.

The Leaders also agreed that in the interim RAMSI will continue to operate in its current form and that a Consultation Mechanism between the Government of Solomon Islands, RAMSI and the Pacific Islands Forum is established. The Consultation Mechanism is to be a high-level reference group which provides strategic advice to all parties on the policy direction of RAMSI until the Task Force publishes its findings.

The composition of the Task Force will include deputation from the Solomon Islands Government, being a major partner and the most directly affected stakeholder, in accord with the Forum Chair and the Forum Secretary-General who will be tasked to appoint the Task Force to undertake the review.

### Purpose

The purpose of the review is to assess and recommend a way forward to guide the future operations of RAMSI which, represented by the SIG, is in the best interests of the people of Solomon Islands. It is also expected that the review propose substantive recommendations across a broad range of RAMSI's activities which affect the Government and people of the Solomon Islands.

# Scope

To fulfil the mandate by the Leaders and complete the review of RAMSI, the Task Force will undertake:

1. To review the operation of the Facilitation of International Assistance Act 2003 and the multilateral Assistance Agreement (2003) ATS 17 between participating countries.

2. To establish the original basis for RAMSI's intervention in the Solomon Islands in 2003 and clarify general contingencies surrounding the intended partnership arrangements at the time between RAMSI and the SIG.

3. In consideration of progress made, to evaluate since its arrival, the overall impact of RAMSI on the sovereignty and integrity of the Solomon Islands Government in relation to:
   - the integration of RAMSI into Solomon Islands Government institutions
   - operational aspects of the RAMSI partnership which overlap with functions of the Executive Government.

4. To examine RAMSI's focus, objectives and its key guiding principles in the context of the Solomon Islands Government's Six Point Plan.

5. To examine the role, responsibilities and objectives of RAMSI, including existing coordination and partnership mechanisms with the SIG, in the following key areas:
   - economic governance and growth (including financial management, financial accountability, economic reform and development)
   - law and justice (including the legal, judicial, law enforcement and correctional sectors)
   - government sector (including accountability of institutions, the public service, cabinet and parliamentary processes)
   - compliance with existing legal requirements including Public Service rules and regulations affecting the appointment and facilitation of personnel under RAMSI
   - the employment of externally based commercial private sector companies to provide administrative and logistical support to government orientated programs that include policing and security operations.

6.  To identify areas in the Government's 'Bottom Up Approach' Policy on Rural Development which could be supported and implemented by RAMSI.

7.  To appraise whether the progress made by RAMSI on capacity building is aligned to SIG development priorities and policy objectives in ensuring government agencies are staffed and funded appropriately, and to also consider:

    • goals for strengthened capacity building including towards the localisation of positions
    • specific benchmarks to measure progress of these efforts
    • improvement in Public Service Systems.

8.  To examine current aid and policy coordination between RAMSI and the Solomon Islands Government in particular, to establish a clear demarcation between the RAMSI and bilateral AusAID programs by separately defining the joint cooperation of both organisations on contingencies specifically related to programs supported by RAMSI.

9.  To examine processes by which decisions are made to change existing arrangements relating to RAMSI programs and personnel.

10. To examine the role of the Pacific Islands Forum in RAMSI, including Forum–RAMSI–Solomon Islands Government consultation mechanisms and the possibility of creating a Forum Ministerial Standing Committee to be established as a governing body designed to regulate the operations of RAMSI.

11. To consider the recommendations made by the Pacific Islands Forum Eminent Persons' Group (EPG) in its 2005 Review of RAMSI, determining its relevance in the context of present circumstances and what possible action might be taken by the Solomon Islands Government and RAMSI.

12. Appreciate the ultimate necessity for the eventual exit of RAMSI and to determine the timetable and withdrawal strategy.

## Methodology

In carrying out its mandate, the Task Force is requested to:

•   peruse the documents leading to the establishment of RAMSI which shaped its spirit, accent and values such as the 34th Leaders'

Declaration on the Solomon Islands in Auckland 2003 and the Biketawa Declaration

- consider the current roles, obligations and responsibilities of both RAMSI and the Solomon Islands Government

- consider relevant SIG, RAMSI and Forum documents including the SIG recurrent and development budgets, SIG Policy Translation and Implementation Document, SIG departmental corporate plans and annual reports, the draft RAMSI Medium Term Strategy, RAMSI Performance Framework, RAMSI 2006 Performance Report, Capacity Building Stocktakes, the Financial Management Strengthening Review (FMSP) report, Economic Reform Unit reports, existing RAMSI reports to the Forum and the Forum EPG report also including the Oxfam report on Bridging the Gap Between State and Society 2006 and other documents describing the social, cultural, economical and historical background of the Solomons for the 10 years preceding the Social Unrest years which informed and shaped events leading to military intervention

- consult with the Solomon Islands Government Members of Parliament, provincial and local governments, constitutional office holders, government officials, the Solomon Islands Police Force and Solomon Islands Prison Service, judicial bodies, traditional leaders, business and professional representative organisations, representatives of civil society, women's organisations, youth organisations, religious leaders, media organisations, RAMSI participating governments, the RAMSI leadership and personnel on the ground including development partners

- invite submissions from any interested or affected persons or organisations on their assessments and perceptions of the role, record, performance and future of RAMSI.

## Outputs and reporting

The Task Force will compile its findings and recommendations in a Report. In line with the 2006 Pacific Islands Forum Communiqué, the Report will be presented to Foreign Ministers, who will make further recommendations to Forum Leaders.

# Index